D0272381

Conspiracy of Secrets

Conspiracy of Secrets

'For years, the illicit love affair between Prime Minister Herbert Asquith and Venetia Stanley was concealed. Shocking events in our family led me to uncover the story of their forbidden love.'

Bobbie Neate

JOHN BLAKE

Published by Metro Publishing
an imprint of John Blake Publishing Ltd
3 Bramber Court, 2 Bramber Road,
London W14 9PB, England

www.johnblakepublishing.co.uk

www.facebook.com/Johnblakepub facebook

twitter.com/johnblakepub twitter

First published in hardback in 2012

ISBN: 978-1-84358-372-1

All rights reserved. No part of this publication may be reproduced, stored in a retrieval system, or in any form or by any means, without the prior permission in writing of the publisher, nor be otherwise circulated in any form of binding or cover other than that in which it is published and without a similar condition including this condition being imposed on the subsequent publisher.

British Library Cataloguing-in-Publication Data:

A catalogue record for this book is available from the British Library.

Design by www.envydesign.co.uk

Printed and bound by CPI Group (UK) Ltd, Croydon, CR0 4YY

1 3 5 7 9 10 8 6 4 2

© Text copyright Bobbie Neate 2012

Papers used by John Blake Publishing are natural, recyclable products made from wood grown in sustainable forests. The manufacturing processes conform to the environmental regulations of the country of origin.

Every attempt has been made to contact the relevant copyright-holders, but some were unobtainable. We would be grateful if the appropriate people could contact us.

I wrote *Conspiracy of Secrets* for my mother.

Fond memories of my mother urged me to clamber over what seemed like Herculean mountains in order to achieve my aim of redressing the past. I like to believe she would have been proud of my efforts. As family was of deep significance to her, I believe, she would have liked to be remembered as Jean Owen, which was her maiden name.

'Perhaps all detectives learn their curiosity in childhood and remain absorbed in the past.'

Britain's first detective, Inspector Jonathan Whicher

CONTENTS

Prologue

Names have always fascinated me. I don't know why. Was it because at each family mealtime Louis Stanley, my stepfather, had acquired another famous individual to add to his elite social circle? To my childish ears each celebrity appeared to have a strange sounding name. Fancy being landed with the name 'Aga Khan' or 'Beaverbrook'? I teased myself with the images the names invoked as I sat at the kitchen table bored with adult conversations. Or did I have a fascination with names because my own surname had been summarily dismissed. Nobody ever explained and I was too fearful to ask why I used to be at the top of the school register and then suddenly to my utter dismay, my position plummeted to the nether reaches of the roll call. However my childhood fascination with nomenclature was to help solve an intriguing adult mystery.

Lurking in my childhood were suspicions. What was I uneasy about? I don't know. There had always been mysteries. Things I knew not. Things that were not to be asked. The mantra of childhood was never to question, and slowly this secrecy drifted into my maturity; but there always lurked those dark suspicions. Suspicions too deep to raise, too disturbing to examine. So why disturb the calm? Little did I know when I was five that fifty years later I would be forced to confront my fears and start delving into the lives of others.

The event that sparked my change of mood was my mother's deep stroke when she was nearly ninety. At this juncture in my life, my stepfather began to act bizarrely. His unsettling behaviour compelled me to enter into the labyrinth of secrets and conspiracies, which were so carefully concealed for one hundred years. I had to ride the pain of reconsidering my early home life, and it was not until I started asking questions that I had confirmation about my parentage.

My mother divorced my father, an Anglican vicar, in 1955. At that time, and unbeknown to me, the divorce was a *cause célèbre* and even featured in the tabloid press. In May of the same year, my mother remarried and her new husband, and our stepfather, was Louis Stanley. He had previously been known to us as Uncle Louis.

I was the youngest child and must have unwittingly absorbed sufficient clues to initiate my truth-seeking voyage. Once afloat, I retrieved the two most vital titbits my stepfather had accidentally divulged about his past. These clues dangled tantalisingly in front of me as I steered myself through a storm that blasted away the scales that once covered my childhood eyes, enabling me to see my port of call with a more detached heart. My first job was to recall Stepfather's words to us all as I sat teetering on a tiny stool at the kitchen table. Family talk about his two female relatives, which my stepfather had been so quick to persuade my mother to house, added fuel to my search.

As I made progress with my sleuthing I applied more rigour to my reading. Intrigue was not enough, nor were my childhood memories. They needed to be fused with historical data. There was no one particular detail that helped my conjectures. It was an accumulation of minute pieces of evidence – particulars that were inconsequential to those who had not lived in the same house as this devious man. There was no decisive paper trail, no one piece of research, just numerous connected suppositions. Some historical facts were of immediate relevance to my conjectures while others appeared immaterial. Each time I filled one section of my puzzle I had to revisit the paperwork as a place, a date or a political name that I had previously ignored now became uppermost in my mind. Each step, rather than helping me progress, pushed me into another trail of discovery and yet another list of names and potential clues.

Years previously, when I had first spotted a photograph of Prime Minister H. H. Asquith, I was hit with unease. There I saw a man who looked just like my stepfather. The images were so powerful that I was never going to forget them. How fortunate it was that father and son were so alike. It is not always so. Historians of the 1980s knew Herbert Henry Asquith had been 'close friends' with Venetia Stanley, but because of the age differences they speculated it was an unconsummated affair. They made no conjectures about a lovechild. It was our unusual and distasteful upbringing that allowed me to prise open the conspiracy of secrets and remove them from the political safe.

When I started writing I had no idea that this tale would develop into my own personal detective story and a whole lot more. Questions from childhood emerged sleepily from the deep recesses of my brain and then gathered pace as each piece of my genealogical jigsaw took on new meanings. My sleuthing and investigative work dragged me down into a shadowy scheming world.

Just as in other spheres of detective work, my journey raised many questions. I can provide a satisfying explanation for some but for others there are no neat answers. At times my solutions are not the only possible ones and, as so often happens in research, as soon as one question is answered another arises. So you, my reader, might like to surmise possible solutions to my many imponderables, since, in my view, the loose ends only add to the mystery. Even now after all my efforts to place my story on paper I still find parts of the tale barely credible.

CHAPTER 1

THE MYSTERY OF STEPFATHER'S CHILDHOOD

I was miserable. My mother had died. Her funeral had been on Friday, and now, on this cloudy Monday in July 2002, was her interment. For a brief moment I allowed childhood memories to come flooding back as I approached Sutton Coldfield's Cemetery Road. I saw myself huddled in the back seat of the Morris Oxford estate car, with its distinctive yellow slats of wood dividing the doors and windows from the pale-green chassis. It was a large vehicle for the 1950s but it soon became too small for four children and a poodle, dachshund and terrier as our growing legs took up more of the available space under the back seat of the car.

Mum would, of course, be driving. Stepfather never drove. In my recollections, my three older siblings had left for boarding school and I, as the only child left at home, was alone on the back seat. Beside me sat the handsome wreath that Mum had organised. On each anniversary of the death of her mother, father and younger brother I accompanied her on her pilgrimage to the family grave. It was my job at the age of seven or eight to stop the wreath falling to the floor if she braked hard. Woe betide me if my stepfather spotted I had failed in my duties and it had slipped from its position!

The previous day she had been on the phone, sitting in her usual position: leaning on her left elbow, the phone pressed to her ear while she allowed the pen in her right hand to doodle on the notepad. She knew all about the florist's home life, just as she knew all the triumphs and disappointments of her favourite shopkeepers. As with everything else to do with her family, she gave the floral arrangement a great deal of care and attention. The end result was always an unusual but fitting tribute.

As we approached the cemetery Stepfather put on his supportive-husband act: deferential, courteous and speaking in quiet tones. Mum would reply with subdued remarks about her dearly departed family. She would recall vivid memories of her graceful mother and her talented dad. He was an engineer who built a thriving company that supplied car parts to the motor industry and died when my mother was only 17. He passed away so young that he achieved hero status within family folklore. Whatever time of year, the churchyard custodian stood waiting to greet us beside the lychgate, brush or fork in hand, ready to sweep leaves or to pull out any brave weed that dared to encroach on one of his paths.

But on this disturbing day, over fifty years later, I was the adult and I was the griever. I knew that the burial service would be harrowing, not just because we were burying my darling mother, but because of how we were to deal with our manipulative stepfather. I had been pulled through an emotional mangle and I longed for some peace. But the biggest shock of all was still to come.

It was on a cold Sunday in December 2000, 18 months before my mother's burial, that my life fell apart. I was in my early fifties and a divorcee myself, in sole charge of three teenage children. Tom, my elder son, had been visiting home for the first time since starting university. We had spent the weekend doing all the old things that we used to do when he lived at home. While we were out, Stepfather had left an unclear message in his low resonant voice.

'Mum has had a mild stroke,' he relayed in his haughty voice. 'It's nothing to worry about.'

What? Mum's suffered a stroke? Mum was nearly ninety but she was invincible. I was in deep shock. I tried to ring him back but the phone was engaged. The dull bleeps reminded me of all those years ago, when the phone at my family home, the Old Mill House, was constantly in use. Thoughts flooded into my brain. Did I have to admit to myself that I hardly knew this man? Was the pretence over? He was the secretive man who had married my mother when I was young, and in those early days he did not go out to work but lingered at home writing in his upstairs study. The same puzzling man later became famed in the world of motor racing when I was entering my teens.

It was Tom hollering from his bedroom that evening that jerked me from my anguished thinking: deep concern for my mother tempered with fear of having to deal with Louis Stanley without her steadying influence. While my elder son crammed his tatty clothes into a holdall I shouted housekeeping instructions to Rupert, who was studying for his A-levels, and the lively Hannah, who was 14. I called to Tom to jump in the car and we left so quickly I didn't have time to wave goodbye. Little did I know as we set off that this would be the first of many stressful drives to Cambridge.

My mother had been inspired to look for a larger house in Cambridge when I, her youngest, arrived. She immediately fell in love with the old miller's house that stood on the corner of a main road leading into the city. She would sit at the kitchen table, staring at the heavily netted kitchen window, searching for a glimpse of her delightful courtyard, and recall buying the place.

A small part of the house dated back to the sixteenth century, but Victorian additions made the building an attractive if chaotic structure. However, this did not stop my mother's love for the old miller's abode. It was she who arranged for the gate to be painted blue. Later she bought a brass bell with an arched clanger and had it fixed so that, when the blue gate opened and exposed the enclosed courtyard, it merrily jangled.

'Do you know, I paid ten thousand pounds for the house?' she would say.

We did. It was one of those oft-repeated family stories, one of the few she was allowed to retell that predated the arrival of Stepfather.

The kitchen was the hub of the household, welcomingly warm with steamy windows, the air filled with scrumptious smells. The aromas permeated through the thick heavy door and out into the cold passage beyond. Even on the coldest windswept Cambridgeshire days, the coke-burning boiler generated a cosy background heat. It sometimes produced pungent odours, overcoming the bouquets of roast dinner, apple pie and steamed greens, but, even if the acrid vapours hurt my lungs, it made the Mill House home.

In those early days, if I had fallen down the greenhouse grating, been hit on the head with a rounders bat, argued or just could not do my homework, I would expect to find her in the kitchen, with an attractive apron strategically placed over her fashionable clothes. She might have kicked her high heeled shoes to one side and be in stockinged feet, but she would be there. The radio would be tuned to the BBC Light Programme (the network that became Radio 2), *Housewives' Choice* would be blaring out, and there would be remnants of flour on her hands.

Years of dedicated and loving culinary work had made the surface of the old oak table irregular. It was similar, in many ways, to a butcher's slab with its ups and downs of wear and tear with the pitted wood revealing the many chops and gouges of various cutting implements over the years. But the kitchen table was not just the place to chop meat, peel endless potatoes, and roll out pie after pie. It was the place to do your painting by numbers, to play the latest board game and the floor was always the best surface for any car game.

Car toys were always popular with me. In the winter I set up a permanent Scalextric track in the playroom and I would play for hours putting oil on the back tyres of the model cars to make the steering harder.

Then on warmer days there was the garden to practise my cycling. I pretended I was driving a BRM and I had to get the fastest lap. The washing line had been moved to above the asparagus patch, and if I reached up from the saddle I could fix my stopwatch with a peg so that it dangled from a height. Grabbing it and clipping the button as I skidded in to beat my previous best lap time was all part of the fun. The garden had a maze of paths, so there were lots of corners to be taken at speed and many were lined with low box hedges or hidden flat bricks.

In those early days when I got home from school on summer days my mother would fling open the front door so that the flagstones of the veranda became an extension to the oddly shaped hall. The Victorian ironwork pillars that held the slanting glass roof made a superb backdrop to where Mum had organised a gigantic arrangement of tall blooms in one of her massive vases. The white tray tables would be in use again. We would carry them from the kitchen loaded with bread and cakes. Then, when we got into the right position, perhaps over Stepfather's knees, we would press the handles carefully, so that our fingers would not be trapped in the mechanisms that lowered the legs. A teatime treat might be strawberries from Mrs Hacker's farm, collected on the way home from school. Then we would sit in deck chairs eating and watching the birds peck at the flowerbeds.

As we ate, my mother might allow herself to recount how she loved sorting Baxter Prints with her adored father on Sunday afternoons. Then she might recall the stories of the punt her parents kept on their moat and how she paddled them around among the reeds. On happier days she did not hear Stepfather's heavy huffing and puffing, which indicated that she had reminisced enough, for she might add the story of her teenage brother, Ernest, and how he grabbed the boat from under her nose and set off without her, then lay in the punt listening to his records on his wind-up gramophone, while eating quantities of the richest Sutton Coldfield chocolates. He deigned to give her an occasional wave from behind the horn of the gramophone, as she stood stranded on the lawn. But by now Louis was tapping his teaspoon on his cup and she drew to a halt. He had grudgingly agreed to these stories from her childhood but she appeared to be barred from reminiscing about her earlier adult life when we were very young.

It seemed so strange that Stepfather never recounted any incident from his early years. If I turned and asked about his childhood he never replied, so I soon learned that questions about his previous life were unwelcome. Even a mild 'Where did you go to school?' might provoke a thunderous look, but if I ventured to ask, 'Where did you live?' his mood would darken further. Yet his silences only increased my curiosity. Was childhood too demeaning for such a great man? As I grew older and perhaps a little braver, while my knees still knocked I would ask the two questions that utterly infuriated him: 'What did your father do?' and 'What did you do in the war?' These often made him strike out in rage.

On one occasion after I challenged him hard about his past he finally snapped angrily at me, 'My father was a cotton broker.' Those few words stopped me prying for some months. Then, years later, when we boldly pushed him about his lack of relatives, he lost his temper and swung his arms out in a mock, or perhaps real, attempt to hit us. 'I had an Uncle Oliver. You must have heard of him.'

For all that, Stepfather could not resist occasionally tantalising us with a boast about his past years. If *Question Time* was on TV he might brag, 'Of course, it's not as good as when *I* appeared on it. The programme was called *The Brains Trust* and was on the

Light Programme. In those days, just after the war, everybody listened.' When I was older the question of why he had been selected was on the edge of my lips, but I resisted the temptation. I didn't want to hear another torrent of bragging stories, which always appeared too fanciful to be true. However, years later he could not resist showing us a huge antiquated audiotape in a metal circular box with 'BBC' written on it. Stepfather also seemed to know many TV personalities. He rarely liked them. The journalist and author Malcolm Muggeridge had once been his friend, but not any more; and when the politician Roy Jenkins or the historian A. J. P. Taylor appeared he always made some derogatory remark.

Stepfather's name fascinated me. Why was he called Louis? It was such a strange-sounding name. None of my friends' fathers had French names. Why did he? And why did nobody address him as Louis? Even my mother avoided using it. And pronunciation of his name caused all sorts of problems to others.

My stepfather was a romantic and always seemed fond of my mother, and she shyly returned his affections. He bought her endless bunches of flowers, showered her with expensive presents and never let her leave the house without a kiss. He always watched her walk through the painted blue gate from the landing window if she was nipping out with us children.

Of course that does not mean they did not have quarrels. There were lots, especially in the early years. When I was older, the rows were either about our behaviour or about a woman called Auntie Mamie.

When I was little my mother went shopping every day; of course, Stepfather came too. She rarely went out on her own. Our first stop was the baker – Mum would chat to the lady behind the counter as she passed me armfuls of bread to carry home. But there were other, more worrying, conversations that I overheard on the Cambridge pavements.

'Yes, of course, I'm still going to do the baking for the Mission to Seamen. Some of my charity works will stop, but not the one most dear to my heart.'

Even when I was that young, all did not seem right. Why did she have to repeat this to so many people? I wondered if my mother was somehow disgraced. There were other whispered asides that I didn't understand.

It was my mother who had to deal with the running of the house. She paid all the bills. There were times when Louis wanted more control. This always proved disastrous and he ended up exploding with anger with one of the poor individuals who were trying their best to help. My mother would then be called upon to use her charm to encourage the tradesman back to his job. But Louis's behaviour lost us the services of many local businesses for ever. Builders, plumbers, florists, stationery and book stores all experienced his wrath, but the biggest loss of all was the large department store Eaden Lilly. They banned him. It proved a great inconvenience to us all and slowly my mother began to do more and more of her shopping in London. But he even managed to destroy some of her fun there. There had been some sort of argument with the Harrods management about money owing. As a result, Louis refused to shop there any more. Little did I know that he had been refused their credit.

In the afternoons when I was very small Louis used to cycle into Cambridge. He first topped up the air in the tyres of his extra-sturdy bike, fixed with dynamo lights and three thumb-click gears, then he would wrap the bottom section of his russet corduroy trousers into tight tidy folds and clip each ankle with a black sprung clip. If it was colder he would wear his fawn duffle coat and Emmanuel scarf. As he opened the blue gate he would turn and wave at my mother who stood at the landing window. When he came back, I remember, he reported to my mother he had collected his post from his old college, kept in a strange box in the porter's lodge. He would also tell of visiting his mother and strange sister in Newnham, where they lived before they permanently moved in with us.

For, unlike like my friends' fathers, Stepfather did not leave for work in the mornings and return tired in the evenings. Instead, he lurked at home writing about golf. Then, as he became more interested in his wife's passion for motor racing, he developed his already well-honed photographic skills to publish a yearly account of the season's Grand Prix races. Each year he became more adventurous with his pictures and text and the racing circus began to fear each new edition, in case an individual was featured in an unflattering or derogatory manner.

Mum had been a proud housekeeper and Stepfather greatly increased her work. She always had a freshly ironed tablecloth at every mealtime. In those early days she must have washed and ironed a mountain of linen every week. She had needed a survival strategy. It evolved over the years. She subtly looked and waited for the opportune moment when Louis might be in a good mood – it would eventually come and then she would pounce.

One Thursday, after she had come home from her weekly shopping trip to London, she produced a big parcel, which she had bought at one of the smart stores she visited. She allowed us to unwrap the packet and, as we opened it, the unaccustomed waft of an oily product hit our noses. It was a plastic tablecloth. Stepfather looked thunderous. 'I'm not eating with that sleazy object on the table,' he said.

'We're trying it out while I iron the embroidered tablecloth. There isn't a clean one at the moment.'

I can remember mum's sheer joy at only having to wipe away drops of gravy, the odd piece of roast potato after it had shot off our plates, or spills from the water jug. Slowly the plastic cloth replaced the embroidered ones. She had won a small battle. Her victories were subtle, but they began to work for her. I watched her manoeuvre him to her advantage and I believed that, when I needed help, she would always do her best to win a small contest against him, for me. He was manipulative, so she became crafty.

Now I can write quite confidently that Louis Stanley was my

stepfather, but as a child I was perplexed. And there was nobody I could ask. He insisted on telling everybody else that we were his children and, as nobody ever mentioned a father other than this stranger, who had once given me a huggable teddy to replace my stiff-jointed monkey, I was confused. I don't remember asking questions when I was told that this massive, balding, thick-set man was suddenly to be known as Papa and not Uncle Louis. Nobody liked the name 'Papa', so Mum tried to use Poppy. But nobody liked this version of his name either.

I was always too frightened to ever ask questions about a real father. But I remember querying with myself whether I really had a proper father or not. I wondered where I had got the notion he might have been a vicar. There were times when I overheard gossip about a father having a possible fling with a maternity nurse. Was this my father? I asked. Then there were the whispering shopkeepers talking in lowered tones after we left their stores. Even then I felt everybody else knew more about the truth than I did. It was not until I started my investigations that I was to find out more.

When I was five or six, I started school. Byron House was based in a rambling Edwardian house with extensive grounds. Every morning we filed into the hall so that Miss Gimmingham, the headteacher, could take the register. Later on, if ever I was in doubt about having a 'real' father, I recalled my previous position in the register. Surely my surname had started with a 'B'. The voice of my teacher was an auditory reminder that I had once been at the top of the school register and now I had plummeted to the nether reaches of those children whose surnames began with 'S'. I kept the recollection to myself. There was nobody in whom I could confide. Stepfather controlled us with the divide-and-rule principle, so I felt unable to talk with my brothers and sister.

Stepfather was frightening. He was so severe I never even dreamed of disobeying him, even in the smallest way. The perplexing problem was that sometimes he tried to be nice. Looking back, I guess this was only when my mother was around. He could be brutal in his comments. He soon put a stop to my noisier games and banned me from my favourite sport of Grand Prix circuit antics on my small bike in the garden. He certainly did not want to hear any of us and if we hid ourselves away he was more than content. My brother was turned out of his large bedroom and put into a box-sized room so that Stepfather could have an upstairs study. There he hid away for most of the day, appearing only for meal times. Sometimes I could hear the tip-tap of his Olivetti typewriter but more often than not I heard popular music of the time blaring out, 'Moon River' being one of his favourites. Years later he shut himself away in his room with the telephone.

Stepfather's study was his sanctuary but he also used this private space to entrap the few visitors he had. There was something disturbing about that one step into his room. I had to pluck up courage to cross that imaginary boundary and sometimes I was asked to lurk. Guests were always deferential. Stepfather did not have friends. As they entered his study they were instructed to view the series of golf books he had written, then they were guided to admire the garish colours of the dust jackets of his motor-racing titles. Next, the visitors were asked to turn their backs on the shelves and marvel at his gallery of black-and-white snaps that were placed on the wall facing the door. They were his celebrity close-ups. Most of them also featured Stepfather. I remember the close-up of W. H. Auden, whose face was grooved by deep facial lines, and his pride when he added Elizabeth Taylor to his wall. Then there were Cecil Beaton, Orson Welles, Harold Macmillan and Gilbert Murray. I knew nothing about the people, and his interest in photography sent shivers down my spine, so most of the images remain grainy in my mind.

But I have a clearer memory of his haughty voice repeating the names of the people he was meant to know: Lord Birkenhead, Jo

Grimond, Eric Lubbock, the Aga Khan, the Du Maurier family, T. E. Lawrence, Duncan Sandys, Douglas Fairbanks, a man whose surname was Masterman, Oswald Mosley and the Mitfords, Lord Beveridge, Malcolm Muggeridge, Gilbert Murray and somebody strangely called Trevelyan. (We will meet some of these characters later.) He had repeated these names so often, how could I ever forget them? I wasn't interested in the fame of the people. I was fascinated by their nomenclature. Augustus John: fancy having the surname 'John'! I thought. The other name that amused me was Bertrand Russell. I was interested in its rhythm, but it stands out in my memory because Stepfather liked to call each male acquaintance by just his surname. So for years I thought Bertrand Russell was a double-barrelled name. Surnames such as Pitt Rivers and Goodenough amused me. Then there was the fascinating name that Stepfather always mentioned when he came home from London, which conjured up all sorts of geographical images: Beaverbrook.

Friends were something our family did not do easily. My mother was a social individual, but when she married Louis nobody dropped round. The blue gate outside our house became a kind of barrier to deter guests. If a neighbour was brave enough to open the gate and walk through the courtyard, more often than not Stepfather would get to the door before my mother and the poor visitor would leave crestfallen having had a thorough grilling. My friends suffered the same experience. Even when invited they were sent away from the front door without explanation. Often I never knew anything about their humiliation until years later.

My earliest experience of friends being banned from our house was around the time of my birthday. My mother enjoyed planning my party. She was adept at organising games. But as each birthday approached I became increasingly worried about whom I would be allowed to invite because in previous years I had cringed with embarrassment. Stepfather rudely forbade the same particular names. There was something strange about it. Even in those days I asked myself if it was something to do with his secret previous life.

My party always came to a nervous end, when the doorbell started to ring and other parents came to collect their children, my mother began to change character. I picked up vibes that she was embarrassed in some way. She stood uncomfortably on the threshold with the women who had once been her friends before Louis came into her life. To me as a little girl it all seemed so contrived. As I grew older things did not change. Stepfather's attitude to my friends was frankly rude. I lost precious pals and potential boyfriends. It was too scary to challenge him.

Thursday had always been a special day in my mother's life – it was the day she spent in London. As a treat I would be allowed to go too. It was always the same routine but the success of each trip depended on Stepfather's mood. As we drove down Park Lane I used to get butterflies in my stomach: what would happen when we reached the Dorchester's forecourt? Often there was a fuss, as Louis demanded to take one of the bays right outside the hotel entrance. We sat in the car as Stepfather spoke with the smart commissionaires with their pristine white gloves. They would shake hands and then, smiling broadly, one of them would direct my mother into one of the six prime spots. As time went on Louis did not even pretend to use the hotel, for, after leaving the car, he immediately called upon the same commissionaire to call a cab and we went off to lunch at Bendicks coffee bar in Wigmore Street. After the meal two taxis would be called and we went our separate ways, Louis to meet his publisher and my mother to the salon in Knightsbridge created by Mr Teasy Weasy.

As a treat Mum might arrange to meet Stepfather at five outside Fortnum's Quick Bar, but things would often go wrong. He would be late. We would wait for so long that my mother would suffer the indignity of the shop closing behind our backs as the assistants pushed us further away from their steps. Even then I suspected he liked to play 'waiting games' with those he could.

As I grew older the Dorchester Hotel featured more and more in Louis's life. He could not resist repeating every so often that in his previous life he had lived permanently there and that he had driven around in a Bentley. Again, to me as a child, this seemed an odd boast, as he never drove anywhere. Occasionally he went to London on the train and took lunch in the Dorchester's Grillroom, usually with a publisher he called 'Collins'. In later years there was no doubt in my mind that Louis had a passion verging on obsession about the Dorchester Hotel. He insisted Mum's car use one of its six precious parking bays for the whole of Thursdays. He also tried to use the hotel lobby as his own personal space – and often succeeded – and was constantly trying to convince us that the new chef, the head waiter or the manager was a personal friend.

Then, when I was much older and he was allowed to take more and more control of the motor-racing team of BRM, he held his meetings in the hotel's long elegant lounge. Then he progressed to hiring one of the hotel suites. My mother was very against this squandering of money and she persuaded him to lean on the hotel management to bend their strict rules. He did indeed exert his power over the manager and he allowed him to hire the suite by the day. But this did not stop his continuous boasting to the racing circuit that he had a permanent suite in the Dorchester Hotel.

It's difficult to work out how old I was when I think about some events in my early life, but I do remember Coronation Day in 1953. It was the first time I can recall having Louis Stanley around. I was five. The royal day proved for our family, as for many in the nation, to be the incentive to buy a television set. My mother bought everything for the house. He never paid for anything.

I clearly remember the excitement of watching the engineer set up the strange-looking contraption. There were wires everywhere and deep narrow holes to be made in the walls.

Later in the day, on the spur of the moment, Mum and my new stepfather decided to take us up to the Royal Mall. Mum loaded up the back of the red-and-white Hillman Minx with pillows and bedding and made a bed for my brother and me. As we left

Cambridge it was great fun pretending to go to sleep in the back of the vehicle.

It seemed no time at all before I was surrounded and squashed by tall excited adults. The crowd on that warm summer's evening was in a jolly mood. Clinging to Mum's hand, I was washed along with the happy throng, seeing only trousered buttocks, buxom hips in floral dresses and clasped hands.

As the royal couple emerged onto the balcony of the palace, everybody cheered at the same time. The noise was electrifying. The masses pushed forward and Stepfather picked me up and put me on his shoulders, but his hand moved up my legs. I waved my Union Flag with its balsawood stick, but the excitement was gone. The bed in the car was not so cosy on the way home. Stepfather frightened me.

Chapter 2

Those Women

When newly married, my stepfather imposed a more fundamental change to my mother's life than tougher domestic duties, for she was to receive two uninvited guests who occupied the best rooms in her house for many future years. She had to wait another thirty years to get her suite of rooms back.

I was probably only six, so I don't remember the details. I only know that one Christmas Stepfather's mother and elder sister came to stay, and that during the visit the senior woman apparently fell ill. I could never quite work out why the two women stayed, because they had a flat of their own in Cambridge, but I hasten to add there was a kind of rumbling, from where I don't remember, about how sick the older woman actually was. But Mum adapted and quickly changed our old nursery, a long tapering room that dominated the downstairs, into a flat for her new in-laws. As my siblings had been recently sent away to boarding school, my mother had looked forward to converting the newly available space, the best room in the house, into a sitting room. But her plan never came to fruition because Stepfather persuaded Mum that his two female relatives needed the downstairs washroom and pantry as well. My mother also lost her attractive Edwardian conservatory, as this provided the two women with their own front door.

I never heard her complain about the lack of rooms, but she found Auntie Mamie difficult to deal with. So did we all. She had no idea how to treat children. I soon learned to keep my distance. At the kitchen table my mother would occasionally lose her temper, telling Stepfather that it was his job to keep his relatives in order. Auntie Mamie told my mother tales that made Mum angry and occasionally she would declare she was a troublemaker. I never understood why. Now I suspect I can guess what the nature of the tales might have been, but even now I'm not sure. It was not until I was much older that I realised just how exasperating Auntie Mamie must have been.

My mother always encouraged her younger uninvited guest to take more care of herself. She was always giving her presents to cheer her up. On Sunday afternoons the two women walked across the hall from their side of the house to ours and joined us for afternoon tea. I don't know what I called Stepfather's mother. It may have been 'Home Granny', as she lived in our house, but, since she never became part of my life, I have few recollections of her. Conversation flowed easily between my mother and Home Granny but, as to her looks, I am hazier. I have no family snaps to remind me. Sadly, those were all thrown into a skip. But I get ahead of myself.

Little did I know then how important Home Granny and Auntie Mamie would become in my detective story. Just like Stepfather, they never talked about any relatives or their past lives. Home Granny never talked about her lost husband, nor did she ever mention the antics of Stepfather as a little boy. As far as I know neither she nor Auntie Mamie ever had any visitors. They just kept to their side of the house. The agreement struck between Stepfather and my mother was that, after Home Granny died, Mamie would move out. But of course she didn't. Stepfather was a great persuader and Mamie acted up her incapacity by painting her face with white talcum powder. The trick worked, so our dining room continued to be our sitting room and Mum only ever had half of the ground floor of her house.

Each morning as I got ready to go down to breakfast, I asked myself if Stepfather would be nice or nasty. I was now living in an uncertain world and I had to learn quickly that he could turn in a flash from being agreeable to being unpleasantly cruel.

Throughout my childhood it was an important part of Stepfather's morning ritual to walk across the yard to the letterbox, which was fixed to the inside of the blue gate. Eventually, when the weather turned foul, he let me retrieve the post for him, with strict instructions not to pry. Among the pile of letters often nestled a magazine or a journal in a strong brown cover, occasionally rolled like a newspaper. Each morning he balanced the hefty pile on his side plate. Then he poured 'today's' milk (the rest of the family had yesterday's offerings) over his Rice Krispies. He sorted the post into three heaps: one to be opened at breakfast, another to be taken upstairs, the third for my mother. She rarely showed interest. Her post was the bills.

I used to watch him slit open the envelopes from his breakfast pile, wrapping his thick fingers around the kitchen knife. He had huge hands. Occasionally I glanced at the back covers of the journals. Many of them had the word 'Economist' in their title, but the journals that caught my eye were the organs of The Royal Institute of International Affairs and the United Nations. There was another document with a bluish-grey cover that seemed to be about political affairs. I wondered why he had these journals, for they didn't seem to fit in with his life as an author on golf.

There was always trouble with the postal delivery to the Old Mill House, or at least that is what we were led to believe. I can remember numerous times when accountants or relatives told us they had sent letters. It always seemed that it was the post for my mother that never arrived. Tickets would go astray; letters from my mother's company would not arrive. Even those that had been sent by recorded delivery went missing. Louis's tactic was always ruthlessly to blame others, and on these occasions it was the bemused postal workers.

When I was older I recognised the journal with the greyish-blue cover. It was Hansard. One day, even though I knew I was encroaching on dangerous territory, I could not resist asking, 'Isn't Hansard about what they say in the House of Commons?'

'Yes,' came the flat reply.

'Why do you have Hansard?' I nervously asked, but he must have been in a good mood that day because he smiled. 'I just like collecting them,' he joked; 'I don't read them.'

Years later I was to discover that hiding the post was one of his games, but again I am getting ahead of myself.

Stepfather and I had one common interest: sport. He told me he was a leading authority on golf and, as there were many books on this subject with his name blazoned on the cover as the author, this seemed likely to be true. Stepfather appeared to understand my childhood thrills of running faster and hitting a ball further and harder than anybody else. When he was new to our life at the Old Mill House he encouraged my mother to enter me for the 'brothers and sisters' race at my brother's school. I won with ease. My prize was a huge powder-blue box of chocolates, with a matching ribbon and floppy bow. Later I was teased because, rather than share my prize, I went down to my den in the garage and ate the lot. However the box remained a treasured possession, which I hoped to show to my own children one day. Stepfather was proud of the action photograph he had taken of me as I rushed for the finishing tape. At the time I had no idea he had worked as a photographer. Sport gave us a certain affinity but it was a strange kinship. I didn't trust his motives for getting close, and desperately hoped I wouldn't find myself alone with him. If I did, I knew something horrid would happen.

Stepfather's past remained a mystery even when I was older. When I started to talk of school exams he told me that he had achieved a double first in English at Emmanuel College, Cambridge. I never doubted that this was true, for in those early days he always wore the college tie, while the scarf was part of his winter uniform. The colours were navy with cerise stripes. I disliked them and thought them garish. Stepfather seemed to be a walking encyclopedia on the cities of Cambridge and London, so again I never doubted anything he told me.

There was a time when I began to wonder whether Louis had been married before. Until then it had not concerned me. One night when I was about 12 my sister went to answer the phone. She came back into our sitting room in a state, saying, 'There's a man on the phone. He says he's Poppy's son.'

Everybody stopped what they were doing and looked at each other in shock. Louis pulled himself out of his deep chair and struggled to his feet; he had been in a half-slumber. But he was wide awake when he glanced at my mother on his way out. After the door closed behind him there was a long awkward silence, which nobody broke. We had been too well groomed to discuss any delicate matters among ourselves. Each person was left to ruminate on the significance of the call, as nothing was forthcoming on his return.

There were other embarrassing times when Auntie Mamie tripped up and called my brothers by the wrong names. At the time it was too unsettling to consider why she might do this. So we all ducked the issue. Just as I did with the memories of my own father, I buried them.

It is only now that I can allow myself to recall some memories of my biological father.

A three-flame gas fire had been fixed into the angular chimney-breast that dominated the room I had as a toddler in the Old Mill House. Mum had insisted on retaining the original floor tiles with only a low, raised brick rail, warning of the potential hazard of the heat of the fire. My real father must have left the family home in the colder months of the year, because I recall that my cot was placed parallel to the fireplace, which meant that it was at a peculiar angle to the long rectangular bay window that overlooked the sprawling lawn.

In those days children slept in their cots until they were four or five, so I can easily recall mine. It had solid legs and a sturdy frame with dropdown sides, and it was painted off-white. On the inside of the two curved wooden ends were hand-painted images of angels and clouds. I remember listening and waiting for the clickety-click of a side panel moving down over its ratchets – the signal that I would soon escape from my secure containment.

I don't know how long the tall greying man in the dog collar had been standing over my cot. My recollection was not of fun but of tears – tears that splashed, from a height, onto my upturned face as I tripped on the ends of my long nightgown, reaching up with my arms. His tall, thin body heaved and whimpered in his effort to disguise the pain. When he finally held me, the tears abated, but then a voice called from some eerie distant place that interrupted our moment. We heard the high-pitched, almost distorted, voice.

'Leslie, it's time to go. Come on, you must go.' He held me tight, looking over my shoulder.

The voice became more shrill.

'Leslie, it's time to go.'

I felt him shake as he gently kissed me on the cheek. Then he hurriedly put me back in my cot. I had no idea that he was leaving for ever but, as he left the door ajar, I heard his measured steps retreating down the back stairs.

Other memories of my father were scant. I could recall what must have been the Christmas Eve before his final departure. There were many excited adults and children in our large nursery. I remember a glittering Christmas tree placed in a wooden box in the huge bay window, and people were attaching clip-on candles to the lower branches. A lofty man whisked me up high in the air and flung me over his head. I sat perched on his shoulders way above the rest, so high I felt I could reach the beam that swept across the ceiling. I was thrilled with his jiggling shoulders that danced me around the tree. Exhausted, he settled down in a comfy chair and sat me on his knees. I was warm and secure in his arms as we looked at the elegant timepiece that he had on his left wrist. It had a worn and stained brown leather strap. We both gazed at the ticking of the tiniest hand, in its little sphere, a circle within a circle. The movement jerked as it jumped from one little division to the next, while the other larger hands had miniature arrowhead tips that tediously moved towards the Roman numerals and my bedtime.

At times I ventured into wondering if my memories had been wrong. But, if I was right, why was Stepfather so keen to introduce us as his offspring? Children are often uneasy with introductions, but for years I continued to find them embarrassing. The greatest discomfort was experienced on the motor-racing circuit. Through my mother's interest in Formula One, racing cars and their drivers were a normal part of our lives and Stepfather insisted that everybody be told that we were his natural children. Nobody ever dared to argue with him, and even when we were older fear kept us from ever using the term 'stepfather' even with our best friends. He had ensnared us in his lie and I carried this untruth into my schooling. Boarding-school friendships, like any others depend on honesty, so I never felt completely comfortable with my pals. To them this bulky man whose appearance was so frightening was my father. Each time he accompanied my mother and arrived in the school driveway I felt pangs of betrayal. I had let myself down. I parried if friends asked about his role in my life. I did not want anybody to know how much I distrusted him. What had started in youth continued into later life. I had been party to a lie and I knew no way to escape. What was my fear? I am not sure I can explain.

As we grew older we probably probed with our questioning a little more. Stepfather had no sympathy with teenage angst and, as he never mentioned his own father, we began in concert to be a little braver. On one memorable evening he rasped that his father had been a 'cotton executive', as he had told us on one occasion before. But when we asked a further question about his father we put him into a terrifying mood that lasted until the next day.

There was another time when I got into trouble asking about names. One evening Stepfather and Mum were talking about somebody with the surname Bonham Carter who had been mentioned on the Home Service (which later became Radio 4) on Mum's kitchen radio. 'Bonham Carter, that's a strange name,' I ventured.

'Yes,' said Mum in a supportive tone, her voice reaching me from around the corner where she was doing the pans at the old butler's sink.

'Fancy being called Bonham Carter!' I giggled.

But this was one step too far for him. 'How dare you?' he scowled. 'You ignorant little tyke!'

His retort was so harsh I felt as if a ton of rubble had fallen on me. Mum tried to defuse the situation and talk about our dogs, but the damage had been done. I was never going to forget the name Bonham Carter. But strange names kept cropping up in Stepfather's vocabulary. I was desperate to make some comment about the Aga Khan, Masterman or Trevelyan, but I had learned my lesson.

Beaverbrook was a surname that captured my imagination. One evening I was grateful to Bette Hill for helping me out when she and her husband Graham Hill, our entertaining racing driver and a world champion, came to dinner.

She was sitting in one of the broad chairs in the dining room, when Louis started to name-drop: 'When I saw Beaverbrook last week in the Dorchester Grillroom, he told me he was enjoying life but he asked my advice about what to do in a difficult…' 'Oh, so, you know that tycoon, as well, do you, Mr Stanley?' Bette Hill was one of the few people I knew who were brave enough to interrupt Stepfather. Perhaps she knew Stepfather was more civil to those who were useful to him. The evening must have been going well, because Mum was also in a jovial mood and allowed herself a sideswipe: 'Oh, Bette, Louis knows everybody, don't you, dear?'

He sighed at her but from his demeanour it was clear he took her words as a compliment.

Louis obviously thought we should be impressed, but the name Beaverbrook meant nothing to me, just like his other brags. But, as I got older, there remained a fascination about his mysterious past and I began to invent motives for why he refused to chat about his previous existence. I decided he and his mother, Home Granny, were suffering from unresolved grief. As neither of them ever talked about his father, I was sure this mysterious figure must have died when Stepfather was very young.

Mum used to try to justify to us why Stepfather was such a fussy eater – he wanted only plain food and always refused to try anything new. She explained, 'He had been a very spoilt child. His mother absolutely adored him because he was the baby she had always longed for.'

But her words did not justify to me why he couldn't drink the same milk as we did and why his toast was eatable only if it was one special shade of brown, with no crusts.

Sometimes my mother would elaborate: 'You see they wanted a baby and no baby arrived. That's why they had Auntie Mamie.'

She talked of 'they' and I had no idea who 'they' were, so I assumed she meant Home Granny and her husband – the man nobody ever talked of.

'What do you mean?' I would ask.

'Well, they were desperate for a baby and when none arrived Home Granny took Auntie Mamie from a hospital.' She paused. 'You know, she is much older than Poppy and she's his adopted sister.'

I still didn't understand the situation but she always finished her story with these words: 'What a thrill it must have been when Poppy turned up. How exciting it must have been.' And Mum always threw open her arms in empathetic glee. It did not explain why we all had to run around pleasing Stepfather, but as a child I accepted what she said.

I can recall many incidents that involved my stepfather's love of golf. He also enjoyed going out in the car and in those early days we dreaded his directing my mother to take him to another golf course. Here, he would walk to the golf professionals' hut, and all of us, including my mother – who had kindly driven him there – would be left sitting in the car with nothing to do but wait.

When we visited his hometown of Hoylake on the Wirral he told us he had been a scratch player. He boasted that all he had to do was cross the road from his house to play on his local course, the Royal Liverpool. At the time I thought he must have an exceptionally good player, as he had written instructional books such as *Swing to Better Golf*.

Then there were the many visits to golf championships. One day he and my mother collected me from primary school and sprang the surprise that, instead of going home to tea, I was going to the Open Championship at St Andrews. Mum, of course, drove all the four hundred miles far into the night. The town was like another home for Louis. He loved the Scottish settlement. Another golfing town we often visited was Lytham St Annes. It was fun to be out of school but I was beginning to miss vital lessons, and the fascination of walking on miles of flat sand soon lost its edge as Stepfather talked endlessly with his golfing friends in the failing light. On a rare occasion of honesty my mother whispered that she was bored as well.

Much later, I recall, when I was not living at home any more, he gloated that he was paid £10,000 for one golf article. I couldn't think why his words were worth so much, but I accepted that he had earned that amount of money, otherwise how did he keep up his lifestyle? It was not until much later that a cousin suggested to me that perhaps he was wildly exaggerating how much he earned. But, as life got busier and we became older, my mother finally put her foot down. She'd had her fill of striding around golf courses rushing to keep up with the players. She cleverly persuaded him to watch the competitions on the TV from his armchair. So he wrote golfing articles without actually being present at the tournament, which was quite an achievement in those days.

If he wanted to, Louis could be witty, entertaining, humorous and charming. It all depended on his mood, and more importantly the social status of the person he was with. If they were important to him he was almost a good host; however, if he thought the man would be of little value to him he would be treated with distain. Women were regarded differently.

Mum was allowed to tease him on the odd occasions. One Easter Sunday was especially memorable and relevant to this story. Louis had plonked himself down in his armchair after a chocolate filled day with one hand stuffed in his pocket, the other playing with the armrest. He had been in a reasonable mood all day and Mum decided to risk a little tease. 'It's hard to imagine that the Great Louis T was ever a baby.' She watched for a reaction before continuing, 'You are just too huge, too distinguished, too illustrious.'

'Go on, show them,' said Mum, making bigger waves with her arm in the direction of his seat. He was slumped low, his left hand was still jammed in his blazer pocket. Could I detect unease? We caught Mum's bravery. 'Show us,' we demanded. Cautiously he drew a small card out of his pocket. It was unlike Mum's photos, not shabby or curled or stuck with ageing corners. This print appeared pristine. An Edwardian baby sat in a pot-bellied perambulator wearing a lacy jacket and a frilly bonnet with ribbons tied under his chin. We took turns to study the picture but he never let go of the card. 'The great Louis T started as an exceptional baby,' Mum joked.

'So big for a one-year-old,' she giggled, 'really exceptionally large for an exceptional man.'

The Old Mill House had grown haphazardly over the four centuries it had been a family home. There had been three Victorian extensions with no architectural planning, so this meant the flooring upstairs was irregular. At the top of the steep back stairs was the long landing. Then two further steps led up to the bathroom, the toilets and the guestroom. At the top of the steps there was a loose floorboard.

Stepfather's hobby was photography, and when he first moved in he used to bury himself in the old scullery with a large collection of chemicals and trays of fluids. It was a large room. He used to give me undeveloped rolls of film, on which, I could etch a story sequence. Also there was a certain fascination watching the images emerge in the chemicals. With the noise of constantly flowing cold water washing the new prints, mixing pleasantly with the noises of clanging saucepans, chopping knives and family chatter from the kitchen, I felt safe. However, because his relatives had moved in and taken over the pantry he was soon relocated into one of the upstairs toilets. He now had a designated room. The toilet bowl was taken out and replaced with the large sink taken from downstairs. Cold taps were fitted and shelves made for all his materials. It was equipped with a high stool, a draining board, various trays for developing fluid and the latest photographic machinery including a large contrivance with a bulge that enlarged the image. There was a thin rope strung above the shelves for hanging prints to dry. The room was tiny. It could only be described as a cupboard. He was a large man, so there was little room for anybody else. The window, with its bubble-frosted glass, criss-crossed by shadows and outlines of wisteria branches, was lost for ever, as he had fixed a thick black roller blind over it. The only glimmer in the dark was the low-wattage bulb that had been painted red. The glow made the machinery look menacing.

The only lavatory in the house was located around the corner to his cupboard. To reach it I had to step on the loose floorboard that was at the top of the two steps outside his den. Luckily, his cupboard door had a noisy roller snap fitted. The slipping roller ball made a loud distinctive click as it was opened, and this sometimes gave me the opportunity to hide before he enticed me into his hellhole. And I mean a hellhole.

When I was small my mother always found time to visit my long-widowed maternal grandmother, of whom she was very fond. After the long journey from Cambridge I looked forward to spotting the two tall manorial columns that announced we had finally arrived on the New Hall estate. Built of large blocks of seasoned red sandstone with mullioned windows, the house resembled a fairytale castle. The name New Hall confused me, as it was so old. The house was originally built as a hunting lodge in 1071 but after an extension was added in 1340 it was called 'New Hall' and had retained the name ever more. With its many bold extensions over various periods it made a stunning country home. The moat held a particular attraction. As soon as the car stopped I used to leap from it and run across the tile-covered bridge, stopping for a split second to confirm that it still had crystal-clear water.

I was as enchanted by the moat as my mother had been. It retained its original depth and width, being fed by seven nearby springs. The clear water flowed through the moat and down to a millrace, where there had once been a working watermill. Large carp, pike and smaller freshwater fish had been caught by my uncles and were displayed as trophies on the walls of the billiard room. Obscuring the edge of the moat grew damp loving plants in abundance: marsh marigolds, buttercups and bulrushes.

But it was the water lilies I loved. Olive-green leaves formed huge matted clumps while the lilies' fibrous roots reached into the unsullied waters. The firm, elongated buds unfolded into leathery petals as the sun's heat warmed them. Some of the flowers had pencil-line brushes of pale pink.

But not all my memories of New Hall were so pleasant. One day when I was eight my mother hurried me into the car and told me that New Hall had been burgled. Both Granny and my mother were deeply upset when the police suggested that an intimate knowledge of the house had been required to carry out the crime. Hilda the cook and the butler, Green, had been there for twenty years, so Granny was sure they were not implicated. Even in those days I had vibes that Stepfather could not be trusted. I am not sure why but I didn't want to spend any time thinking about him.

A few months later two youths were found in the grounds mucking around in the outhouses. Stepfather wanted to take control and called the police. As the boys were too young to be charged he insisted they be taught a 'real lesson'. Granny's health was deteriorating by then, so she grudgingly agreed that the boys be given a beating. Stepfather made sure that my brother and I heard over and over again his plans to beat the lads. I have no doubt his gloating of the success of the thrashing was designed to terrify.

My mother was grief-stricken when my Granny died. Mum's tears fell in deluges on me whenever I saw her. She explained that I was not old enough to go to the funeral service.

'You're lucky Papa volunteered to look after you,' she said. She explained there was nobody else available to care for me.

I watched from my stool in the far corner of the sitting room as my uncles, aunts and cousins congregated. They spoke in muted voices and then slowly gathered to leave the house. Green had aged and was a lost soul. His mistress of forty years had gone for ever. Eventually the heavily clad door with its massive iron hinges closed. I heard the noise of the many car wheels roll on the gravelled quadrangle and then fade away as they made their way up the rutted drive. There was nobody left. I was alone with Stepfather in the massive house.

But I was happy enough. I had the tantalising solitaire board all to myself with hours to play. Stepfather was in the breakfast room next door, reading a pile of papers. Each marble had its own character and I had plenty of time away from competing siblings to admire their individual markings as I laid them in the hollow cups. When all the holes were full, I plucked out the central marble and placed it expectantly into the circular track. It displayed all its charm as it rolled in its groove with the friendly rustling sound of marble on polished teak.

After many a game, nature called and, as I came out of the lavatory, he was sitting waiting for me on one of the chairs in the large hall, which was up one flight of stairs. I have never felt more alone. My cosy bed and teddy bear could not protect me as they had done when 'things' had happened before in my bedroom. Abuse in the daylight was far more frightening and now I knew that he had abused my mother's trust.

When I was 24 and about to get married, curiosity got the better of me. It was, I decided, a suitable time to venture into unknown territories and find my father again. It had been easy to find the details of a man called Leslie Civil Baber in *Crockford's Clerical Directory*. It confirmed that my father had indeed been a man of the cloth. More importantly, it gave his address, so I wrote to him and was invited down to the New Forest.

But it was hard. I did not want to find out the dodgy truth about Stepfather's involvement in the divorce. Nor did I want him to know I had broken rank with his lie about parenthood. If I got found out I would be in for some well-chosen derogatory words. His succinct phrases spoken in his lowest tones would ruin my serenity. I knew his game and my proposed visit made me exceptionally anxious. But this was not my only worry. Maybe to rub salt into the wound he would have an indiscreet talk with Mum. It would ruin her equilibrium and I didn't want that.

The ageing stranger was ten years older than my mother. However, for a seventy-year-old he was tall and straight with his height exaggerated by his black shirt and clerical collar. It was his watch that caught my attention. It was an emotional moment when I spotted the same timepiece he and I had studied so many years ago

I sat by his tiny gas fire. Had I ever called him Dad? I realised at that moment I had never experienced having a father. Louis had fallen well short. My father must have been a man with energy: he had only just retired from his demanding insurance job in the city but spoke longingly of renewing his professional interest in religion and taking services in the local church. His enforced early release from the Church of England was a subject I did not bring up, but on my third visit, as my father attempted to light a fire with wood collected from our walk in the forest, I ventured into the past.

'Did you love my mother?'

'Yes,' he replied as he reached behind his long legs to find the unfashionable and uncomfortable sofa. He sat down, the slow movement allowing him more thinking time. 'Yes, I think we loved each other.'

I tried to envisage my mother as a vicar's wife. There had been times in my childhood when she had allowed herself to make what for her were quite cutting remarks about the uncharitable nature of women churchgoers. What provoked them? Mum was rarely rude about anyone. Maybe her local community hurled hurtful comments in her direction when she divorced. Had my father experienced cruel comments as well? I persisted in my questioning, 'Did my mother enjoy being a vicar's wife?'

'Yes, very helpful. She…' He paused for some time. I had jerked old memories. Now I had to pluck up courage to ask about the nature of his divorce and I realised I didn't even know where their parish had been. While he stared at the kindling as it spat out its dampness I persisted against his hesitancy. With his eyes still on the last few flickering flames, he spoke in a softer voice. 'I did something wrong, very wrong.' He paused. 'I can't tell you: you're not married.'

He sat back defiantly into the faded sofa. It was my turn to think hard. Was I to surmise that his wrongdoing had been of a sexual nature? If so, the rumours I had overheard as a child must be true. But which rumour? Was it an affair with my maternity nurse or the married woman? Or was it some other sexual act? I resolved to pursue the matter on a later date. But I never brought up the subject again.

CHAPTER 3

EARLY DAYS

On my last visit to see my mum she had been on great form. Nobody would ever have guessed that she was eighty-nine years old. She never needed to visit the doctor and her sharp brain had not dulled. She was still able to make her hair look as if she had just returned from the hairdressers but now she favoured a new softer less back combed style. A bouffant hairstyle had been my mother's trademark but she had not achieved this without a great deal of effort. She never went to bed before one in the morning. Stepfather never allowed her go to bed before he did. So at midnight and often much later, I would find her sitting on her bedroom stool in front of her three-panelled mirror with the radio blaring out any kind of music. She vigorously brushed her hair to remove the hairspray. Then carefully she combed sections onto her homemade cotton wool rollers. Her backcombed hairstyle was held in position by spray for 'hard to hold' hair. In the days of Grand Prix racing Louis insisted she backcomb her hair to silly heights to fool people that she was tall. Over the years she increased the amount of lacquer with 'extra firm hold' until even a strong breeze left her hair unscathed. Stepfather forbade us children to touch her hair but if I accidentally brushed it, it felt like a rough netted bag with a squishy inside.

Shoes also helped Mum disguise her lack of height. She wore the highest shoes she could find with the most tapered heels. She could wear them all day and when she became fond of gardening she even worked on her herbaceous beds in them! The leather tip on her highest stiletto shoes might only last one or possibly two outings. Her taste in shoes allowed for some amusing family tales: frequently her stiletto was caught in a drain, or a crack in the pavement or worse still a manhole cover. She had too many narrow escapes to ever agree to stand on an escalator.

As we became older we realised that Stepfather was able to whip Mum up into an emotional state. Occasionally something would bug her and she would sound tense. Each time we discovered that Stepfather had been winding her up. It worried us but there was nothing we could do. Then Stepfather demanded we buy her more and more costly presents for her birthdays. It was a powerful tactic.

As the couple grew older we began to be anxious about what might happen in the future. However, when she became worried about the state of her finances a warning bell rang inside my head. I decided that her trusted accountant, Mr L, ought to know. As I talked privately to the man I had met many times before I surprised myself by blurting out that I had suspicions that my mother's money might be going missing. I even surprised myself by asking this adviser if Stepfather could be the subject of blackmail. His reply bowled me over as he said, 'I've learned over the years to rather like Louis.'

Why did he say this? This man was Mum's trusted guru and was acting for her. So, rather than act on my vague suspicions, the accountant ignored my warnings.

I tried to forget about the meeting. I was powerless.

We had all individually pondered, when we were children, over Stepfather's behaviour with our mother, but none of us had noticed how odd it was. It was our partners who appeared fascinated as to how and why our lovely mother had married such a problematical man while we had accepted the facts that no friends called on our sociable mother and she never went out on her own. Sporadically, sometimes over a glass of wine, our spouses encouraged us to conjecture what Stepfather had done in his earlier life. We had not thought him worthy of speculation.

There was a memorable time when I first suggested that perhaps his father had been an MP. 'Why do you think that?' asked my siblings. I had no absolute answer but they accepted my justification. 'He seems to know so many politicians and people in that field,' I replied. My siblings agreed it was possible and even half-heartedly searched for MPs with the surname Stanley. There had been a number of 'Stanley' MPs, and I found a photograph of one called Arthur, but none seemed of the right age, and, as we were not particularly interested, we never continued our search. One day, much later, I had turned to a historical text and spotted a photograph of Prime Minister Asquith. It had made an immediate impact on me. But, as I had no real reason to enquire further, I left the book unread and tried to forget the unmistakable likeness.

In those early days, golf and steeplechasing were Stepfather's preferred interests, not Formula One cars. Mum eventually persuaded him to enjoy the motor races and when I was just six she took us children along too. So even as a very young child I visited the rarefied atmosphere of the racing paddock and became fascinated by the huge complicated engines. It is the noise of the sport that has left its legacy with me. Even now when I hear a souped up car in the distance I relish the noisy power of the engines reverberations. Every time my ears pick up the sounds I am reminded of the powerful roar of the V16 BRM and my childhood.

I am not alone. Motor racing enthusiasts still reminisce about the pitch and volume of the BRM's 16-cylinder scream. Motor pilots of that generation recall that the engine roared its power with such ferocity its noise distracted even the most seasoned drivers as they waited for the flag to drop.

How did my mother come to be so involved in a Formula One racing car in the days when women rarely had careers?

Two enthusiastic and idealistic men called Raymond Mays and Peter Berthon wanted to emulate the might of the partially state-funded German motorcars of Auto Union and Mercedes-Benz, which had dominated racing up to 1940. So after the war the British Racing Motor Company was created. Its racing cars were to be known by the initials BRM. With great national excitement the first model, called the V16, was unveiled later in the year. Everybody agreed that it was handsome and hugely powerful. However, raising enough money in austere post-war Britain was always to prove a problem. Mays decided to contact companies involved in the motor trade. Rubery Owen, our family's firm, was one of his targets. My two uncles took the bait alongside a large number of other motoring companies.

However, too many people, too soon, had wanted to see the car race with too little money. After much national hype, the first all-British Grand Prix car painted in patriotic Brunswick Green rolled onto the Silverstone grid for a demonstration run on 13 May 1950. The shrill V16 exhaust excited the crowds. But the world's press wanted the car to race, so in August of that year the *Daily Express* funded a Silverstone race. The paper hyped up much public interest in the patriotic car. All the engines roared while the drivers waited for the flag to drop to announce the start of the first heat. All British eyes were on Raymond Sommer, perched in the cockpit of the BRM. To add to the tension, the royals looked on from the grandstand. The starter's flag fell and the race began. The BRM lurched forward to start its great career. But calamity struck! The drive shaft broke and the huge machine failed to move further than a few metres. To the humiliation of all involved, the V16's race was over before it had begun. The crowd in the grandstand jeered and catcalled the mechanics when they appeared from the pits to push the car back to the paddock. The British press condemned the car's dismal failure. One paper headlined its front page with FLOP and another lined up the letters with BRM calling it a BLOOMING ROTTEN MOTOR!

I can remember Mum hiding her eyes in shame as she told me the story of the car with its chassis made by her family company, failing to leave the grid. Even though they were only part of a consortium of companies, she and her brothers had felt the nation's shame on their shoulders.

After more outings that demonstrated that the cars were too unreliable to win races, the BRM Trust was disbanded and put up for sale. My Uncle Alfred and to a lesser degree my Uncle Ernest retained faith in the car's potential, so the family firm, having recently expanded to be known as the Owen Organisation, bought BRM. It was a rash decision.

The modern industry of sleek, sponsor-endorsed, computer designed, semi-automatic cars, racing on pristine tracks with every possible facility, bears no resemblance to the fun loving sport of the fifties recovering from the traumas of a world war. It is now a billion dollar business for the ever-expanding racing teams and has little to do with a 'sport' in the original sense of the word.

In the fifties and sixties motor racing was colourful and exciting, full of dash, verve and characters. The rash youths of the day, frequently the sons of the world's wealthiest families drove for pleasure, often recklessly and at breakneck speeds. There was little or no sponsorship with many of the cars financed on a shoestring. Mechanics from each team were friends and lent each other vital tools. In those times each part of the country had its own racing tracks; most were nothing more than old wartime airfields converted to form a circle. Safety for both drivers and spectators was rudimentary or in some cases nonexistent. Circuits used farmers' straw bales to line the track or a tricky chicane. Their combustibility caused many unnecessary fires. Trees and telegraph poles were left to stand beside the track without a thought of their treacherous ability to kill.

Post-war cars were powerful. Even in the fifties racing motors could reach the type of speeds Formula One cars race today. But race technology was in its infancy. Engineers tried to apply lessons learned in the war from the performance of jet engines to racing cars. However the rest of the mechanical workings of the cars had not developed in line with the sheer pace of the engines.

Fire-protective clothes had not been invented so the drivers wore ordinary cotton overalls. Their gloves might have leather palms but were often string-backed and bought off the peg. They may have worn soft-soled shoes but there was nothing to protect them from the scorching heat of the cockpit. When I look at old photographs I realise their hard-hat style helmets provided little protection. As they sat high up, almost out of the vehicle, I loved to watch them change gear and struggle with the vibrating steering wheel. If the car should turn over they had no roll bars to protect their heads and no seatbelts to hold them in on the bouncy tracks. The only way of communicating between engineer and driver was by a metal board held out by a mechanic for the driver to read a coded message as he screamed past the pit lane.

Each car represented a country and they were painted accordingly: the German cars which had dominated racing prior to the war were silver, the French cars were blue, the Dutch orange, the Italians had their red Ferrari and Maserati, and the British cars were green.

Stepfather hated being an appendage. That's why he hated motor racing in those early days. BRM was part of my mother's family company and it was her hobby. He didn't want anything to do with it.

It seemed incongruous that Stepfather did not drive – especially later, when he stealthily eased himself into becoming joint managing director of the BRM racing team with my mother. We knew he *could* drive, but he never did.

I hardly dare recall the terror of the afternoon when we, as children, had goaded him to prove to us he could drive. I was very small and he had driven like a maniac through the villages of Cambridgeshire. It was so terrifying we dared talk about it only once and that was in earnest whispers. We never teased him again about his rejection of the driving seat – we had learned our lesson. But this did not stop him repeatedly telling us stories of his adventures in fast-moving cars. His favourite tale was about driving his Bentley through the London backstreets, racing and betting with others as to who might reach the Dorchester first. His stories never made sense. Why did he have a Bentley? If he could drive, why demand that my mother do all the driving? He was a man who always liked to show off, so why did he ask his wife to drive in prestigious situations in front of Formula One world champions? I even remember sloping around in the back of Mum's Isis with Jack Brabham. He was beside me and leant forward over the seatbacks earnestly listening to the conversation from the front. Mum drove while Louis took the front passenger seat. He would not allow even that year's world champion to take his seat.

Could Stepfather have been banned from driving? It all added to the dark mystery of the man. But there were so many strange things about this stepfather of mine. He had huge amounts of energy and anybody who could not keep up with him was always referred to as 'a wimp'. Nobody was allowed to say they were tired. He had no patience for anybody who might be frail or infirm and he could change in seconds from a jolly mood to a persistently black one.

My earliest memory of motor racing was the race for the Silver City Trophy at Snetterton. It was the poor relation to the more prestigious Brands Hatch, Silverstone and Goodwood, but it was the nearest of the five big circuits to Cambridge and we supported the track whenever the BRM was entered.

The day did not start well. Our tickets did not arrive in the early-morning post, so we had to wait for the late-morning delivery, hoping for our entry passes and parking discs. Tempers were frayed before we left the house. Once again Mum would be in the driving seat. As we sat in the traffic jam outside the track we heard the menacing machines leap away from the distant grid. We had missed the start and our automatic right to enter the Paddocks. This led to a most embarrassing altercation outside the main gates. Stepfather pointed his thick fingers in a menacing manner at a group of men and demanded that we be allowed to enter. But he was not well known at that time and they refused us entry.

'If you won't let the car in, get your snot-ridden youngster with his acne spots to run to the BRM pits to collect the tickets for us,' he snapped, while Mum shuffled uncomfortably in the driver's seat, leaning over the gearstick and trying to smile at the steward but to no avail. For once there was no option but for Mum and Stepfather to split up. My mother and I were directed to park in a desolate area on the furthest side of the track.

The route back to the paddock lay along a tufted grass path running alongside viewing banks, often so high they blocked my view of the racetrack. As a group of cars roared past I scrambled up one of the hillocks to see if I could spot the familiar green bonnet of the BRM. The noise was thunderous as they first braked and then accelerated around the corners. At the next bank Mum joined me, slithering unceremoniously in her heels. I steadied her, as a tightly packed group of cars roared past. In the bunch were two BRMs tussling with a Cooper. We squeezed each other's hand.

The finish was perfect: the cars accelerated for the line and Ron Flockhart took the chequered flag. The P25 BRM had won the Silver City Trophy. Flockhart, a dashing Scotsman, grinned from ear to ear as he struggled to undo the chinstrap of his helmet. He wiped his hands on his sweat-stained cotton overalls and there were handshakes all round. To my delight he insisted on shaking my hand. Even Stepfather clapped everybody on the back and spoke in loud tones. I remember little else of the day, but winning had been intoxicating. The joy was infectious. Other drivers, their mechanics and team managers all made their way to congratulate the BRM team. I became entranced.

For one single hour at that racetrack, Stepfather was not by my mother's side. I was her only companion and she enveloped me in her new world. Before my eyes, my mum became the impassioned supporter of a green single-seater racing car in which daredevil men, in battered helmets, drove around circular roads with tight bends at death-defying speeds. After all the disappointments of the past years I understood that BRM could win races!

As years went by, tickets became a source of fun for Louis. He always wanted get to more prestigious places on the grid where he would normally be barred. So he brazenly forged himself a counterfeit fancy arm-badge to deceive all the foreign authorities, and, when travelling abroad, he insisted on an opulent vehicle that would impress the many gatekeepers who had previously wanted to keep him at bay. Once Louis found a German chauffeur who was willing to use his huge hired Mercedes as a battering ram through the crowds and past the lines of irate marshals in his own country, he never let him go. Later, this chauffeur was driving him down a series of Alpine hairpin bends when they met a bus full of schoolchildren. The bulky Mercedes was unable to squeeze through the gap, and both drivers refused to move. After an altercation, Louis got out of the limousine and into the bus. He took the keys out of the ignition and threw them down the ravine, leaving a bus full of children stranded on a mountainside.

Most of the major races were held in the school holidays or on bank holidays. I never tired of watching the BRMs being unloaded from their transporters and pushed around the paddock and eagerly waited for them to roar into life. The cars had to be 'push' started so every time a motor needed to be fired up two strong mechanics stood behind the machine and shoved with all their might for ten or twenty yards until the momentum allowed the driver to ignite the sparks. The last minute trouble-strewn hasty scrambles to overcome mechanical gremlins were all part of the fun of racing.

I remember Silverstone circuit as little more than a windswept airfield with basic facilities. The paddock and pits were located on the island of land inside the circuit and so each year the organisers had to build a temporary access bridge to provide pedestrians access to each side of the track. This was the fifties and the bridge was just made out of scaffold poles and planks. As each car roared down the home straight the ill-equipped bridge shook terrifyingly.

Being allowed into the pits never lost its thrill. It was where everything happened. They were just narrow concrete bays with no facilities but once practice started they became full of life. From my corner I watched the race mechanics carry to and fro their metal toolboxes crammed full of essential implements. In the less important races the mechanics allowed me to find the metal number tiles that were slotted into the drivers' message boards.

I probably enjoyed the thrill of being close to complicated engines more at Oulton Park circuit than anywhere else. It was not a championship course and everybody was more relaxed, as the races were treated as experimental outings. Because the circuit was in Cheshire, we usually stayed up North, in either Chester or Liverpool, the two cities Stepfather loved. In fact, looking back, I would say he changed character when we in the vicinity of the Wirral. He was more relaxed, took control of navigation and was always trying to tell Mum some story about the history of the towns.

The Adelphi Hotel in the heart of Liverpool was no treat for youngsters. It was built of large sludge-coloured stones and had grey-coated commissionaires who attended its revolving doors with a bored disposition. The hall gave me the impression that only the staid and serious were welcome. Stepfather tried his best to be on cordial terms with the local staff and he made it quite obvious he wanted to share his knowledge of the city with them. Sometimes while we were up there I recognised a hint of a Merseyside accent appear through his plummy voice. Even though he was secretive about his childhood, once up North, he loosened up and admitted that Cheshire was his home county and he loved the city of Liverpool because he was brought up in a small seaside town, Hoylake, on the other side of the Mersey. Liverpool Football Club was his passion and at every opportunity he anxiously looked for their results on news agency's tickertape. When we were in the area he usually wanted to stay a night at Lytham St Annes, another seaside town with a famous links golf course.

However, it was at Aintree trackside that we heard him brag to the BRM team, 'Well, of course, my family is related to the Stanleys of Liverpool. Stanley Park is named after them and the Earl of Derby is a relative.' The boast seemed very odd. Why had he chosen to tell strangers about his family and not us? So when he was in a good humour I asked, 'So who were the Stanleys of Liverpool?' To my utter surprise his mood changed dramatically.

'You know nothing,' he snapped, trying to finish the conversation.

'Yes, but I want to learn – who were the famous Stanleys?'

'They owned most of Cheshire.'

I felt anxious, as Mum had left the room, but my childish curiosity was too great, and once started I was not going to let go, so I continued with my questioning.

'And the Earl of Derby, who was he?'

'He was rich and famous, a politician, owned many racehorses and swathes of land in Liverpool.'

But that was as far as I got because Mum reappeared. I had got him exasperated and he now had a good excuse to send me away with a flea in my ear, telling my mother I deserved a good hiding. As always, I never discussed my questioning with my siblings. We were cultivated not to. But his behaviour did not stop me thinking. Why did he have no relatives other than the two women who lived in our house? If his family were so well known, why didn't he boast about them? He never stopped crowing about knowing celebrities, so why didn't he show off about his family? Once, I was taken out of school (he was always trying to persuade Mum to do this because my schooling limited their movements) and I joined them for the famous Aintree steeplechase. On the night before the horse race I had been allowed to stay up to dinner because I was frightened of my drab, dark hotel bedroom, and I sat and watched as Stepfather romantically took Mum off to the dance floor. When I returned to Aintree later that year it intrigued me that I had previously seen the magnificent jumpers go anticlockwise while the racing cars went clockwise on the same piece of land.

An earlier meeting at Aintree motor circuit is etched in my memory because of its ironical nature. On that day Stepfather risked all our lives, but years later he became well-known in his fight to improve motor racing safety.

Mum had dragged Stepfather along and he had bought a couple of Leica cameras with all the accompanying paraphernalia: light meters, holdalls, hundreds of rolls of fast film. He took his shooting-stick on which he precariously perched his huge frame. Over the years the metal frame had became so cluttered with sporting entrance tickets that the seat refused to close. On the first practice day he marched my siblings and myself round the course, where he stopped at various places. He sat for hours on the tiny seat, absorbed with the viewfinder of his Leica, practising moving the camera in synchronisation with the car as it flashed by.

During the afternoon practice session he would want to be at a position near the track, where there were no spectators to disturb the swing of his camera. As the cars started to appear for practice, we walked around the course and based ourselves at the end of the Sefton Straight near the Melling Road. In front of us were some rusting poles, bending in unison, when the brisk wind blew across the undulating land.

I jumped out of my skin when the first car came hurtling

towards us. I tried to make my legs run for my life but the shrieking of the tyres and the engine cackling transfixed me. I closed my eyes, as the driver appeared to head straight for me and thrashed with the gearstick. After he had disappeared around the double-twisted turn, I turned to find Mum, equally terrified, pulling at Stepfather's jacket sleeve.

'We can't stop here, we're right in their path. I have to take the children to safety before another car comes.'

'You're my wife. You're not going anywhere without me.'

'I think the children are frightened and there's nothing to stop the cars coming straight into us.'

'Don't be wimps,' he shouted at us, trying to be heard above the noise of the next car approaching. 'This is an ideal place for photographs of the cars in action.' The noise abated and he rasped in his usual way: 'Come on, darling, there's nothing to fear, they're just making a lot of noise. You're not taking the children away. We're watching expert drivers here. They know what they're doing.'

Mum made more protestations, but all he said was, 'There is this protective line of poles in front of us. Come on. You'll soon get used to it.' He was clearly enjoying himself. He turned to me and said, 'This is something to tell your friends about at your primary school.' How little he knew me! I rarely told any of my friends about my home life.

As the next car stormed towards us, I noticed the driver had difficulty controlling the rear wheels as the back of the car swayed into the chicane. I gripped Mum's hand tightly– it was cold.

She tried one more time to lift her voice above the scream of the next car: 'I'm sure this is far too dangerous for us all…'

'Don't be silly, dear, this is fine,' Stepfather replied, not lifting his head from the viewfinder. 'You're getting an amazing view from here. You'll soon get used to the cars coming straight for us.'

In the silences, I listened for the distant rumble of the next car as I searched the horizon for what appeared to be a tiny black fly that climbed the hump, before it came bearing down on us at over one hundred and eighty miles per hour. I grimaced each time, but I no longer closed my eyes, as I was fascinated by the cars, often with one or more of their wheels off the ground.

From a distance all the cars appeared to be the same colour and shape as they sped towards us, and I could only identify individual cars when they were upon us.

Mum and I felt more reassured when we recognised the BRM was out on the circuit with Harry Schell, our charismatic driver, at the wheel. Stepfather continued to concentrate on his photography as we watched our hero find the last possible braking point before drifting through the double bend.

Mum, with stopwatch in hand, predicted when the American would appear over the brow of the hill. It seemed less alarming now we had the BRM to watch. At the allotted time I scanned the horizon for his car. Then, there he was, the uneven surface jostling him from side to side as the car bounced up and down. As he approached, I anticipated the noise of the jangling gears and screaming brakes but I did not expect the gesture: Harry raised his gloved right hand and gave us a big wave!

'Did you see that?' I yelled over the screech of the departing brakes.

Mum was as amazed as I was. Stepfather had missed the excitement as his capacious nose was still pressed tight into the sights of his camera.

The lap time of one minute thirty seconds appeared more like one and a half hours as I waited for Schell to reach the top of the small incline again. Finally there he was, bearing down on us, this time I was ready with my hands in the air. As more cars joined the practice session the noise became continuous, so conversation was only possible during brief pauses between cars. The pungent aroma of the shredding tyres hung in the air and I could taste the spent fuel. Finally the session was over and the track was quiet. My legs were like jelly. My mother, obviously relieved, was full of chatter.

'Oh, Harry Schell is such good fun, isn't he?' she chirped. We all agreed. 'Fancy having the time, on that corner, to give us a wave!'

Back in the paddock, Harry was grinning, happy with his practice times for the day. Mum congratulated him, 'That time is brilliant for the first day. Fancy having the time to wave at us on the Sefton chicane – the fleas [a term she liked to use for us children] really enjoyed that. You've made their day; they can't stop talking about it.'

'Oh, that's all part of the fun,' he replied, 'but I was also trying to warn you. That's a treacherous position to watch; if any of us had lost control, like a car did last year, we would have ploughed straight into you.'

Suddenly Stepfather had slunk away. Mum stuttered, 'But there's those iron protective railings…'

'They'd fall like a pack of cards. That's not any protection for cars, that's for the horses. They wouldn't stop a Hillman Minx at ten miles an hour.'

Two further stories concerning Aintree race track show Stepfather's persuasive powers in the city he had loved as a little boy. There had been a last minute disaster (BRM was good at late night dramas) and the mechanics who had already worked through one night, were facing the prospect of doing so the following night. Mum felt sorry for them so asked Stepfather to do something to help. He was in home territory and was on good form so he found the local beat policeman. Then he cajoled this neighbourhood 'Bobby' to unceremoniously knock up the local publican and demand he provide beers for the BRM mechanics at two in the morning!

The other story was on the morning of the British Grand Prix. Unusually Stepfather had gone out on his own, visiting some of his old haunts. He was late returning and Mum fretted wondering how they were going to get to the track in time. He walked out of the Adelphi Hotel and to my mother's utter dismay 'hailed' a police car. He presumptuously told the local traffic cops that he was urgently needed at the circuit. Needless to say the local coppers agreed to give my mother's car a police escort. The persuasive powers of this most extraordinary man had worked once again.

After our experience at the end of the Melling Straight we never watched from unprotected corners again but motor racing in those days was lethal. In those days drivers died. It was a common experience for those you knew to die or be injured so horrifically they never raced again.

Wolfgang Von Trips died before Stepfather became involved in safety – he helped fight the track authorities to make circuits safer and organised with others the provision of the first fully equipped mobile hospital for drivers – and his death made a big impact on me. This German was one of my favourite characters, because, alongside his dashing good looks, he made a point of talking with me when I was only very young. He never drove for BRM but wanted to keep his options open.

In 1961 he demonstrated that he was a top-flight driver and was leading in the championship points table. All he had to do was to win the Italian Grand Prix and he would be named as world champion. It was lucky for me that I did not attend, because disaster struck. At full stretch his sizzling red Ferrari was hit by another car. The momentum of the crash shoved his Ferrari up a steep bank and into a group of spectators. Fourteen of them were killed along with von Trips, known as the 'uncrowned world champion'. His death was poignant for us all.

From then on my mother lost more nervous energy every time BRM raced. And, whether we had won or lost, she would exclaim, 'Well, thank goodness the race is finally over.' We all knew what she meant and after each new death her comment took on a new poignancy.

Years later, after I had left home, my mother experienced two traumatic deaths in one year. First there was Pedro Rodriguez, an attractive Mexican who had proved a wonderful tonic for BRM, driving superbly at a time when team morale was low. But disaster struck in 1971, when he was injured in a sports-car race in France. All contracts in the late sixties included a clause that forbade drivers to compete in races other than Formula One unless they sought permission. When we first heard of his accident we discussed why Rodriguez had risked driving in such a minor meeting without seeking authorisation, while Stepfather started to compose Pedro's ticking-off. But a few hours later we learned he had died. From that moment my mother began to emotionally pull out of the sport. It was not just the grief but also the huge disappointment. After a lean time things had been looking up and now her hopes were dashed. She also had a difficult diplomatic time, as Pedro had a wife in one continent and a mistress in another.

My mother's greatest fear had always been that a driver should die in a BRM. It was not long after Pedro's death that the inevitable happened. Later that year, Jo Siffert, the moustached Swiss driver, hit a bank in a minor race at Brands Hatch. He suffered only a broken leg but his car burst into flames, demonstrating the inadequacies of the safety systems of the times. My mother was emotionally devastated and resolved to ease out of her involvement with BRM.

Stepfather was not heartless but he dealt with the deaths on the track in a very different way. He must have been affected. Talking about a death made him stern, but I never saw any sign of emotion. He was an enigma.

My mother's role in Formula One was an odd one. Stranger still in the 1960s, she was in the macho world of motor racing. She chose to be the ambassador for her family company. In the early years, when we were all young, she was a passionate supporter of her team. She advised but she had no official role. However, as my uncle got busier and more races were held on Sundays, she and my stepfather took more control. When it was clear that Uncle Alfred would not be able to retake the reins of the company after he suffered a debilitating stroke in 1969 my cousins agreed that, as my mother knew so much about the Grand Prix circuit, she should take on the running of the team. But what were they to do with Louis Stanley? He had been causing trouble for the company for many years, so much so that my uncles employed a gatekeeper to confine his bizarre ideas for development to paper. Not only that, but he had taunted my uncle by writing libellous articles about him. However, the family took his antics on the chin. A compromise was made and it was here that my cousins made my mother and him joint managing directors of BRM. At least that way they could keep their 'uncle' off their backs while they dealt with the parent company.

I return to the day I first drove to Cambridge after hearing my mother had suffered a stroke. Stepfather's short message reported she had suffered only a mild stroke, but my legs felt weak as my body responded to my brain's commands to get out of the car. What was I going to find? It was a nasty feeling that would return, time after time, over the next two years.

The bell still jangled merrily over the blue gate but as soon as I entered the courtyard things felt different. It was gloomy. There were no powerful kitchen lamps lighting the way to the back door. There was no Mum at the butler's sink looking out through the netted kitchen window for me. Nobody came to the back door, so I had to ring the bell. The back door was actually the front door now but it had kept its wrong nomenclature since the increased traffic made it uncomfortable to sit under the veranda and the front gate was boarded up for lack of use. This left the blue gate the only entrance to the yard and, beyond that, the house.

Inside, there was no noise and the air was cold. The four forceful gas hobs that were always burning in the kitchen were turned off. The radio was silent and there were no remnant smells of cooking.

Mum was lying on her double bed, awkwardly placed on her back. How had she got there? Why was she not in hospital? She was unable to move but her glazed eyes gave me slight hope, as there was some semblance of recognition. Suddenly I realised I knew nothing about the care of stroke victims but it seemed odd that she was lying on her own bed with no medical attendance.

Stepfather kept repeating, 'Everything will be back to normal in a few days' time.'

His face held a grim expression and was serious but he was friendly enough.

'What can I do to help?' I asked.

'Thank you, but no thank you,' he replied. I had heard him say that many times before.

My siblings had all turned up and there was general murmuring as to the when and why of my mother's health. It appeared she had been getting ready for bed the night before when she suffered her stroke. The faithful weekly cleaner had said she had been unusually stressed. We whispered together as to why Louis had waited until eight the following morning to call the GP. It was all very peculiar. But I told Stepfather that I would stay the night and went to bed in the narrow bedroom next to theirs. As I tossed and turned, I could hear mumbled voices through the wall. I willed myself to believe that my mother's speech was a sign of her early recovery. But it was not long before the quiet footsteps of Louis came to rest outside my door. I wanted to pull the covers over my head. The door handle turned. I heard him ask if I could help.

The sound of his approach had reminded me of the terrifying nights of my childhood…

When Mum came into my bedroom to say goodnight I demanded to be tucked in tightly. She saw it as a game. Sometimes, when she was reading me a bedtime story, the whole room seemed to joggle up and down when Stepfather came to give me a goodnight kiss, his footfalls evident from the protesting floorboards outside my room. More undesirable were his 'other' visits. Mum would have gone downstairs to prepare his supper, as he eased the door softly open. The hinges creaked, but only quietly, and his footsteps made the ornaments quiver, not shake.

He found an excuse to talk and, after cocking an ear, he would reach down under my blankets. I didn't like it. I did not know why I couldn't confide in Mum. I just knew I couldn't.

The abuse progressed. He started showing me his penis and how it grew to be a different shape. He never wore underpants. He demanded I touch it and I was pleased when he allowed me to escape this task by turning the other way. It all seemed very eerie and unnerving. He would grunt a little and then get his handkerchief out of his jacket pocket to clean himself up. I was desperate to keep my eyes closed because all the action seemed very close to my face.

I tried to shut down my brain, but then the nightmares began. I was possessed by a recurring dream. I had a passion for Matchbox toys. Every Saturday I looked forward to buying a new vehicle with my two-shillings-and-sixpence pocket money (12.5p in decimal money), but in the nightmare instead of dreaming of the Matchbox containing a miniature steamroller, I woke with a deep apprehension that it might have a tiny living baby inside.

The visits kept getting worse. Even though I was innocent of even the most basic facts, he started to talk about watching Mum and him doing something in their bedroom. The depth of my nightmares increased and with a heightened sense of survival I knew I had to stop him.

Then one night he said he would arrange for me to be hidden in one of the cupboards in their bedroom. This sounded petrifying and I was rigid with fear. I kept thinking and scheming: there *must* be a way of stopping him. My final plan was simple: I would shout as loud as I could. It was something I *could* do. Once I had my plan I was full of resolve and keen to put it into action. But, the next time he walked furtively across the bouncing floor, the resolve ebbed out of me. I was furious with myself for my inability to stick to my scheme.

I don't know how many times I let myself down. Each failure created more self-doubt and frustration. When I opened my mouth all I could hear was my breathing. I decided practice was needed, so I went down to the bottom of the garden and let rip.

The next time he entered my room I screamed and screamed and screamed. He turned to leave, only to meet Mum rushing towards my room with her apron awry and her hands covered in flour. She looked aghast.

'What on earth has happened? Are you alright? Have you had a bad dream? What's happened to you?'

Her words came tumbling out. I sat bolt upright up in bed, looking out of the window, with the orange street light falling across my covers. I had tears in my eyes but I wasn't crying. I had done it. Mum never asked me again why I had made so much noise. But, from that night on, the abuse stopped.

Chapter 4

Why Act Like This?

The morning after my mother suffered her stroke, a cheerful district nurse came through the blue gate. She had organised a rapid-response team of nurses to call at various periods in the day and night, and she went off to find Louis to tell him the good news. I worried about the series of nurses finding their way around the rambling house in the dark. So, despite leaving my two younger children to fend for themselves, I declared I would be staying another night and busied myself with jobs around the house as I waited for each new set of nurses. I allowed myself to lie down and wait for the team that would arrive between two or three in the morning. I listened for the familiar bell above the blue gate to warn me they were here. When it jangled I looked down from the landing window as the team hesitated in the yard, I flung open the narrow window with its blue shutters but they failed to see me as they bent their heads low to avoid the wisteria branches. I had never leaned out of that window before. Mum or Stepfather had always used that upstairs position to wave goodbye to each other if either was leaving the house for an hour or two. Stepfather did not like his wife to go out without him. She went only when she was buying essentials for our schooling. Standing at my mother's back door welcoming the nurses was even stranger. I had replaced my mother. I prayed it might be only days before she could reclaim her role.

Relief spread through my tense body as I welcomed the two smiling nurses, one male and one female. I admired their cheeriness at such an hour as they chortled their way up the stairs. It did not seem kind to break their relaxed mood but I felt it important to warn them that Stepfather could be difficult.

'Oh, don't worry. We're used to that. Nothing fazes us. You wouldn't believe what we have to face,' the fresh-faced young man replied, catching the eye of his colleague.

As I pointed out the door to my mother's room, he sent me to find a suitable basin, which could be filled with hot water. When I returned they were still standing outside the bedroom door.

Stepfather's domineering voice came from within. 'I expected a nurse, not some namby-pamby who calls himself a man. Get out and leave us alone.'

I looked at them nervously. The youth was the first to recover his composure. 'I'm the only qualified nurse. My assistant has not even done the basic training.'

'I'm not having a man in this room. Just keep out.'

I poked my head into the doorway to start to negotiate but Louis pointed his thick fingers at me. 'You can go away.'

The male nurse was not going to give up so easily. He kept up a continual chatter through the doorway, eventually negotiating that his unqualified assistant and I should be allowed in the bedroom with the door being left sufficiently wide so that we could hear his directions. The water I had collected was now cold, so I went to fetch more.

There was more trouble on the following morning and I hung my head in shame when the cheery district nurse was sent packing. She had dared to suggest that Mr Stanley had to accept the nurses who were on duty, whichever their gender. Things were looking grim.

The consultant in geriatrics arrived at the house the following afternoon. His prognosis: my mother's swallow reflex was weak and in three days' time she would be dead. She would drown in her own mouth fluids. Stepfather reacted calmly.

I was in utter shock. She appeared to be making progress but I had to accept the expert's verdict. I thought of my first night in the house. How had she managed to swallow the painkillers with our drops of water? As the consultant had ordered her to receive nil by mouth, I worried whether our helping her swallow paracetamol had done her damage.

The district nurse took me and my siblings aside. She said the words I hoped I would never hear: 'If your mother was to start to fail would you want her to be kept alive?' The words were hard but the decision was easy. We told the nurse about my mother's living will.

I wanted to help Louis as much as I could. I knew it would be hard but my mother would have wanted me to be by his side. I rushed home to my own family and grabbed some essentials, sorted out my children's arrangements and was back on the road within minutes. As I drove back to Cambridge, I thought soberly of what a tough few days it would be.

Two days later I had another shock. On the stairs I met Pauline, one of the nurses, and asked if I could help her, but she backed down the steps away from me holding a tray covered by a teacloth.

'Can we go somewhere quiet?' Puzzled, I took her into my old playroom. 'I found this under the bed,' she said, and she lifted the teacloth and showed me a menacing pistol.

'Oh, it's the gun!' I responded, trying not to sound as shocked as I felt.

'Did you know about it?' she asked. 'I was going to show it to my managers.'

'Oh, Mr Stanley always told us he had an air pistol. He told me he kept it beside his bed in case of uninvited guests. It's nothing to worry about,' I said, hoping I sounded convincingly light-hearted. I looked at the gun again. It didn't look like a harmless air pistol to me.

My mother's fighting spirit proved the consultant's prognosis inaccurate and she began to make some sort of recovery. But my problems were only just beginning.

For, although the district nurse had persuaded Stepfather to order a lifting hoist and a hospital-style bed, within an hour he had changed his mind and cancelled the orders. The ordering of the bed and hoist in the next few weeks was to cause the nursing staff numerous problems, because Stepfather would not stick to any fixed arrangement. He was back to his old forceful self.

I thought about him and I realised I hardly knew the man. But over the years I had watched my mother cajole him to behave, so maybe this was the best way to deal with him.

The NHS struggled to organise more suitable nursing care and the rapid-response team continued to call, but things were not going well. By Week Two, Stepfather was not listening to family or medics and just repeated, 'Thank you, but no, thank you' when offers of help were made.

Unfortunately, my mother's stroke had occurred at the busiest time of the year for the NHS. They could not supply a steady rota of nurses and, as the shock subsided, Stepfather began to throw his weight around. Worryingly, he was not listening to medical advice, nor was he listening to us. He was making decisions on his own. When our offers of help were made he just repeated, 'Thank you, but no, thank you.'

First, he announced that he was going to employ a private nursing agency but at that time we, as our mother's children, still felt involved. The nursing agency's manager approached my siblings and me, and asked for our views. It was agreed that the ideal arrangement for my mother was to supply one trusted capable nurse so that a friendly bond could be made between patient and carer. Little did I know that this would be the last time we would be asked our opinions.

However, the time of the year was working against us again and the agency could not find any permanent live-in nurse who could start before Christmas. So, strictly as a temporary measure, they supplied nurses in an eight-hour shift rotation throughout the day and night. But, as the festival approached, gaps began to appear in the nurses' rota, so my siblings and I agreed among ourselves to cover for the times when there was no care. As we were not medically trained, it soon became obvious that more consistent help was needed.

Stepfather was moody and he had taken one of the burgundy tub chairs that had sat in the hall for years and placed it on my mother's better side. It was cumbersome and its placement made it difficult to get close to my mother. I also noticed there were grumblings from the visiting nurses about having to cook proper meals for Stepfather, who was becoming ever more demanding. So I suggested to Stepfather we find a live-in carer who could cook and would supplement the visiting temporary nurses. We children would fund her. Stepfather happily agreed to my plan. So, even though he had rebuffed me, at times like this I felt the team spirit was not entirely lost.

After ringing round a number of the caring agencies I struck lucky: an experienced Scottish lady had become unexpectedly free and was happy to stay over Christmas and New Year. 'Your mother will love her,' the agency owner enthusiastically briefed me. 'She can travel down tomorrow.' With a burst of energy, I went to prepare Janet's old bedroom. For forty years the room had not lost its original nomenclature. Janet had been our mother's help all those years ago. As I tidied, I looked at the décor. My mother had converted it into a fun room her grandchildren adored. It was up two short flights of steps and it was like visiting a turret. A fireplace took up much of the room. Blue wallpaper covered the walls and on the ceiling she had painted gilded and bronze flying swallows, which circled ever closer to the central light rose. Over the mantel hung a hand-painted mirror. Around the looking-glass pond my own grandmother had painted bulrushes and swans hiding among the meadowsweet. I could still hear my mother's voice explaining the artwork to my children as they snuggled under the turquoise duvet covers. As I smoothed the cover over the freshly made bed I hoped the carer would love this pretty little room.

From the bus station, I collected our carer, Bonnie, who had travelled down from Edinburgh on the overnight bus. As she dropped her duffle bag into the boot and climbed into my car, I warmed to this spirited Scot. She enquired sensitively after my mother's health and it became obvious as we drove that she had a keen sense of humour. I was sure Mum would grow to love her. Her broad Highland accent reminded me of Louis's past boasts about living as a resident in Edinburgh's Caledonian Hotel. He knew the North Berwick coast well and talked knowledgably about the seabirds on the Bass Rock.

Christmas had always been the highlight of my mother's year. She made every effort to make the house and especially the table look gloriously overburdened with tinsel and crackers. Christmas 1962 was highly memorable as it was the year BRM won the Constructors' World Championship. That year the last race of the season was to be held in South Africa on the day after Boxing Day. There was no live TV coverage, just radio updates and phone calls. My mother decided to keep the tension at bay by pretending it was a 'second' Boxing Day. So the dining table groaned with food and crackers as we sat waiting for news. Luck was with us that day and Graham Hill cruised home in first place.

But Christmas was very different this year. Mum lay paralysed on her bed, so, instead of much to-ing and fro-ing through the blue gate by family laden with presents, it was nurses arriving and departing. Mum had already decorated the dining room and had prepared the decorations for the table before she was struck down. So I cooked a Christmas lunch and Stepfather came down from my mother's bedside and joined us for the meal.

In many ways it was an awesome Christmas as Mum was making such good progress: her speech was good, her face had no signs of paralysis and her personality was unchanged. I enjoyed helping Bonnie look after her. That evening she smiled at me as I helped turn her from one side to another. She was almost like a Christmas rose blossoming. 'That's a good smile, Mum.'

'Well, you gave *me* such a good smile I had to smile back.'

I felt I was getting my mother back. As the New Year arrived, she was in less pain. She could sit propped up and her brain was active. Her left side was paralysed but the doctor was hopeful she would recover most of her movements with manipulation from a physiotherapist. The system of three nurses visiting for eight hours each was clearly not ideal, because they were not consistent, but, since the holiday period was over, I was hopeful Stepfather could find a quality live-in nurse who could be ably assisted by Bonnie, now everybody's darling. Stepfather liked her and she had developed a fine strategy with him, for she knew he liked to talk about Scotland, especially the seaside town of St Andrews. Louis knew everything there was to know about this town.

However, Louis had been in foul moods with the visiting nurses and kept changing arrangements. Most worryingly he had changed his mind about a permanent live-in nurse. He had rung the nursing agency and made the excuse that there was not enough sleeping space, even though there was plenty of room. Instead, Louis wanted to continue the emergency arrangement of three eight-hour-shift nurses. I was upset. The various visiting nurses were pleasant enough, but they were not the same as having one friendly face for my mother. Also, the nursing organisation warned us that the cost difference was massive. Instead of one salary, Stepfather would be paying nurses by the hour on the 'emergency rate'. The managers of the agency had never been under such pressure before and collapsed into agreeing to the bizarre agreement.

My siblings had all been working hard in their own way to help the situation and we all started to resume normal life, but we began to wonder why my mother had not been taken to hospital when she was first struck down. The hospital was less than five minutes away, so what had happened that night?

I began to ring the house both morning and evening to relieve Mum of her boredom. Stepfather gruffly answered the phone, just as he had always done. It was clear the nurses had been instructed not to touch the receiver. For the first few months after my mother's stroke we had a courteous conversation before Stepfather passed the phone over to her. But then the excuses started. The reasons why I could not speak to my mother increased in variety and frequency: she was eating, having the bed changed, being dressed, the physiotherapist was visiting, she was sleeping. He asked me quite charmingly to ring back, but when I did the phone was engaged or went through to the answering machine. Siblings and cousins started to report similar problems. Just as with me, Louis promised he would ring them back but he never did. What did my mother think? Had he told her that family called? Or was she left to imagine we had all abandoned her?

Each month the difficulties increased. I was slow to realise it was a strategy. He asked me to ring at a certain time but when I did he refused to answer the phone. The following day he would innocently claim that Mum had needed attention when I called.

Every time I redialled the Trumpington telephone number, I was reminded of days when I was much younger. The phone had been a vital weapon in Stepfather's armoury. The timing of his calls had been the bullet. He loved to make surprise night-time calls when more sensible people were already asleep. For his most seriously manipulative calls he employed his lowest tone of voice.

I decided that, if I could not speak to my mother on the phone, I must visit more often. Each time I made sure I took him a small gift and looked after his needs as well as my mother's. All went well to begin with and there were times when Louis was pleasant. When he was in a good frame of mind I often stayed with them both until the night nurse arrived at ten o'clock and saw Mum settled down for the night.

But then things became more worrying. I could not get physically close to Mum. At first I just thought it was the awkward arrangement of the bed and his chair, but as things deteriorated I wondered if it was all part of his plan.

I had no option but to share Mum's 'good' side with Louis. As she could not turn her head, sitting on the other side of her bed was not possible. Even giving her a kiss was awkward from this angle. Stepfather's tub chair was always in the way, so holding hands was impossible, and across the void holding any sensible conversation was hard. He sat there like a large pudding, blocking my way. I had two options: to stand at the bottom of the bed and lean over so she could hear me or to sit on a stool at the foot of her bed. Leaning for long periods soon became very uncomfortable and when I was on the stool my mother had difficulty seeing me. Concentration was difficult, as both of us had to work too hard to hear each other with the TV in the background.

Louis dominated the situation. He sat in the tub chair, his long legs stretched out, obstructing me from pushing my stool any closer. My protestations were unheard. He just smiled or glowered according to his mood as if I had said nothing. He adamantly refused to move his seat. Nor did he ever leave the round chair. When I prepared to leave he would ask, 'When can you come next? It's so nice to have you here.'

But when I rang the next day to tell him I could come the following Sunday, he said it was not convenient and that I would have to book further ahead. A month later, weekends were not convenient and he said I would have to visit on a weekday. It began to be very stressful. It was a long drive and the traffic queues were appalling. To my work colleagues I was becoming unreliable and forgetful. I began to feel helpless and sleep eluded me.

Then at other times Louis rang me up to chat. He often sounded like a broken man. My emotions were in tatters. I didn't know how I felt about this man. At times I wondered why he wanted to talk to me so intimately. Others were beginning to suggest he did not have our mother's best interests at heart, but I continued to try to support him. I felt sorry for him. I did not realise I was caught in a trap.

I was upset that my mother did not have one regular nurse, as we had originally planned, but I was pleased that Mum had begun to build up some sort of relationship with her three eight-hourly nurses. Of course, she loved the bright character of Bonnie, who was allowed by Stepfather to help the nurses in the mornings, but he did not permit her to sit with Mum and chat.

Five months later, Mum was displaying her determination to rise to the challenge with her physiotherapist. She was struggling to walk again. As Mum could now take teetering steps around her bed with her frame, she would constantly ask when she was going downstairs. However, the more she recovered the more she began to feel trapped in her bedroom. A plan was devised so she could move downstairs. Here she would have the best room in the house, the one my mother had lent to Stepfather's mother and 'Auntie' Mamie, both of whom are by this time, long dead. Once she was downstairs Mum would be able to be move from room to room and go into her beloved garden.

Meanwhile, Stepfather's behaviour was more outlandish.

CHAPTER 5

WHAT TRICK WOULD HE PLAY NEXT?

One day my phone rang minutes before I was to host an important AGM. Stepfather told me that, while the household had slept, Old Mill House had been burgled. The news ruined my concentration, so instead of socialising with my colleagues after the meeting I made my excuses and drove straight to Cambridge. Louis was so ultra-careful about security, and each night he carefully locked every door. Why had he forgotten? There were other mysteries. Why had the replacement night nurse who was meant to be alert to all my mother's needs not heard the burglars? They had walked up and down the corridor outside my mother's door. How could this have happened?

The double bay windows in the dining room had been smashed open and the thieves wandered from room to room stealing a number of items. Stepfather told me the police had interviewed the nursing staff. The temporary night nurse sitting beside my mother agreed she must have dozed off while a carer whose bedroom was above the dining room heard the crash of broken glass from her bed but had done nothing about it. It all seemed very odd. Louis was so strangely calm. Did he know this burglary was going to happen? I thought of the burglary that happened when I was small at New Hall, my grandmother's house. What did he know about that? Or had Stepfather now employed so many different nurses that there had been a bad egg among them?

Stepfather used the burglaries as a catalyst to employ more staff. Joe, an Irishman, whom he had recently asked to drive him around locally, was now to work full time. He was to be a jack-of-all-trades in the day and was asked to remain overnight and stay in the kitchen. The situation sounded weird. But Stepfather had more plans. He now set about ordering wildly expensive individual electronic deterrent grilles for all the downstairs windows, and when I visited he appeared even more distant with me. Each visiting day became a trial. Joe's job was to vet each person as they came to the door. He was acting as Louis's bouncer.

Eventually, the day came when my mother could escape from her bedroom prison as she called it. All was ready to initiate her move downstairs and on this occasion Stepfather did call everybody to help. But when I arrived the atmosphere was tense and I was not allowed into my mother's bedroom. All the furniture had been moved while the nurses had prepared a special carrying hoist, which would allow her to be manoeuvred down the L-shaped flight of stairs. At one o'clock Stepfather told everybody to wait in the kitchen. As we waited, the original shift nurses chatted like old times and told us our mother was excited. However, as time went on we anxiously watched the clock and, as the hour hand moved slowly round, we started to run out of topics of conversation. At four o'clock the message came from 'on high' that we were all to go home. Stepfather had destroyed another working weekday and we had failed to see our mother.

As soon as I reached home, I rang him. He did not explain why the plans had changed but just said a lift was a far better idea.

So he now had a new project. He rang every lift company in

the country, refusing to discuss the matter with any of us. I had lost any control over him and felt increasingly isolated. The nurses appeared nervous and spoke with more reserve. Pauline whispered that she was concerned that he had ordered a top-of-the-range wheelchair that was highly unsuitable for stroke victims, while he boasted to me that he had bought a flashy new Chrysler car. We questioned his decisions but he left us feeling there was nothing more we could do but wonder at his ever-growing need to throw his weight around.

On some days he played almost the model man; polite, loving, gregarious even humorous at times. I managed to have another word with the GP. I told him I thought his behaviour was bizarre and questioned his sanity. The GP dismissed me with a flourish, "He's not mad but may have a personality problem." I was once again stymied.

The system of visiting nurses was not working. More and more nurses I had never met appeared for their eight-hour slot beside Mum's bedside and each new nurse had a rude awakening when they addressed my mother for the first time. Stepfather responded in the same manner to each of them: 'My wife has not invited you to call her by her first name. Wait to be invited.' Over all the years he had insisted she be called Mrs Stanley on the racing circuit, which had often produced some embarrassing moments when colleagues had tried to address her differently. But his own name caused even more problems, for an individual might try to call Stepfather 'Lewis', 'Lo-is' or 'Lowees'. Stepfather would rudely turn his back and snap, 'My name is not that; I am called Mr Stanley.' If the person was a woman he was more accommodating.

It was the fun-loving American racing driver Dan Gurney who could not get to grips with having to call him 'Mr Stanley', and it was he who coined the name 'Big Loo'. The name caught on fast around the circuit. While the American commentators at Watkins Glen noting his chauffeur driven limousine decided he must be an

English baron. Much to Mum's embarrassment Stepfather did nothing to contradict them. Louis was canny. At least in the early days of motor racing he always made sure he was on good form in racing drivers' company and he could be quick witted especially at others expense. He enjoyed belittling others by addressing them with just their surname. Graham Hill, after many years, was one of the few who managed to cajole Louis into allowing him and Bette to call my mother Jean, but Stepfather made Graham wait until he had won the championship for this privilege.

Jackie Stewart also drove for us but he never became as close to our family as Graham. However, when he was severely injured at Spa, Stepfather accompanied him in the back of the ambulance. Jackie was semiconscious and talking nineteen to the dozen about anything that came into his head. What happened next became one of Jackie's favourite after dinner jokes. In the confined space of the vehicle Jackie said, 'Lewis, what do you think Helen, my wife, will say?'

'Look, Stewart,' replied Stepfather, 'if you insist on calling me by my first name, at least call me Louis, as the French pronounce it. LOO-ey.'

Jackie jokes that his inappropriately timed ticking off was so severe that it brought him round from his semi-conscious state, so much so he was no longer worried about his massive injuries or what his wife might think.

The two months it took for the lift to be fitted was an eternity for my mother. The doctor thought her progress remarkable and she was thrilled to be finally downstairs. She could sit in our old playroom, where as children we argued over the differently coloured Penguin biscuits at teatime. The room had more recently been redecorated in one of my mother's brave styles. She had chosen black-and-white check wallpaper but the chests in the alcove, crafted to store my toys, were still there. And so were my toys.

The problem was that now I could not go upstairs, for a nurse was instructed to make me wait until Mum was ready to see me. Mum had to be dressed and safely ensconced in a chair with her feet raised. Long gone were the days when I was allowed to help. He organised a similar chair to the one he used upstairs, but this time it was square, velvet and plum-coloured. It was of course placed on her better side. With her feet set at an angle it was again hard for me to get close. Conversation was difficult. On the next visit Louis told me he was organising an impressive launch party for his latest book on motor racing at the Dorchester Hotel. To rub in the grandness of the event he made one phone call after another while Mum and I sat looking at each other. As we tried to speak across the empty space and over the noise of his voice she admitted that to amuse herself she was counting the checks on the walls. This was serious. She was becoming more and more isolated from any kind of proper care and I had lost any control over the situation.

For over six months the Cambridge agency had been charging Stepfather on an hourly 'emergency' basis for its nurses. Their fees, we thought, must be over £8,000 a week. How were my mother's savings standing up to this? When I tried to raise my concerns Stepfather dismissed my comments, but there were also disturbing rumours. He had not, as we had thought, bought the Chrysler and a new Daimler outright: a Cambridge car company had lent him the money. The odd-job man found out that he had been driving uninsured cars. The thought hit me: had Louis refused to pay the garden wall repairers not because of bullishness but because he had run out of money? Had my mother's savings already gone?

Even more worrying was the fact that my unfortunate mother was one of the 16 per cent of stroke cases who become subject to epileptic fits. We learned this not through the proper channels but through the nurses' grapevine. Luckily, experienced nurse Pauline was on duty when my mother had her fit and, even though Stepfather had refused to allow her to call 999, she had the presence of mind to overrule him.

Now a feeling of hopelessness came over me. My mother's quality of life was wretched and she was on drugs for the first time in her life. We knew she had not wanted to finish her days like this. We renewed our efforts to fight for her dignity. Each day we fought with the professionals that now encircled stepfather. None were prepared to listen to us.

His glamorous party began to be Stepfather's only topic of conversation. Each time he would go through his list of guests. He now intended to invite four hundred guests, many of them celebrities. Even more worryingly, he was insisting my mother attend.

As the bright and breezy Bonnie had been such a success, my siblings and I agreed we should continue to pay for her. If our stepfather did not allow us to give practical help, at least we could provide funds for somebody who could. The caring agency's contract for the employment of Bonnie had been signed by me and I organised to collect the monies from my siblings to pay for the invaluable household help she was providing for my mother. But trouble was round the corner. Stepfather had his own devious plans, of which I was totally unaware.

After a few months I noticed that the caring agency's fees had steadily increased. I checked their figures and they told me Bonnie was now working longer hours. But the following month the fees escalated again, and before they could provide clarification the next month's accounts arrived and they were double what I had expected. As Stepfather prevented me from visiting the house I was not able to ask Bonnie what hours she had worked.

The Old Mill House's phone was constantly engaged but when I did finally speak to Stepfather he told me the agency must be at fault for the escalating costs. 'I can't understand why they are demanding more money from you all,' he said, sounding completely innocent.

Two days later he rang in a particularly sweet manner. 'I hate to say it,' he said, 'but your agency rang me up to say you have not paid your bill. They'll stop providing Bonnie if you don't pay.'

I was perplexed. What was Stepfather talking about?

I rang the agency but they only got bad-tempered with me for querying the bill once again. Each month they were now demanding double the amount I had initially agreed to pay. As I could not contact Bonnie I was beginning to feel I was going mad with confusion. Whenever I managed to speak with Stepfather he kept telling me the agency was at fault. This caused the manager of the agency and me to have some bizarre conversations, in which each of us could not understand what the other was talking about.

Finally, I had the answer. Louis had double-crossed me. Behind my back he had found the details of my agency, talked with them on the phone and asked them to send another carer, even though he already had Bonnie and the three nurses from the Cambridge agency. One carer, he told my agency, was not enough for his situation. This same organisation obeyed Stepfather without contacting me, as he had instructed them not to involve me. Stepfather was so assertive with them that they did not question this strange request. By this devious behaviour Stepfather had manipulated us into paying for two full-time live-in carers while he already had too many nurses kicking their heels with little to do. It was a cunning ambush.

This was not the end of his trickery for, soon after the first fiasco, I started receiving phone calls from a third caring agency, who had been told we wanted another (a third) carer. Luckily, the manager of this new agency was more level-headed than the others. Once he heard the weird nature of the situation, he pulled out.

But what were we to do about my agency, who supplied the wonderful Bonnie and whose manager had fallen for Stepfather's duplicity? Were we stuck with paying the bill for the two carers, one of whom my mother clearly did not need? He had manipulated us into an emotional conundrum. If we did not pay the full bill the wonderful Bonnie would have to leave. I could not allow that.

Stepfather had lied and manipulated me, but I was still not willing to believe he could be so wicked to purposely damage me both emotionally and financially with his tricks.

I had to be strong enough to throw off my childhood fears and investigate Stepfather's background. If his life was so mysterious, maybe we could reveal something that might help our mother in her hour of need. My siblings and I had all been working hard in our different ways to help her but now we needed concerted action on how to deal with Louis. We agreed to pool our knowledge of his past life and asked each other penetrating questions. The first time we had ever done such a thing. To be discussing Stepfather behind his back in such a serious manner disturbed me. We had been groomed not to. Each of us agreed there must be dark secrets in his past. We tried to look at our childhood memories with adult eyes. It had all seemed peculiar. Even though his mother and 'adopted' sister had lived in our house he seemed to lack a family. Why did he never talk of his own childhood?

Then there were questions about his previous life. What had he done? He gave out annoying boasts of driving Bentleys and living in hotels but no firm evidence of any real work. We had to investigate further. We pooled our knowledge on his own father. Each of us had heard him say in the distant past that he had been a cotton merchant. But that was all. Perhaps he had never had a father. Was he illegitimate? We laughed. I reminded my siblings of my previous thoughts on his employment. Then from out of my mouth popped the words, 'Perhaps he's the illegitimate son of an MP.' The words seemed to fall out of my mouth like a knee-jerk reaction.

At first, I think, I was trying to make a joke, but then I became deadly serious. I don't know whether it was the increasing pressure of Mum's predicament, the fact that this was the first time we had opened up together, or whether the subliminal thought had been in my mind for years, but I surprised myself. My world was immediately turned upside down for, as the words left my lips, I felt a deep conviction that my proposition could be right.

Stepfather loved to drop political names into any conversation whenever he could. I recalled his return from trips to London when over his late-night bowl of Rice Krispies he would endlessly brag about whom he had met, and who had come over to his table in the Dorchester Grill Room. It had not crossed my childhood mind that they were politicians. I was bored by it all. Birkenhead was particularly interesting name because I never knew if he was talking about the place or the man. I never dreamed he was a politician.

When I decided to ring my mother's cousin Daphne, who had been Mum's closest friend when they were both at school, I wondered if I was doing right. I was breaking a family code. It was a difficult phone call but I finally got round to saying, 'We suspect that Louis may not be quite what he seems.'

There was a long silence, and then she uttered these words: 'Your mother was my dearest friend. Louis destroyed our friendship.' I gasped. 'There was a time,' she continued, 'when the four of us met up in a New York hotel. Your mother and I went to the ladies' room and in there we had a good old natter. As we were leaving the washroom your mother said, "Oh, Daphne, this has been such fun – you see, I'm not allowed any friends." '

My worst fears were beginning to be confirmed and I realised that Daphne was right. My mother had been denied any freedom. Her only social contacts were the hairdresser and the baker. No neighbours ever called.

'I'm not sure if you want to know this or not,' she said hesitantly, 'but there was a commotion in the hotel lobby. Louis had bribed the doorman to organise a cameraman to photograph him with Charlie Chaplin. Chaplin was beside himself with rage.'

Henrietta, a local friend, continued to be a staunch listener. She was one of the few people I had confided in. She knew about our theories that Louis might be illegitimate. The next time we met up, she asked me how things were going. I told her of the words that had tumbled out of my mouth.

'I know it sounds crazy, but I think he might be the illegitimate child of an MP. It just seems to fit. I can't tell you why.' We chatted more and I told her of our previous hunt for all the MPs with the surname Stanley who had served in the House of Commons in the early part of the twentieth century. I joked that one very famous politician whose surname had not been Stanley had been the spitting image of Stepfather.

The situation behind the blue gate did not improve. Food was becoming a major issue. A battle was developing over what my mother was given to eat. Bonnie had started to cook puréed vegetables for her once the doctor had said she was able to eat them, but after two weeks Louis said that my mother was turning into a rabbit. He demanded she be given 'proper food'. The duty nurse demurred but he insisted Mum be given meat. The strong nurse stood her ground and called the doctor. Stepfather was furious and gave further instructions to Bonnie that, if Mum had to 'eat mush', it must be presented exquisitely. He stipulated that four different-coloured vegetables were to be presented and they were to be of the standard of the Dorchester Hotel's nouvelle cuisine. This was the end of the line for our brilliant carer. Bonnie, who had threatened to leave a number of times before, finally escaped for a well-earned break; sadly, she never returned, so the cheerful rock that had held the household together was gone. No amount of new staff could ever replace such a sensible jovial soul.

Then, on another occasion, I heard his voice at one in the morning. He said, with no apologies for waking me up, 'Can you come on Thursday? Mum has to have a minor incision to remove a small growth on her neck?' I was horrified. Was this really necessary? 'Be here at six o'clock,' he insisted. I hastily reorganised my arrangements.

'No, be here at one o'clock,' came the next call. At least this time I was allowed into Mum's bedroom without fuss. I looked around. While I sat beside my mother I thought of past times.

My mother's bedroom had always appeared like a haven of luxury when I was a child. The palest rose-coloured nylon covered the dressing table, the imitation lace hiding tiers of drawers at the end of each wing. The dachshund would be curled into a tight ball at her feet. Placed on the nylon was a layer of thick glass on which Mum kept a peculiar mixture of cosmetics and cans of hairspray with quantities of egg-shaped wads of cotton wool.

An ornate three-panelled mirror took centre stage and over the hinges grew a collection of costume jewellery: long heavy necklaces and various strings of imitation pearls always larger than the real item. As the years passed the carpet around the dressing table area became grey and tacky from excess hairspray (or 'lacquer', as she would call it). I noticed that things had changed. There were no more cans of hairspray and the table was much tidier than I ever remembered. As the doctor made his incision, my mother and I chatted as in times gone by. I treasured the moment.

My mother recovered swiftly from this minor surgery but Stepfather just kept on employing more people. The doctor recommended a physiotherapist who could treat my mother. Louis clearly liked the rather attractive woman, so, instead of the recommended twice a week, he asked her to attend every day. I wondered whether this amount of treatment was good for Mum, but she had determination. She was keen to get her all her movement back and she talked of overcoming her lack of movement like her hero, Graham Hill. Then came the next bombshell.

'I've organised a beautician for Mum,' he announced. 'She's going to give her a massage.' I didn't say anything but I knew Mum had never liked the idea of massage. 'You'll meet her when you come at the weekend,' he intoned.

By the time I arrived, the beautician had increased her role. When I entered the room she was ensconced on Mum's 'good' side and as I went to hug my mother she did not have the grace to shift her position. Then she began trying to claim Mum's attention by turning over the pages of a fashion magazine, turning me aside like a piece of lard. But my mother was sharper than the beautician realised. She turned to me and asked, 'What do you think, Bob? Do you like that dress?'

I looked at the ageing female. She was not my mother's kind of woman. I know what Mum would say of her sort: That woman is false – false face, false nails, false thoughts. But the beautician had not given up. She was as determined to exclude me as Mum was to include me.

Stepfather smugly told me my mother loved the visits from this woman, so he increased her time with her. She was to attend for two full days a week. There was something deeply suspicious about this glamorous and gushing female. Luckily, she slipped up and didn't stay the course. Much later, the nurses told me that she was well known in Cambridgeshire for her husband bagging. She had been married four times and they were sure she was on the lookout for wealthy number five. She can't have been more than 40 and her latest husband had recently died at the age of 88. It had not been difficult to pick up her duplicity, so I was delighted to see the back of her.

One Wednesday night I arranged with my stepfather that I should stay over. Early next morning the bell rang and I found myself pulling back the yellow striped net curtain above the butler's sink just as my mother used to do when she heard its jangles above the blue gate. Across the yard marched a spruce, uniformed nurse, with smartly cropped hair, wearing fashionable spectacles. I did not recognise her. When I opened the back door for her she failed to introduce herself. As I knew the carers were busy elsewhere I wondered if this new nurse might need my help, so I approached my mother's bedroom. It was unusual to find the door ajar and through the gap Mum flapped her good hand to welcome me. I made to enter over the doorway but the new arrival abruptly shut the door in my face saying, 'Your mother isn't ready for a visit.' As I stared at the door in shock I heard my mother's voice. She was speaking in her emotional high-pitched tone, 'I don't trust you. Why are you here?'

I went slowly downstairs, thinking hard. I heard Stepfather come down the big step into the kitchen. He was carrying the post in his left hand, just as he had always done.

'I've changed things round with your mother's care. I've made a private contract with one of the nurses from the nursing agency.' He spoke in his soft, more scary voice. 'The daily nurses are not consistent so I'm appointing this one as head nurse; she'll be in charge of all the arrangements.'

My head was spinning. My mother was making progress again. Why did Stepfather need to increase her care?

Taking no notice of my perplexed silence, he continued, 'Unfortunately, your mother has taken a dislike to this nurse because of her name.'

This was turning into the maddest conversation I had ever had with him.

'Her name is June.' He paused.

Fiddling with the cutlery on the table, I asked innocently, 'What's wrong with that?'

With these words I had fallen straight into his trap. He sat up straight and started to noisily butter his toast.

'Well, your father had an affair with a married woman from his parish. She was the mother of two little boys and her name was June!'

He looked at his toast as if deciding whether to bite into it or not. But he had no interest in the food. He had just paused to increase the tension. I found myself gripping the handle of the spoon so tightly it was making my palm hurt.

'Your mother has lost touch with time. She thinks this June is the same woman as the married woman your father fancied. She has boys that are of the same age.'

I was in such shock I wondered if I was dreaming. After all these years of his pretending to be my real father, here I was listening to him tell me that I really had a genuine dad. Why was he telling me this now? Was it because my mother could no longer keep him in order? Had my father been an adulterer? How had Stepfather controlled his urge not to tell me earlier?

My world whirled around me as he started again. 'Your grandmother found them together in the vestry.'

I was saved by the telephone. As he talked to the caller my grip on the spoon relaxed and I started to rub the imprint it had made. He rose from his chair and took the walkabout phone with him. Had he told me the truth? Mum's comments and behaviour earlier in the bedroom had struck me as very odd. My poor mother had lived with an adulterous first husband. Now she had a permanent day nurse she did not trust but who had been given the authority to control the household.

Stepfather's unsettling comments over the breakfast table had motivated me and I felt stronger and more determined to look further into why my parents had divorced.

What was story about this married lady called June? I needed to know more. Was this the truth? And, if so, what role had Stepfather played in the breakup of the marriage? I went back to the New Forest and asked the lively church secretary that my father had married in 1957.

She told me that my dad had been the only child of an austere father. As a quiet studious boy he went straight from school into marine insurance, where he won numerous prizes. However, when he had saved up sufficient funds he took himself off to Oxford to study theology. Later, he was appointed as the curate in Sutton Coldfield, where he met my mother. After my parents married they moved to an Oxfordshire village parish. Little more was known except that in the 1950s divorce lawyers had to present sufficient and clear condemning evidence, so it was frequently the case that both sides agreed to fabricate facts. Many couples paid a willing subject to pretend she had spent a night with the married man and allow herself to be photographed leaving a hotel with the guilty party.

However, it would have been unlikely that my father would have agreed to this type of plan, as I knew he had been desperate to be allowed to continue in the ministry. The rumour was that my mother's lawyer had not behaved well in the court case. My mother had changed her petition at the last minute from separation to cruelty. This dramatic change of events ruined my father's chances of continuing to practise in the church. My father had felt let down by the court. Rumours were rife at the time that Louis Stanley had told my mother to change her petition because the new type of appeal meant Stepfather could marry my mother sooner.

As to what my father had done wrong, Joanna believed there had been talk of a crude letter that Dad had written to Mum on the eve of their wedding day. She suggested I read the local newspapers for the time when they divorced. A vicar's divorce in the 1950s, I thought, would be headlines in the local papers, so I searched old copies of the *Cambridge Evening News* but I found no reference to it at all. I eventually found details in the national press, *The Times* had a small article with the heading NOT FIT TO HOLD HOLY OFFICE while the *Star*'s subheading was WIFE SUBJECT TO UNNATURAL SEXUAL PRACTICES. The newspapers reported that Judge Tudor pronounced my father 'a sexual maniac', adding, 'The quicker he is out of the church the better.' Judge Tudor declared my father unsuitable for holy orders.

I found out later that my uncle had persuaded other national newspaper proprietors to keep the lurid case out of their publications.

It was now 18 months since Mum's stroke. Easter had always been a special weekend in Mum's calendar. Stepfather agreed that my children and I could visit for the whole weekend. But then he changed the plans. He only wanted us on Sunday. When Sunday morning came he had changed his mind again. He wanted us to arrive after lunch. To make sure there were no delays on the motorways we set off early loading the car with Easter goodies.

It turned out very wet so we took shelter under the wisteria tree as we rang the doorbell. The entrance was much darker than normal as there were no lights on in the kitchen. My heart sank further when nobody came to the door. I felt awkward in front of the children. How many times could I ring the bell? I tried the knocker. Finally Carol, the more regular weekend nurse came to the door. She appeared embarrassed, turned her back on us and scuttled away.

We went to get the dining room suitable for Easter tea arranging hazel twigs as the centrepiece as they were one of my mother's favourite signs of spring. However within minutes the door burst open. Louis was not going to play the game of a loving grandpa today.

'Happy Easter,' I blurted out quickly, catching his eye for the briefest of moments.

'Stop all this nonsense! Don't do anything until Mum comes down.'

'I'm just making the table look Eastery; you know how Mum likes…'

But he just ordered us out with a thunderous voice. The children in their hurry to leave the room became entangled with each other as he went to bolt the door behind us. I tried to ask about the care he had over the weekend but he made no reply and just pushed me away. The kitchen was out of bounds so the only place to wait was in the hallway. It had always been a draughty place but that day it seemed particularly cold. Conversation was stilted as we all dealt with the shock in our own way. Hours later we heard the familiar clang of the lift. Stepfather shoved Carol out of the way and grabbed the handles of the wheelchair. I went to greet Mum but he was not going to give us any opportunity for a kiss. He whisked her past me so fast he missed the doorway and stubbed the chair's front wheels into the skirting board. The usually composed nurse looked flustered and left the room.

Stepfather arranged the seating so that there was a distance between my mother and I. Carol was on my mother's better side and he occupied the other. Mum tried to bridge the void. 'You have made the table look wonderful,' she said, trying to speak past the nurse who leant back in her nominated chair so we could at least look at each other. But Stepfather refused to let us talk.

'Mum, I've a new leaflet out.'

'What's that? I can't hear.' I repeated myself, trying harder to articulate each word

'She says she has got a new leaflet out, Mrs Stanley.' Carol shifted her position nervously as she repeated my words.

'Oh, do show me.'

'Not now,' Stepfather thundered, writhing in his chair. 'We're having tea. You can see them later. You need to go upstairs.'

'Leave me alone, I'm fine. Now, I want to talk to Hannah.' Mum's voice was becoming stronger and she was sitting up straighter. I had forgotten the years of practice she had in diverting tricky conversations. But when she asked me to get the family photos out things deteriorated rapidly.

'Nurse, take her upstairs,' he snapped.

'I don't want to. I want to talk.' Mum continued to chat, but before she knew what was happening he had taken hold of the chair's handles and barged out of the room towards the lift. As Carol worked out how to arrange Mum into the confined space, I delved to the bottom drawer of the heavy bureau and retrieved one of her battered albums.

'Oh good, I won't be long,' said Mum, 'Tom and Rupert will

enjoy seeing them. The other album with Uncle Alfred and Uncle Ernest is underneath the frayed…'

The lift closed and stepfather pressed the button for its ascent.

'See you soon…!' I shouted and waved through the low window of the solid white door.

My mother was proud of her family and liked on the odd occasion to rifle through the heavy bottom drawer of the dresser where the battered albums were kept. We waited, pretending that she would come back to Easter tea, but the heart had gone out of the meal and nobody was hungry anymore. Then three hours later, when Carol needed to take some food into the bedroom, I sneaked in behind her. I held the faded shabby album out to Mum. Louis's left arm lunged at the album and it dropped to the floor. If Mum noticed the frosty atmosphere, she did not show it as we tried to gather around and laugh at pictures of when we were all younger. We left with hugs and kisses promising to be back soon with more old photos.

As we were leaving the room, she said, 'You never showed me your new leaflet, Bobbie.'

'Next time,' I said. There was nothing wrong with her brain, I thought to myself.

'Come and visit whenever you like,' she chirped as I blundered out. Her last words echoed in my ears as we faced the long journey home.

Soon after, Stepfather employed a lawyer who, he told us, was to act for him and our mother. We guessed he wanted the solicitor to help him raise money by all means possible. Much to our distress, we decided we also needed a family lawyer who could advise us through our predicament. We went for a London-based lawyer who was used to treading on eggshells in delicate family matters. We gave further thought to the position of the family accountant. What was he playing at? I recalled the meeting I had with this man ten years previously. Why didn't he listen to us?

Louis's weekly expenditure was huge. He now employed a head

nurse, a rota nurse, two carers and Joe, the chauffeur and odd job man. But the advice from our lawyer was not to provide him with short-term financial help: 'This would only put the crisis off for another week or so.' Pauline whispered that Stepfather had frittered away so much money that our fear he could not pay the nursing agency's fees was becoming a reality. We could not find out because the managers had been told that they were not to talk to Mrs Stanley's children, as we didn't care about our mother. However my brother, Edward, was working behind the scenes trying to rescue the financial situation but all to no avail.

During some visiting days Stepfather desperately pleaded with me to stay for supper. It often did not turn out well. So many carers had come and gone that now he was left with women who really couldn't cook. One night when my son, Tom, was with me Stepfather ditched the meal made by the carer for us all, calling the carefully planned dish 'utter rubbish'. He promptly rang the pub next door and ordered a pheasant meal. 'You'll stay, won't you?' I hesitated. It was already ten o'clock and I had 126 miles to drive.

CHAPTER 6

FAMILY LIKENESSES

I was feeling particularly depressed, having been denied another weekend visit to my mother, when on the Monday evening at about six the phone rang. I summoned the energy to answer the call and was pleased when I heard my friend Henrietta's quiet supportive voice.

I wondered if I should tell her just how depressed I was but she didn't wait to hear me. She had her own agenda.

'Bobbie, I don't know whether we're right, but we have a theory. Can we meet up tonight? I can't tell you on the phone.'

We found a quiet corner in our local pub. Henrietta could hardly wait for me to sit down with the drinks. She was so bursting with news. 'You know last time we met? We compared notes about how appalling politicians are.'

'Yes, and I said that Stepfather fitted into their mould,' I said.

'Well, did you know that a politician in the early twentieth century wrote lots of letters to a Miss Stanley?'

As soon as the words fell from her mouth, I knew that Louis was not just an MP's illegitimate son. He acted too superior for that. He was a Prime Minister's offspring. I recalled Louis's habit of using the word 'offspring' when he spoke of children.

'It was Asquith,' I said.

It was Henrietta's turn to be stunned. 'What? How did you know?'

'I've seen a photograph of him. I was stunned by his likeness to Stepfather. They looked identical!'

It was as if a light bulb had been turned on in my brain. Everything slotted into place. I had no evidence that Louis was illegitimate or even the son of an MP, but from that moment onwards I never had any doubts that Venetia Stanley was his mother and Asquith his father. Now I had a purpose – something to fight for. For my own satisfaction I would prove it.

Henrietta raised her voice trying to get my attention.

'It's just a guess,' she said. 'I don't even know if the years fit.'

I was hearing her but not listening. I had my own questions.

'How did you find out about this love affair? Wasn't it all secretive?'

'There was a book lying on my mother's coffee table,' said Henrietta, 'and I started to read it and spotted the name Stanley. Last week you told me about your childhood and that your stepfather was called Louis Stanley, so it was all fresh in my mind.' She took a breath, realising that I was now deeply engrossed in her words. 'My mother devours biographies and she's gripped with the life of Asquith at the moment.' She allowed herself a pause to sip her red wine.

'Bobbie,' she said, 'you'll have to get the book.'

My exhaustion vanished as a surge of energy shot into my veins and relieved my weary blood. The libraries were shut but I could still search the Internet for the name Asquith. I gulped down my drink and thought of how little history I had learned at my boarding school.

Henrietta understood my desire to rush home to look at my

computer screen. She knew I was desperate to make sense of all this before it was too late. My search started well for my eyes hooked onto the third paragraph of a website page. It read, 'There can be no other man in the country who could have juggled so many balls in the air but still had time to write these letters.'

'Oh, really,' I thought.

> Asquith was known as 'the busiest man in Britain'; he was controlling the country during the bloodiest part of World War One, he had dissent in Ireland, and he was presiding over one of the most powerful and cleverest cabinets ever in British history, only H. H. could have found time for love letters.

'Yes!' I shouted at the computer screen. 'Like father, like son.'

'Only H. H. could have found time for love letters' were the words that drove me over the next months. For this phrase almost more than any other evidence convinced me he was Asquith's son. Only Louis had the same high level of energy. Only Stepfather could tell so many different yarns to several people and keep all the stories boiling without making a mistake. But I had to prove it.

In the early hours I finally came across a clear photograph of Asquith at the age of perhaps 65. The black-and-white image loomed out of the screen at me. I was scared. It was not the eerie light of the winter dawn that frightened me: it was the immediacy of the likeness. I was staring at the stepfather of my childhood. Asquith's protruding tummy, broad shoulders and slumped posture were immediately reminiscent of the slouched upper body that had sat opposite me in the pink-and-white chintz-covered armchairs at Old Mill House. Asquith had more hair than Louis at a similar age but there was no doubt the politician had huge hands. The eyes and the exceptionally large face were so familiar. The accompanying brows and sagging eye bags were, too. So was the shape of the ears. However, it was the nose that sent shivers down my back. Asquith's nasal passages were less gross but they created the same broad arched shape. The mouth was set in the pose Louis used for his photo calls – serious with a hint of a smirk. Stepfather always insisted his profile be taken from his left. Asquith's photo was also taken from this direction.

In the early hours I waited for the public library to open. I needed to read the book *H. H. Asquith: Letters to Venetia Stanley*, edited by Michael and Eleanor Brock, but it was not in stock, so I had to wait an agonising three weeks. In the meantime, I resorted to more research on the Internet, which gave me an insight into Asquith's politics but gave few personal details.

One website described how 'Venetia Stanley was to trigger an astonishing stream of letters from a man whom many would have thought had the most taxing job in the world.' I discovered that Asquith was one of Britain's longest-standing leaders, having served for eight years and 241 days. The Liberal Party's website claimed that his years of premiership were among 'the most challenging' of any recent stewardship. He was no 'ordinary leader', but a Liberal hero making some of the greatest liberal achievements of the twentieth century. Asquith led a radical party that pledged to help the ordinary man in the street. This reflected his own roots, as he was the first prime minister to come from a middle-class background.

Finally, I found a webpage that confirmed that this great politician had written love letters to a young woman. 'It was in 1912 that Prime Minister Asquith fell in love with Venetia Stanley.' I read more. He was 'besotted' with this woman, writing letters and poems to her at least once a day, even during Cabinet meetings! The American *DC Bar* website suggested the Prime Minister had been indiscreet in 1914 and discussed his war plans and political manoeuvrings with this young woman. The site claimed he had even disclosed to her 'the most secret military information', covert plans that even his own War Cabinet had not heard. I found this hard to believe but I read on, fascinated. How could this married prime minister have 'seen' this woman, and not been found out?

Surely, these frock-coated gentlemen in top hats acted with more decorum than our twenty-first-century politicians, or was I being naïve? But the website spoke of Venetia Stanley's involvement with Asquith and another politician who was 'interested' in her. It read like a modern-day gossip magazine. I thought this website must be sensationalising history. Then I found the most interesting fact of all: Venetia had been friends with Asquith's own daughter, a girl of the same age!

In the ensuing days I thought more about the older woman who had lived in our house. I was beginning to be more confident she had not been Stepfather's birth mother, but who had chosen her to bring up Louis, and why? I had to investigate her background and the strange daughter, Mamie. These women might give me vital clues.

I tried hard to recall Home Granny's facial features but I remember only an aged female frame. She wore her long dreary hair away from her face with her copious skirts reaching the floor. Thinking back more, I remembered her aged spaniel, her talking turquoise budgie, which was allowed to fly from one end of her long room to the other. She was also talented in crochet work, but that was as much as I could recall.

Looking back, I decided that Stepfather must have been a loving son. On Mother's Day he bought her bunch after bunch of daffodils, and whenever we were out he would buy her a small keepsake. When she became frail he bought her new Mohair shawls. Mum helped him choose so they were always bright: crimson, orange, turquoise or garishly multicoloured. At six o'clock, after we had finished our own tea, he almost tiptoed – he was so light on his feet – across the hall to their part of the house. I watched him reach for a key from his right-hand jacket pocket and let himself into their flat. When the door closed behind him he escaped into their world. I never knew what he did or talked about. Home Granny and Mamie belonged to him.

I have a stronger image of Auntie Mamie, as she lived on another ten years. She was always short but as she grew older she seemed to shrink before my eyes and she developed a hump back. She was slim but appeared dumpy. She took little care of her appearance. My mother tried to help by paying for her to have a perm and a blue rinse, but when this soon washed out she was left with straight, wispy, white hair. My mother loved shoes and so often gave Mamie money to buy new ones. As she got older, however, she suffered from large bunions and wanted to wear slippers, but Stepfather forbade them. There were huge rows if he discovered she had kicked off her shoes and hidden them under the chair. Her conversation was limited and she knew little of the world around her, but she was adept at creating rows between Mum and Stepfather.

My work interrupted my searches on the Internet, as I had to go North with my friend Maggie, so I grabbed Colin Clifford's biography, *The Asquiths*, off the shelves of my local library and stuffed it into one of my bags. We found ourselves staying in Doncaster in a shabby bed-and-breakfast. Having prepared our work for the following day we chatted over a fish supper. I explained that I was going to attack the biography as soon as we had finished our meal.

'But Bobbie,' she said, 'how will you ever make any connection between Louis and Asquith, when your stepfather has been so secretive over the last fifty years?'

'Well, the first thing I want to do is find a connection with Cheshire. He was proud of that county. Then there's his connections with Liverpool and the town of Hoylake on the furthest western tip of the Wirral. He told us he was brought up there, maybe there's a link.' As I talked, I realised that I didn't have any plan of campaign; I didn't know what I was looking for. But, as I talked, the county of Cheshire remained important to me.

'Won't it be hard?' Maggie asked, knowing the effect of Mum's deteriorating position had on me.

'Well, it'll give me something else to think about,' I replied, rather too positively.

As I picked the book up, I noted it had more than 400 pages and, having little patience, I decided to scan it first. The word 'Cheshire' leapt out at me from the page. I homed in on the surrounding words: 'Alderley Hall in Cheshire was the home of Venetia Stanley.' I couldn't believe my eyes. 'Look at this.' I thrust the book under Maggie's nose. 'It tells me Venetia Stanley's home was Alderley Hall in Cheshire.'

'Oh, yes,' rejoined my Yorkshire-born friend. 'Alderley, I've heard of it. Alderley Edge is a National Trust site, but I don't think there's a hall any more.'

Finally I had a ray of hope in my distraught life. As I tried to get some sleep I realised that Cheshire had to be a major part of my story or my whole theory was wrong and, as I turned over in my uncomfortable bed, I thought of how Louis Stanley loved everything about Liverpool. He also had a strange familiarity with the area around Stockport.

Each day, I scrounged a few minutes in my busy schedule to read the biography. Deep down, I knew I must be right, but I was also confused. Who else knew? I could not be the only person to suspect that Asquith had fathered Louis.

My research continued when I got home. I learnt that Asquith's father, a wool merchant in the North of England, died when Herbert Henry was only eight. When still young he and his brother were sent to London and billeted with a number of relatives so they could attend school. Luckily, for Herbert, his academic abilities were spotted by his headmaster and he continued to take a personal interest in his progress. He won a classical scholarship to Balliol College, Oxford, where he achieved a double first in law and became president of the Oxford Union.

Later, Asquith's experience of serving at the bar is said to have developed his skill at procrastination and compromise. When he was Prime Minister, his most famous saying was 'wait and see'.

It was where he was first elected as an MP that interested me, as it was East Fife in Scotland. He was to hold this seat for 32 years. Surely this connection with Scotland was vital. Louis's knowledge on that part of Scotland was extensive.

Asquith rose up the political ranks, becoming Home Secretary, during which time he made a name for himself. Soon after, he was appointed Chancellor of the Exchequer.

My research continued. One website told me that the Prime Minister was very popular at the outbreak of war but started to lose his popularity when the frontline troops began to be slaughtered, and the press revealed great shortages of shells in the trenches.

This sparked a recollection of a heated debate in the Old Mill House kitchen about the First World War and the lack of shells. I racked my brain but couldn't recall whom Louis had been supporting, Asquith or Kitchener.

This, in turn, reminded me of another occasion. Another sumptuous roast was resting on the blue sturdy serving dish ready to be carved while Mum stirred the sauces for the vegetables. I must have been about thirty and was elbow deep in the butler's sink cleaning the big pans. We were chatting as mother and daughter about almost nothing, when suddenly my mother said, 'I'm worried about Louis.'

'Why?' I stuttered. I was surprised she was allowing me into her territory.

'Well, he's so quiet and I think it might be because he's worried about Auntie Mamie. You know she's the only relative he has.'

'I thought she was his adopted sister', I said.

'Yes, she's the last of his family,' Mum continued, 'and when she's gone he'll have nobody.'

I seized the opportunity. 'What did his father do?'

'I don't know,' she replied in a tone of genuine puzzlement. 'He lived in Hoylake on the Wirral and treated Liverpool as his hometown and that's all I know.'

'But what about his mother? What did she do?' I quizzed.

'I understand she was a nurse in a hospital, and that's how they came to adopt Mamie. They took home a baby from where she worked.' Then as if thinking aloud she added, 'but she didn't seem to know much about nursing.'

'What do you know about his childhood?' I asked, hardly daring to clank the baking tins in the greasy water. I was so eager to hear every word.

'I know nothing more than you.' My mother's voice was beginning to show signs of annoyance.

'What did he do in the war, or what did his father do?' I persisted.

'I don't know.'

'What jobs did Poppy have before he wrote?'

'I don't know,' she repeated.

'How did he get any money?'

'I just don't know.' She had stopped stirring and was staring into space.

'But how could you marry somebody who you knew so little about?' It was my turn to feel annoyed.

'Bobbie, in those times you just did,' she said. I stared at her. 'You just did,' she repeated defensively.

I realised that I had pushed her further than she had wanted to go. She had broken her silence about past events, so I did not want to probe any more at this time. I thought there would be plenty of opportunities to chat in the future. But as I replaced the saucepans on the high shelf, which had accumulated years of cooking grease, I realised I didn't even know when their wedding anniversary was – another thing we didn't talk about.

I went back to my research. Dates and places were now my priority. I knew how old Louis was, so if Asquith had sired Louis in the years 1911–12 he would have been living at Number Ten Downing Street. I had read no research so far that made any reference to his being a serious womaniser. Stranger still, most of the sources had not even hinted that his letters to Venetia Stanley demonstrated a love affair. His written words provided important historical details, but that was all.

Suddenly the dates of birth of my two protagonists became very important to me. Herbert Henry Asquith was born on 12 September 1852, while Venetia Stanley was born in August 1887 – an age difference of 35 years. No wonder historians dismissed the idea of the relationship as a love union. Asquith was not a likely candidate for an affair. Not only was he Prime Minister, but he was also married with four sons and one daughter by his first wife and two more children by his second. However, it was Violet, Asquith's daughter by his first wife, who provided the opportunity for Asquith and Miss Stanley to meet. 'Vinny', as Asquith called her, was Violet's best friend, the daughter of Asquith's wealthy colleague at the Bar. The two girls of the two lawyers were a similar age and had become inseparable. Had this friendship been the cover for the relationship? Was this why nobody knew?

It was important to find out how long the girls had been friends and I needed to check if 6 January, Louis's birthday, was a possible day for Venetia to have given birth. I could not wait to get the book so I could read the published letters. Maybe, I asked myself, it was even more important to find out what Asquith and his lady friend were doing nine months earlier.

My mother always tried to make Stepfather's birthday special but as the date approached she would often say 'January 6th is a miserable date for a birthday.' She had put so much effort into Christmas that she was often exhausted, and the sixth day of the month was also the traditional day for taking the decorations down. It was dark and miserable outside, restaurants looked tawdry after New Year and, worse still, Mum had run out of ideas for possible presents.

I decided it was prudent to order Louis Thomas Stanley's birth certificate. The child in me felt anxious, as I was prying behind his back, but the need to know who his recorded parents were overruled my concerns. As I waited for the certificate to arrive in the post I racked my brain. Were there any more clues from my childhood memories? I also wondered about the veracity of his birth details, because I now knew that in those times lies were often told on paper.

I searched websites for more details of Asquith's personal life. Eventually I found pages that told me he had been 'happily' married with the mild and gentle Helen, who liked the simple things in life, while her husband had been a 'devoted' father. However, in 1891 things went tragically wrong. On a family holiday on the Isle of Arran, Helen contracted typhoid and died. So Herbert Henry Asquith was left with four young boys, one only 18 months, and a daughter, Violet, who was three. Asquith was said to be devastated but later he married the daughter of the Scottish Tennant family who had made their immense wealth out of chemicals. Her father was a Liberal MP for Glasgow. She had been baptised Margaret but was always known as Margot.

I also read that Lloyd George replaced HH as Prime Minister in a 'palace revolt' and, once his political position had been usurped, Asquith's career and health quickly declined. He died eight years later in 1924. The village where he was buried – Sutton Courtenay – rang a bell in my head. Why did it sound familiar? Familiar-sounding names had started to appear in the biographies I was reading – names that reminded me of Louis's endless bragging.

Another thought struck me. If Venetia had given birth to a bastard child why had she wanted him to have her surname? Was that what the aristocracy did in those days? I needed to find out.

My investigations were continuing. In my head I imagined using a three-pronged fork in some lonely muddy field, digging deeper and deeper to find Stepfather's roots. The first prong was my investigations into H. H. Asquith; the second my search for

Venetia Stanley's past history; the third was Home Granny, Louis's surrogate mother.

Who had Home Granny really been? I needed to find her death certificate and then perhaps I could find out where she was born. I was pleased that Applegate was not a common surname. But I needed all the information I could, as my memory of her as a person was so hazy. I had little idea of how old she was when she died, so how could I start to hunt down her death and birth certificates? To find out more I would have to visit the triangular graveyard in Trumpington where she was buried.

At last Louis's birth certificate dropped through my letterbox. I could tell from the spidery writing that Stepfather had been named after his 'father'. It read 'Louis Thomas Stanley – boy – born on January 6th 1912 – name of father Louis Thomas Stanley'. It struck me as I read the certificate how odd it had been that Home Granny had never mentioned her husband, his grave or any anniversary. As far as I knew she had not even confided in my mother. Surely that was strange.

My eyes went back to the certificate. There was the confirmation that the occupation of Louis's 'father' had been cotton merchant. But these particulars did not hang together. Why had Stepfather, who was so interested in words, never use those related to the cotton industry? My eyes went to the box where his mother's details were recorded. Her maiden name was Mary Ann Applegate and it was she who had registered the birth. The other interesting section was Louis's birthplace: 37 Aylesbury Road, Liscard, in the eastern part of the Wirral.

The entry fitted with the bare essentials Stepfather had told us of his childhood. But I became anxious. It was scary delving into and spying on his past. As I read the document my heart raced as if I had gone to a forbidden drawer and my stepfather would suddenly appear behind me, towering over me as I rifled through his belongings. I put the newly printed certificate away in a safe place but it did not stop me feeling uneasy. I thought of the fairy story that had bewitched me as a child: 'Bluebeard'. It was last tale in a book given to me by my maternal grandmother and was illustrated with the grimmest pictures. Was I now in the same situation as the unhappy wife whose curiosity had got the better of her? The scheming murderer Bluebeard cunningly contrived to go away for a few days and left his wife in charge of a huge bunch of keys; each one opened a different room in his castle. He enticed her by filling each room with more exciting objects, but as he left for his travels he forbade her to open the smallest and most isolated room. She could not resist the temptation to snoop into his affairs and became ensnared in his waiting trap. Was I also falling into a similar ambush?

I knew the investigation of the 'parents' as recorded on the certificate would be time-consuming. Was it all going to be worth the effort? And what would I find out?

I made my first of many visits to the Family Records Centre in Myddleton Street, London, where I turned over the huge tomes full of names. (It was never so much physical fun when the search facilities moved to Kew.) My first search was to see if a Louis Thomas Stanley and Mary Ann Applegate had ever married. Initially I searched for the logical dates but, when I found nothing, I delved into the records for even the most improbable years. There was nothing. I then started all over again and double-checked. I had to be sure.

My next job was to search for the senior Louis Stanley's death certificate. I worked out that if he had existed he could have died any time from 1912 to 1942. But, again, there was no death registered for such a man in the records. I needed help for further investigation, so I turned to a genealogy expert. He confirmed that Mary Ann Applegate had never married a Mr Stanley and no Louis senior had died in this country. However, the only way to be sure that the man never existed was to search for a birth certificate for a Louis Thomas Stanley who would have been old enough to be a father in 1912. This was a much more time-consuming search. The genealogist double-checked my work. But I had achieved a huge breakthrough. There was no birth certificate. Coupled with the knowledge there was no marriage and death certificate I could be certain Louis Thomas Stanley 'senior' was fictitious and that meant only one thing: Stepfather had been born to an unmarried mother.

For light relief I had chosen to read *Black Diamonds*, a book about the wealthy Fitzwilliam family, whose huge estate was Wentworth House and the coal industry. It had been a surprisingly good choice, as it had given me evidence on the various lifestyles at the turn of the twentieth century. I found that the word 'changeling' was still in use. The word was used for babies exchanged at birth while villagers still gossiped about children brought up in their area who were the illegitimate sons of their local lord.

The author, Catherine Bailey, was clear on the future of children born out of wedlock: 'To be born illegitimate regardless of the identity of the father marked a child for life.' Bailey wrote of one of the scandals in the wealthy family. One of the Fitzwilliam females had lied about her birth name, deceived her husband, rarely talked of her own childhood and did not appear on any of the early censuses. Her 'whole life was constructed as a lie'. Bailey makes the point that it is only the electronic search engines of the twenty-first century that make it possible to reveal her real identity.

This information spurred me on and I took another step forward in my reading when I found a review of a book by Naomi Levine. It appeared to be about a man called Edwin Montagu. Levine had written, 'Venetia [Stanley] was to commit the cruellest act of destiny that she could devise: she was marrying his [Asquith's] close friend and confidant, the one accomplice of his secret love, Edwin Montagu.'

Who was this Edwin Montagu? I thought that, if this woman had acted so cruelly to both Asquith and her husband, maybe it was Venetia's genes that Louis had inherited. This made more sense, so

I rushed off to the library to borrow Levine's book to find out more about Venetia Stanley.

The next time I was repulsed at the back door of my old home I made good use of my time. I went back out through the blue gate and walked down to the triangular burial ground where I hoped I might find Mary Ann's gravestone. I recalled her death. I was alarmed when Stepfather had collapsed in tears on my shoulder and made huge gulps. It had made a lasting impression on me. So had the burial. I remembered catching my finger on the gatepost as we left the courtyard, but it was my mother's whispering talk of the depth of the grave that evoked the strongest memory. Later that week after a family lunch, she could not resist asking Stepfather in front of us all, 'Why was Home Granny's grave so deep? You don't expect me to be buried there, do you? I don't want that, I don't like it there.' Her words haunted me for months afterwards. I didn't want my mum to talk about dying. Why had she been so worried about the depth? I hadn't understood.

Trumpington's parish council had made an extensive graveyard between two roads leading out of Cambridge. The streets had always been full of traffic, but the burial ground forty years on was now very different. I remembered that the burial hole had been at a crossing of paths with newly planted yew trees at each corner, but as I entered through the broken gate I found the paths were overgrown. It looked so different that I wondered if I was ever going to recognise her stone, but, despite the dilapidating changes to the gravestones, my memory served me well, for I found it without difficulty. I shaded my eyes from the sun and read, 'Mary Ann Stanley died in her 96th year, 25th April 1963'. So Home Granny must have been born in 1867 or 1868 and would have been 44 when she gave birth to Louis. In those days that was very old for a first-time mother!

I was making progress. Now that I had the year of her death it might be possible to find her death certificate, but I needed to know which quarter she was born in. So I was disappointed that the words on the stone gave me no more clues as to her date of birth. I racked my memory for which month she had her birthday. It would make my search so much easier if I knew. I was fairly sure it was not in the summer and I didn't recall it as being in the winter, as I would have remembered roasting in front of one of Mum's huge fires. I remembered that Mum helped Stepfather choose another brightly coloured shawl that he wrapped her up in when he took her out. Could these mohair shawls be a clue? Could her birthday have been in the autumn?

It was not until I found Home Granny's headstone that I remembered that Auntie Mamie had been buried in the same plot. So I jotted down her details as well. 'Mary Eliza Stanley died on September 24th 1978 in her 70th year'. I was convinced this strange auntie was irrelevant to my search but I was keen to take down all his family details, as I was not sure where my research was taking me.

On my drive home I reflected more. If I was right in my theory, why had the Stanley family selected Mary Ann Applegate to adopt Louis as her child? Had Asquith himself helped select the woman? I guessed not. He had far more pressing duties. However the couple had to find an exceptionally trustworthy person. As thoughts jostled in my mind I became convinced that the most sensible tactic for Venetia's parents would be to select a woman whose family had been associated with the Stanleys for generations – maybe a family friend or an old retainer on the estate. I had to follow every avenue. I was aware that the 1901 census might help me once I knew Mary Ann's date of birth.

Finally, the book of the Asquithian letters to Venetia edited by Michael Brock and his wife Eleanor arrived at the library. It had been a busy week and students' university assignments needed grading but in my lunch break I shoved them aside to allow myself an initial peek at the photographs on and between the covers. The images of Asquith at various stages in his life showed again the strong family likeness. I looked at the battered cover with its tatty protective coat. The library jacket obscured the oval black-and-white photograph of a striking woman. I took the cellophane jacket off and studied her in more depth. There was no doubt that she was impressive with jet-black hair held in place with a band. She wore a close-fitting dress with a plunging neckline and a long jewelled pendant. I don't know why but the magnificent string of pearls around her neck gave me a feeling of *déjà vu*. Was it because my mother loved cultured and imitation pearls or was it something else? I began to examine the text: 'Here are the letters of a Prime Minister in his sixties to the young woman he adored. H. H. Asquith fell in love with Venetia Stanley one Sunday morning in the spring of 1912.' That date, the year Louis was born, was striking. For something was wrong: 'fell in love' *after*, not *before*, the birth of Louis? I reflected more deeply. How did this historian know that the two of them fell in love at a particular time? Why could it not have been earlier?

I read on:

> The letters he wrote are unique because of their scope and their abundance...early in 1914 he started to write [to her] about politics...Whenever Asquith could not see Venetia he wrote to her, sometimes three times a day, sometimes during a debate in the house of Commons, on occasion even in a cabinet meeting.

So that website had been right! Brock's words jerked my thoughts into a different direction. Few of Venetia's letters to Asquith have survived. What was the truth? Had the pages of the *DC Bar* website been full of exaggerations or even lies, or had they written the truth? What is accurate in history? Historians will, of course, put their own interpretations on the letters and maybe other details of Asquith's political life. The research I had done so far had been far too easy – everything had fitted nicely into place. But, noting that the book of letters was 676 pages long, I wondered if my investigations might in future become more tedious. How was I ever going to fit in all this reading?

My other duties in life had to wait. I was drawn to read the introduction: 'The letters constitute the most remarkable self revelation ever given by a British Prime Minister'...however Michael Brock believed that there was no real love between them. He saw the relationship as little more than a lonely Prime Minister's infatuation with a highly educated young girl.

He argued that words such as 'intimacy' 'lover' and 'affair' had changed their meaning over the 95 years since the letters had been written. But how could this historian suggest they were not in love when in 1914 Asquith was writing an average of one letter a day? In August of that year, when war was breaking out, he wrote to her 26 times! There were a staggering 560 letters running to 300,000 words in total.

Michael Brock justifies his policy of including only half of the letters in his book by stating, 'We have been sparing in selecting from what Asquith wrote before he started to write about politics.'

But I was interested in what affection Asquith had for Venetia. I found a few pertinent letters without a thorough search: 'You have sustained and enriched every day of my life.' This was written at midnight on 30 December 1914, as the New Year approached. A fortnight later he shows how significant she was to his world:

> When I got your letter...I at once postponed my interview with the King until noon, that we might have the hour 10.30–11.30 together...I wanted so much at the earliest opportunity, and while the impressions were still fresh, to talk to you, and get your opinions about today's War Council.

It was also easy to find examples of letters where Britain's Prime Minister was asking for this young woman's advice.

> I might create a new office for Lloyd George…and relieve him of his present duties. I shan't do anything without consulting you which makes it all the more necessary that we should spend tomorrow afternoon together…I never loved nor needed you more.

He asked for her opinion on the young and aspiring Winston Churchill:

> How wise I thought all that you said in your letter today on these subjects: especially in reference to the personal qualities of Winston and Mc. K. Your intuition never fails you, and there is no colleague whose judgement I trust so much…

I was shocked. But then my eyes hooked on more disquieting words written by Brock: 'It is almost certain that Asquith never became Venetia's lover in the physical sense…and it is unlikely that he ever wished for this.'

How could he be so sure of this? I had to search for more evidence. It crossed my mind that, if the editors had excluded letters that were of 'a more personal nature' from publication, was there more correspondence that had been written before 1912? If so, where would I find the letters? And what had happened to Venetia's correspondence to Asquith?

The fact that Venetia spurned Asquith to marry another politician called Edwin Montagu made me even more curious. For once it was not the name that caught my eye but the fact that her engagement caused political chaos! Mr Montagu was in Asquith's Cabinet and Venetia had 'searched' for a quiet political week in which she could tell Asquith she was to marry another man. Unfortunately, her letter arrived on Asquith's desk in May 1915, the same day as Asquith faced a barrage of bad press.

I read of two curious letters. One from Asquith to Venetia's sister Sylvia: 'I don't believe there are two living people who each in their separable ways are more devoted to me than she and Montagu: it is the irony that they should deal a death-blow to me.'

The second was written to Venetia declaring that his love for her would not change 'in expression, in intercourse, in confidence, in the thousand things big and little, grave and gay, light or serious which have woven the web of our intrigue and divine intimacy'. Had Asquith been in love? In days gone by men may have been much more flowing in their letters, but to me this did not read like any ordinary flirtation. I even felt a pang of sympathy for Asquith: clearly Miss Stanley's proposed marriage had left him devastated.

Historians agree that in the later part of his premiership Asquith appeared lethargic and his *laissez faire* approach in wartime eventually made him unpopular. I needed to know more.

I allowed myself a thought about Stepfather's possible roots. But what had Louis known? Had he been brought up knowing he was illegitimate? Had he known who his mother was? Had he known his possible father?

Lack of hard work was not Asquith's only fault. He also loved alcohol. Haldane reprimanded him as early as 1904 for his heavy consumption of champagne. Spectators have suggested that Venetia saved him from 'an early sodden end' in 1911, but rumours still circulated in 1912 that he might have to resign because of his need for drink. As I read about a modern party leader's drink problem I learnt that MPs had called Asquith 'Squiff' and that was how the word 'Squiffy' has passed into our language. In those times the music hall performers shouted out, 'Mr Asquith says in a manner sweet and calm, another little drink won't do any harm.' One of his political opponents, Lord Desborough, referred to him as 'a drunken time server with no moral qualities' (Clifford). This reminded me of reading that the young Winston Churchill once had to pick up his drunken boss off the floor of the House of Commons while the parliamentarian brotherhood of the Commons ensured the story never escaped into the press. Louis liked a brandy late in the evening but as far as I knew he never drank to excess.

So far my investigations had concentrated on Louis's possible biological father, but I knew almost nothing about his possible biological mother, Venetia Stanley, who was christened Beatrice but known by her middle name.

What had she been like? How serious was her relationship with the Prime Minister? What had this rebellious young woman seen in a man who was 35 years older than she? Venetia made a fascinating research project. From my first collection of articles I gained a mental picture of this aristocratic young lady. She was described as tall, strongly built and good-looking in a tomboy manner. She had dark luminous eyes and camellia-coloured skin. There seems little doubt that she had a frighteningly fierce intellect. She was also well versed in literature as the family's tutor had been Edward Lear, and Venetia learned much of her extensive general knowledge at the dining table, for mealtimes at Alderley Hall were rumbustious and academically highly challenging. Benjamin Jowett, the famous English scholar, classicist and master of Balliol College, once wrote, 'I am staying at Alderley where the family war is raging.' Often the heated family conversations stopped only when their special treacle tart arrived at the table.

Venetia was born at the family seat. The size of the mansion impressed me. It had forty bedrooms, six large halls, a brewery, laundry, mill house and farm. I thought of Mum talking proudly of her family and New Hall. But it was not on this scale.

Alderley Hall had burnt down in 1931. Louis would have been 19. I imagined him torching the place in a rage, having seen the fury he was capable of. I could imagine him doing it.

Michael Brock claims the Asquithian obsession with Venetia started in April 1912, but as I read further I found there was plenty of evidence they could have met regularly before. I was amazed and perplexed. But I also felt an outside force guiding me to the right discoveries: books fell open at relevant pages, photographs gave me feelings of *déjà vu* and chance remarks by friends led me to uncharted territories. Was my story fantasy or was I really discovering a genuine political tale? Could I possibly be seeing history from a different perspective from that of eminent historians? But time was becoming a huge problem. It was so hard trying to find enough space to gather dates and check what were known facts. I was determined not to leave any stone unturned, but my research was expanding rather than contracting. However, there were far more pressing needs behind the blue gate.

CHAPTER 7

THE SUPREME ARTIST

Our lawyer was working hard on our behalf but there was little she could do without the cooperation of *his* lawyer, who seemed besotted with Stepfather, and talked so little common sense.

Louis persisted in spending silly amounts of money and his celebrity Dorchester launch party was only weeks away. The guest list grew and grew. Each guest had to be a wealthy celebrity. His VIP list included a strange mixture of wealthy men: the Sultan of Brunei, Frank Williams, Mohammed Al-Fayed, Bernie Ecclestone, Jackie Stewart, Max Mosley. Part of his fun was to record how many nurses were now invited. He seemed to have a tally of over 35. To me it was a staggering number of nurses.

'Oh, don't worry about the cost,' he would say. 'The publishers are going to pay most of the expenses.' I did not believe him.

'Of course, *you'll* be invited, Bob,' he would say. I had been invited and uninvited so many times I had lost count.

I tried diplomatically to suggest that Mum wasn't sufficiently recovered to go to London. But he only replied, 'I've thought it out. We'll use both the two new cars. She'll be driven in the Daimler as far as the Edgware Road. There she'll be transferred to the Chrysler.'

When I protested, he just carried on like a well-worn record. 'Two nurses will stay with her all night in the best suite of rooms at the Dorchester.' I was utterly dismayed.

Neither the GP nor Mum's consultant returned my calls, so now I decided it was time to put more of our concerns on paper. The GP did eventually respond, gingerly agreeing with me about my mother's health, but he wanted to show my letter to Stepfather to further his case. I told him this was the wrong approach because my name would be mud, so my intervention must remain confidential. But the GP, either with stupidity or dogmatism, showed Stepfather my letter. Of course, I became sludge and Stepfather upped the stakes. He went into overdrive. As I sat on my lowly footstool miserably hearing the ever more complicated plans, he would say to Mum, 'That's right, isn't it, dear?'

Mum's energy seemed to have finally deserted her, for all she could say was, 'Yes, that's right.'

He was now spending £250,000 a year on nursing alone. How long could he keep this up when his cheques were bouncing with the local traders? And if he ran out of money how was our mother going to be cared for? We had to find a way to bail him out of debt, but how, and where from?

One day as I waited in the kitchen Louis came down the step. 'Catherine Walker is coming to measure Mum for her evening dress,' he said in his most pompous tone.

'Who's Catherine Walker?' I asked, trying hard not to annoy him.

'Oh, don't show your ignorance. She was one of Lady Diana's favourite dress designers.'

I was dumbstruck. Poor Mum! Was she going to be dressed up like a royal doll?

'I want you to meet her. Mum won't be down for some time today.' At that moment the doorbell rang and he ordered me to open the door. I showed the slight woman with her pouch of materials into the dining room and made to leave once she was seated, but, as I did, the designer spoke: 'Mr Stanley, before we go any further, I must tell you that you still owe me eight thousand pounds.'

In shock at the amount, I stumbled up the back stairs. I had a clear aim. If Stepfather was negotiating with the visitor I could talk to my mother on her own for the first time since those early days of caring for her. I found she was extremely anxious about the party. She did not want to attend.

Reality hit me the very next day. Stepfather started to ask my siblings and me for money, but I was no longer so easily fooled. He wanted each of us to part with £10,000. We consulted our lawyer. Her advice was quite clear. If we gave him £40,000 to squander it would be £80,000 next timc and, if he was spending money like water now, he would not stop and we would all be penniless in no time. But the emotional blackmail continued. Calling at midnight he would say, 'Mum has had a bad day another nurse has walked out.' Then he might snarl, 'Do you love your mother or not? Then pay up.'

It was a most powerful ploy.

The bulky, heavy wheelchair became a major issue. The more faithful nurses had clandestinely whispered it was cruelly uncomfortable. It was not designed for stroke victims, but Stepfather listened to nobody.

The only way to secure an appointment with the manager of the agency that supplied the 'emergency' nurses on an hourly basis was to pretend to be a potential new customer. So I appeared at her office under a pseudonym. I knew it was essential they heard our side of the story. When I had finished, the buxom woman looked grave.

'I'd begun to suspect things were not right when the nursing turnover became ridiculously high…' She paused and took a deep breath. 'Mr Stanley has been warning me for some time that you're uncaring, untrustworthy children.'

'Thank you for telling me,' I replied as my heart sank further.

But my bland comment seemed to release her tongue.

'If I'd known who your stepfather was I'd never have agreed to do this contract.'

'What do you mean?' I asked, thinking she meant the motor-racing world.

'Do you remember when your mother broke her pelvis when she slipped in the kitchen some years back?' She didn't wait for me to reply. 'We were the agency used. I remember the time quite clearly because your mother was quite remarkable. She'd hauled herself up the stairs to her bedroom with a double break in her pelvis, an incredible feat, and no doctor had been called until the following morning.'

I was aghast as I heard the details.

'Mr Stanley didn't allow your mother to be treated in hospital. He called us instead. It was also a dreadful case.'

I was about to reply when she started to tell me more.

'At the time our nurses reported that Mr Stanley's behaviour wasn't appropriate.'

'*What?*' I said, my voice almost a screech.

'There was an allegation that he'd been touching one of our nurses' – she paused and looked at her hands – 'in a sexual manner.'

'What happened?' I asked nervously.

'Our male manager asked for an appointment with your stepfather. Mr Stanley tried to call his bluff and insist that your mother be present for the conversation. So, although our manager felt highly uncomfortable' – she paused again, this time her eyes going to the floor – 'he'd no choice but to explain what the allegations were in front of your mother.'

Poor, poor Mum.

This incident meant that childhood memories now took on different meanings. As I drove home, one in particular came flooding back. Late one Thursday night – or perhaps it was so late that it was Friday morning – I went downstairs to greet them. Before I could speak Mum began talking, as if to herself.

'A very strange thing happened today in London,' she said. Louis's huge frame filled the doorway as he watched her.

She stood with her back to me filling the kettle. Then, after pushing the switch down, she turned around to reach for the hot-water bottles and aimed these words at Louis: 'Go on, tell her what happened.' From her tone of voice I could tell she was exhausted. I was old enough to appreciate that she had been driving through the night, while he had slept in the front passenger seat.

Louis reached down to the corner cupboard for the packet of Rice Krispies, his evening habit after he had eaten a full meal in London. He didn't reply.

'Go on,' repeated Mum, 'tell her what happened.'

'Nothing,' he muttered.

'Well, *I'll* have to tell her then.' Her voice was rising.

I was becoming uncomfortable and wished I had stayed upstairs. But there was no stopping Mum. 'We stood on the front steps of the Dorchester as usual and each of us waited for a taxi,' she recounted. 'Poppy took the first one, as he had to see his publisher. I went off to have my hair done. By some strange fluke, when I hailed a cab outside the hairdresser's to get back to the hotel, I had the same taxi driver Poppy had earlier.' Then she said with a meaningful emphasis that I didn't fully comprehend, 'He turned round to me and asked me if I knew where he'd taken my husband. He thought I ought to know. The driver hadn't taken him to the publisher.'

She flung the filled hot-water bottles on the table with a thud. Stepfather continued to pour more milk on his huge bowl of cereal. He had begun to look sheepish.

'Can't we talk about this some other time?' he growled and sent me to bed.

I was perplexed. Lying on my bed, I buried my head in my pillow. What had the taxi driver been implying? As I look back as an adult, my suspicions are clearer. Mum was so emotionally angry that night she must have believed he had visited a woman. Had it been a prostitute?

More stories from previous years came to light when a few of the friendly mechanics who had once been so faithful to BRM agreed to meet me as part of my investigations. At first hesitatingly, they told me things about my stepfather's behaviour.

When Louis was beginning to get more power and to throw his weight around with fledgling drivers, Niki Lauda, was one of those who became attracted to Louis's web. As a well-heeled young man, he flew from the comfort of his urban home in Austria and arrived on a damp winter's day for a two o'clock appointment in the rural flats of the Lincolnshire countryside, where BRM had their offices. Louis insisted that the young man be kept waiting in a small draughty hall with no heating for two hours before entering Louis's inner sanctum. Ex-employees quipped that Louis had a strong light that reminded them of the Gestapo. As soon as the interviewee entered the room, Louis directed the light down on to his own massive hands that he kept firmly clasped on the desk. His low voice came from behind this screen of light and however the employee or interviewee might try to angle their head they could not see Louis' face. It was remarkable that Lauda agreed to drive for BRM, but early in this contract Louis managed to infuriate the young talented driver, so he stormed off to Ferrari. He was later to become World Champion, not once but three times.

When Mum persuaded Stepfather that he would be a suitable person to fight the insufferable authorities and improve the safety of Grand Prix drivers, in order to take action he needed to travel around the country much more. Huge amounts of mileage for little gain became too much for my mother, so Louis employed a part-time driver. This gave Stepfather too much freedom and the mechanics told me that he often never arrived for important meetings at the headquarters in Bourne, but was taken to see a lady in Harrogate.

On other occasions mechanics were asked to replace my mother as Stepfather's regular driver. They told stories of his strange driving demands. One story involved taking him weekly to a woman's house in Ealing Broadway. He would stay for over an hour while she supposedly typed up his notes. But, when they collected him, he would be flushed and during the journey back to London he would periodically throw pieces of paper out of the window. Other stories included Stepfather telling the mechanic to use the car as a billiard ball and bounce off other cars. He directed them so aggressively they never knew whether he was joking or not. Certainly, when a driver cut into Mum's car, Stepfather demanded the mechanic chase the car and force it to stop. Stepfather got the handle of his umbrella and hooked it round the poor driver's neck and told him that he was the chief inspector of Cambridgeshire Police.

It took some persuading for the bashful mechanics to tell me they suspected Stepfather 'had a liking for young boys'. In the early evenings he demanded of whoever was on duty that they take him to a hotel on the North Circular that had a name for acts with young boys. The joint was sleazy and he never stayed long. Again, he returned to the car red-faced. No wonder the mechanics were timid! These stories were far too frightening for me.

As our visits were now severely limited, we often heard stories at second hand from the nurses. We were shocked when they later told us that Louis put Mum under great pressure to attend the dreaded party. Pam, her favoured night nurse, told me she had been fretting about the fancy clothes Louis expected her to wear and feared being paraded around in a wheelchair. The worry brought on another epileptic fit. Before Stepfather could protest, the nurses rushed her to Addenbrooke's Hospital just down the road from the house, but this did not stop him from pushing his weight around once they arrived. He demanded the hospital staff provide her with a single-occupancy NHS room and instructed the managers he was providing his own nursing staff. The medicals looked on astonished as his entourage arrived with posses of nurses and Joe the handyman-cum-chauffeur, who now acted as the watchman. The elderly man with his own sick wife was ordered to sit in the corridor, guarding the entrance to my mother's room for two days and nights. Stepfather had begun to rely on Joe more and more and had bribed him with promises of better times. Long, paid holidays in his native Ireland were offered as an enticement to work ridiculous hours. He never got his money.

There was one good outcome: Stepfather could not sabotage our visits to the hospital. When I visited he was in a particularly friendly mood and thanked me for coming to Mum's bedside. He agreed that I could sleep on the hard floor beside my mother's bed. But his conversation kept returning to the party, which was to be held three days later. It was not to be cancelled. It was not a topic I was willing to discuss, so in a fury he sent me away. As I drove out of the hospital car park my mobile rang. He had changed his mind. Mum was fretting and wanted to know where I was. We must have looked a sorry sight: Joe guarding the room, a night nurse at my mother's left side, I lying on the floor and Louis sleeping in the chair on my mother's right.

In the middle of the night Mum wanted to talk to me but her speech was unclear. However, I worked out that she was hungry, so I made toast in the kitchen opposite. As Louis snored I fed my mother crumbs of toast, which she ate like a little bird as the dawn sun peeped through the shutters. It was good to be able to be with my mother, but now I was sure Louis cared little for her and was interested only in his own image.

I was in a dilemma. Should I attend the party or not? In the end I decided it would be prudent to do so. Sure enough, no expense was spared in the large suite Louis had hired. Wine flowed and ice sculptures of racing cars melted with many motor-racing celebrities attending.

In previous weeks nurses had been enticed to stay and look after Mum with promises of sitting close to a VIP at the celebrity dinner, as the party date approached he started to weed out the less attractive women, but even with this cull he still ordered what he called a 'charabanc' to seat 25 nurses for their journey from Cambridgeshire.

But once again he did not keep his word and his group of favoured nurses were placed in the Grill Room well away from the other guests. I was worried perhaps many of them would have been so disappointed they might never return to help my mum.

At the party I had my objective, so I made a beeline for Mr L, Mum's trusted executor. He *had* to listen to our pleas for help. I pictured how Mum used to walk me round the garden and when we got to the courtyard with our backs to the blue gate she would tell me how much she loved the house. She would repeat, 'Whenever you've got a problem, you must go to Mr L: he knows everything about the family.'

I reminded Mr L of her words. He promised to do all he could but he never contacted us.

Why would Mr L not help? This man had been allowed to run the family trust for the last twenty years. Why was he not protecting our mother's best interests? We started to investigate and dig where we, as groomed children, had been told not to. We soon found out why Mr L hadn't rung. He had been swindling us out of money for years and had allowed Stepfather to 'borrow' large amounts of money from our trust, which of course is against the law.

I was relieved when the party was finally over and my mother was safely back from hospital. Maybe things might settle down now that Louis had had his fun. But my spirits nosedived on my next precious visit to see my mother. Stepfather turned to me and spoke in his lowest tone: 'Hey ho, pity my Dorchester do's over. But it was only the beginning. It's the first of many parties I'm planning to throw.' The grim words cut through me.

Meanwhile, our lawyer told us there was nothing we could do immediately to stop Stepfather getting further into debt, but that did not stop us sitting with him for hours suggesting how he might realise the estate. Then Stepfather seemed unnaturally happy to enter into talks with our lawyer. Again, we soon found out why. He had been telling her he was organising a sensible course of action while behind her back he was making devious plans of his own. He was ringing up mega-wealthy motor-racing VIPs asking if they would be willing to buy my mother's house. None of them was naïve enough to buy the house but Bernie Ecclestone, who must have realised he was getting a real bargain, agreed to buy my mother's only valuable painting, a Millais, which was of a ghostly lady and had hung above the fireplace in the dining room. The input of cash did little to help the situation, with various local firms rattling at his door urgently wanting their huge accounts settled. Stepfather's reaction was to fire his solicitor and seek another.

Having no cash did not seem to worry Stepfather. He announced to one and all that he had money locked up in the value of the house. Rogues appeared with more frequency as he deluded himself he had a bottomless pit of gold. Once, I opened the door to an irate butcher demanding Stepfather pay him £1,467; the last cheque he had written had bounced. When he could not find the money to pay for the food for the household he resorted to borrowing money from the nurses. He never paid them back.

Every time I saw him he had an even better reason for taking out a large loan from the bank against the security of the house. The manager of my mother's bank in Cambridge was completely charmed. She was so entranced she even left her office, to hand over personally the sizeable loan papers to Stepfather, as he sat in the passenger seat of his brand-new Chrysler.

During these distressing times I experienced a strange coincidence. As I was driving to my local shops, I happened to tune into a radio programme about the supreme craftiness of conmen. Intelligent women in high-powered professions retold their experiences of being attracted to men who ruined their lives. Some ended up devoid of all their worldly possessions, others had their bank accounts emptied. But each of these intellectually gifted women insisted that *her* man had been a charismatic person, who, even when her suspicions were aroused, was able to keep her loyalty by using wildly romantic gestures. The programme enlightened me on my present position and explained why Mum had stayed with Stepfather for so many years. I had to agree my stepfather could be charismatic when he put his mind to it. The stories on the radio made me realise how he had stealthily manipulated all the professionals around him. No wonder our many efforts to develop communications with the GP, the nursing agency, the geriatric consultant, his lawyer, the family accountant, the property developer, the physiotherapist and everybody else involved in the case had fallen on deaf ears.

It's hard to believe that even at this stage I did not grasp just how dishonest my Stepfather was. I found the whole issue hard to stomach. I could not get to grips with his fraudulent world but I had to agree he excelled at telling four different stories to four different groups of people. He never slipped up. When he called on the phone and I listened to his arguments I would start to doubt my own sanity, as his viewpoints were always so coherent. When I put the receiver down I was exhausted. His brain was working on a different plane from mine. He was always one step ahead of us all. Most worryingly of all he seemed hell bent on destroying us.

The house of course would have to be sold. Would the property developer pull down the garage, once a storehouse for the windmill? And of course the enclosed garden would be lost. The garden had provided me with a junior archaeologist's dream. As a child I had been particularly thrilled when I found a name crafted by a worker into one of the bricks that had been salvaged from the demolished windmill and used to build the garden wall. Meanwhile, we kept asking Louis's new solicitor, Mr H, if he had seen our mother on her own. Was he sure he was acting in our mother's best interests?

This lawyer seemed antagonistic to us all and only supported Stepfather's more harebrained schemes. Through Diana, our lawyer, we kept reminding him that we believed he had never taken personal instructions from our mother. The lawyer agreed he had not seen our mother on her own but he kept insisting that he was acting for both Mr and Mrs Stanley.

Mr H encouraged Stepfather to sell the house but more worryingly he did not seem at all concerned about what price he might get for the property. We pointed out that at Louis's rate of spending the money from the sale would not last long and once it had gone there would be no more to put aside for the care of my mother.

My relations, who were experiencing their own endless late-night telephone calls from Stepfather, began to realise just how desperate the situation had become. Cousins started to tell stories we should have heard years ago, but they had been sworn to secrecy and believed we were genuinely fond of our Stepfather. Right from the start Stepfather was a jagged thorn in my mother's family's side. He had often caused family strife, writing threatening letters and libelling my uncle more than once. But my uncles and cousins respected my mother and did all they could to keep relationships good. One cousin, called Grace, who had been particularly close to my mother, told me two stories that had happened years before. One day, Grace had bumped into my mother, who was waiting anxiously outside a Cambridge bank; she was unnaturally edgy and asked Grace to move on and not chat. This was totally out of character. The other worrying event was at a family wedding, where my mother tearfully confided to my cousin that she wished she had not bought her new outfit because the large amount of money she believed was in her account had vanished. More stories came from cousin David. Twice in the past, under the influence of Louis, my mother had borrowed money against the value of the house. David worried about this unnatural behaviour, so, when Stepfather borrowed cash the second time, my cousin organised an additional clause in their agreement. If the house or any of the garden was used for development my mother would pay a small additional amount back to the cousins. This, David hoped, would protect my mother from Louis's excessive spending. This same clause might stop Stepfather from selling the house in an underhand manner, the cousins' lawyer advised. This knowledge made us feel more secure but we knew it was only temporary. As an extended family we discussed what tactics we could use, as it was impossible to predict Louis's next move. His most recent ploy was to collapse into tears when it suited him. But at least the whole family were now working in harmony and I did not feel quite so alone.

Pressure was building and the cousins called a meeting, inviting the three lawyers involved, Diana, Mr H and the cousins' own lawyer, who had dealt with Louis in the past. All were invited to suggest ways to provide my mother with the urgent financial security she needed. Stepfather's lawyer explained that he had been working with Mr C, the property developer, on a profitable equity-release scheme with Northern Rock. Everybody thought this seemed a most satisfactory deal and thought Louis should sign.

My attendance at the meeting caused aftershocks. Louis was angry and offensive with me. Then he presented us with the really bad news. He couldn't possibly afford to live on £18,000 a month. Most frightening of all was that his two 'trusted' advisers, Mr H and Mr C, 'changed their minds' and were backing his refusal to enter into this sensible equity-release scheme. His spending continued to be ridiculous and his cheques were of no use. Disaster was only round the corner.

The property developer Mr C had become Louis's 'friend'. He spent much time on the phone with him and even more hours ensconced with him in his study working out yet another equity-release scheme. But we had no doubt this new friend was up to no good. Why would a property developer spend so many hours with this old man if he did not think he was going to make a mint? He was a typical sleazy salesman, but Louis could not see it.

Maintaining a meaningful dialogue was tough. I was in a conundrum. If I was too aggressive and demanded that he address Mum's rights, I feared my outbursts would blow away any sense of goodwill that was left. And then what would we do? I had to keep all channels open. It seemed the only answer. If we lost all contact with him he would stop even our derisory visits. Our mother was already suffering emotionally. She had never seen the many gifts and cards we had sent, as the nurses were ordered to throw them away as soon as they arrived. She needed to know we had not abandoned her. She needed to know we cared.

I was soon to find out other painful truths.

Eleanor, one of the original faithful nurses, who had recently been dismissed for speaking out about my mother's care, asked to see us. She said, 'Mr Stanley's constantly telling your mother that you don't love her.' She continued with her bad news. 'He rings a woman late every night. He declares his love for her.' I must have looked aghast. 'She's called Barbara.'

I remembered phone calls I had made over the years to my mother. She and I had liked to talk about nothing of any great importance, as only mother and daughter can.

Louis had always answered the phone and sometimes he had difficulty hearing my name. The repetition of 'who?' became more intense as the years progressed. I had tried to put this down to his increasing age but I had harboured a nagging suspicion. Who else had a name like mine and rang him at eleven o'clock at night?

Who was this other woman? Had Stepfather been unfaithful throughout his marriage to my mother?

CHAPTER 8

FAMILY PUZZLES

If Louis had been born on or around 6 January 1912, then conception would have been around April or May 1911. Did Asquith know Venetia at this time? In the Brocks' book there was only one published letter before this date and that was written on 10 September 1910. There were no more published letters until 1912. These were dated 1 April, 13 July and 14 August. I was disappointed. But at least I had proved to myself that the two key players in my story did know each other before 1912. The lack of earlier letters intrigued me, but they also flummoxed me. Surely, if Asquith and Venetia had conceived a baby they would have been writing to each other in 1911 and 1912, rather than after their child was born. Doubts started to creep into my head.

One day I awoke to find myself thinking of the photograph of the woman with the long string of pearls. I had a flashback. On this occasion, I was in my early twenties, and Mum had invited me into her bedroom to see her new outfit. The room was hot, with the gas fire burning at full force. I saw that she was a little tense but we continued to admire the purple coat with its huge buttons. Despite my being considerably taller than she was, she insisted I try it on. But as I reached up to take it off its cushioned hanger the floorboards bounced under my feet. Stepfather was approaching. He had a photograph in his hand. My heart sank. Was this another celebrity I would have to marvel at? I was wrong. The black-and-white photograph was of an attractive woman, possibly in her twenties. Around her neck was a long string of pearls.

'It's Poppy's dearest mother when she was younger,' said my mother. 'He showed me the photo last night.'

Was he actually showing me evidence of his past life? My heart pumped faster. My mind was in confusion. The woman seemed so elegant, so striking. Why had stepfather not bragged before that Home Granny had been a beauty?

'Lovely,' I stuttered. I felt an embarrassing silence approaching, so I hastily added, 'When was it taken?'

Mum had moved to the other side of the room. She noisily fiddled with a box of costume jewellery. I didn't move even though the gas fire was burning my legs. There was an awkward moment.

'When she was engaged.' Mum's voice came from afar.

'Engaged?' I repeated questioningly.

'Yes, you know in those days you had your photo in *Tatler* or *Vanity Fair* when you announced you were going to be married.' Her voice seemed to come from even further away.

'Did you?' I managed to say. Nothing seemed to hang together. Home Granny had never seemed to be the sort of person to have her photo in a magazine. I had known her only when she was old, but why had he never made any reference to her early life? As at other times in my childhood when small windows were opened I was unprepared and unable to take full advantage of the grain of opportunity to pry into his past. But for days afterwards I worried about this strange event.

Now, as I pondered again, I remembered a more recent event. In December 1999 my mother rang me up asking what I was doing for the New Millennium celebrations. She did not normally take much interest in New Year festivities but she sounded anxious. I asked why, and she told me that Louis was to receive an honour in the government's annual announcements. I offered my congratulations, thinking she meant a minor award. But then she rang me again saying that Stepfather could not tell from the Downing Street letter which award he had won but Louis thought he was to receive a knighthood. My mother was worried because she did not want to be known as Lady Stanley. I understood her concern but I was amazed by her news. What had my stepfather done in the past to deserve such an honour? I kept the information to myself, as Mum had instructed.

Luckily, I had a previous engagement for the big night but I worried about leaving my mother alone when she might have wanted us all to help celebrate Louis's success. So on the morning of 1 January 2000 I expected an early call, but the phone never rang. I then checked the honours list in the papers. Louis Stanley's name was not there. I felt it was not the right thing to mention the omission and I never brought up the matter. However, I now applied some thought to this strange story. Had the government advisers found at a late hour that he was not acceptable material for an honour? Or had Louis made up the story of the letter? If so, why?

My reading was becoming more time-consuming but Naomi Levine's book on Edwin Montagu proved very useful. I had ordered the American version of the publication called *Politics, Religion, and Love: the story of the love affair that changed the face of politics in the British Empire* I was thrilled to find two enthralling snippets of information in one paragraph. First, Venetia's parents were a prominent Liberal family and her father was an MP. Second, and even more important, were the words, 'By 1907 Asquith had what his wife called a "Little Harem" of young girls.'

As I read on I found there was evidence that Venetia's own

family had been concerned about her relationship with Asquith. Family gossip was clearly upsetting Venetia's mother, Lady Sheffield. Venetia's married sister, Blanche, penned this letter to her other sister Sylvia. 'No doubt she is very fond of the PM – but you don't think there are any signs of her being too fond of him do you?' (I found this letter dated November 1914 in Adelaide Lubbock's book, *People in Glass Houses*). So had the extended family suspected the relationship was unsuitable? Certainly Venetia's mother admitted she had little control over her headstrong daughter and was possibly even afraid of her. The Asquith–Stanley conspiracy was becoming more interesting.

A year had now passed since my mother's stroke and she was beginning to make her own protests. As we have seen, we were rarely allowed to visit, but rumours were circulating that she was refusing to eat. Could she be on hunger strike? It was around Christmas and on my previous visit Stepfather had permitted me to help Mum with her present ordering. The next time I arrived I was armed with homemade Christmas cards for her to open. She was sitting in the drawing room, the large double room that had once housed Home Granny and Auntie Mamie. Even after all these years I had not got used to freely walking through the heavy door that had kept them apart from us. Louis's penetrating voice came from the depths of his chair, which groaned under the transfer of his bulk as he reached forward. 'Just pay up.' He paused. 'All the presents for Christmas have been sent back.' The words cut through me. He certainly knew how to hurt my mother.

After a pause my mother announced in her old familiar tone, 'I am not eating!'

Would nobody listen? Not one professional of any discipline would pay any attention to us. Was our mother at 90 years of age not sending out a clear message by refusing to eat?

Things had already started to 'mysteriously' disappear in the house and nothing was insured. I reflected on our lawyer's advice: we must not provide him short-term financial help, since it 'would only put the crisis off for another week or so'. I knew in my heart she was right but I wanted to help. Louis was deeply in debt. He could not pay any wages and, amazingly, the nursing agency had allowed him to clock up a bill of over £70,000. It frightened us that the same agency was threatening to withdraw all care to my mother unless this bill was settled – and quickly.

Stepfather started to sell off chattels from the family home. But when he alerted local businesses he might have objects to sell, many of which had been handed down from my mother's side of the family, they became vultures, hovering, waiting for the kill. It was painful to watch them play their own part in his downfall. Stepfather tried to dispose of the garden ornaments that Mum had collected over the years. He did not care that the rogue gave him a paltry price. Then my brother discovered that Stepfather was trying to sell family objects without any of us knowing. He had clandestinely put the chattels with a small country saleroom. I did not want to witness the foolishness of the sale, so I spoke on the phone to the auctioneer. He felt sorry for me and allowed me to buy a barograph at a negotiated price. I was pleased I had at least one object to remind me of my old home. But I had little else Stepfather had made sure all the family photographs were thrown into a tip.

Then more bad news filtered through. Joe, the handyman-cum-chauffeur-cum-bouncer, had been ordered to buy handcuffs. What would Joe be told to do with them? But the next story that percolated through from those still ensconced in the house was almost beyond my credulity.

The agency was struggling to find any more sensible employees but they found one last nurse who had not visited my mum before. We gasped as it filtered through a whispering movement from within the house that this nurse had been found engrossed in a sexual act with Louis Stanley. She had confessed in a lengthy letter to her employers how aged Stepfather had induced her to perform. She wrote intimate details of his flirtatious nature and explained how she had been caught out by two carers from another agency who had become suspicious of her behaviour. They had walked unannounced into the room overlooking the garden, where I had once housed my toys. They found the fifty-year old nurse leaning over Stepfather. She had her knickers around her ankles. I was not just stunned: I was frightened. How had this man in his ninetieth year persuaded this middle-aged nurse to execute such an act?

Things deteriorated even further with Mr H, Louis's lawyer. We wondered if he had ever seen the situation clearly but, without a doubt, he was now fully sucked into Louis's web and was losing touch with veracity. He could not tell right from wrong and had failed to get independent advice for my mother. When challenged, he was ambiguous. Then, 18 months after my mother's stroke, he assembled the legal papers so that Stepfather could sell my mother's house. In May 2002, armed with these papers, he then went to the house with Dr F, Mum's geriatric consultant, as a witness. Mum was to be asked to sign them. But Mr H had underestimated our mother! Mum confronted them and refused to sign. My mother's brain was still keen and she was not going to sign anything she did not understand. Dr F later reported that he had been witness to her words. She spoke in the strongest voice she could muster and repeated twice, 'I want my own lawyer.' The medical consultant was shocked and reported it all to our lawyer, Diana. Finally we had the consultant's evidence that she really had been asking for her own solicitor, but we needed to work fast. Her health was failing. We had to find her a lawyer quickly. But how?

The constant ringing of my home and mobile phone numbers over the previous 18 months had been draining. Each time I received a call there was some new drama to be tackled. As I wearily walked through the front door one Sunday night after working in Cardiff all weekend, I dreamed of having the time to wind down, restock the fridge and catch up with my kids and sleep. But this was not to be. As soon as I walked through the door a call confirmed that I had to be in Cambridge early the following morning.

Kim, a carer with a little more inner strength than others, had contacted my brother. She could not stand the situation any more at Old Mill House. My mother was turning against Stepfather and urgently begged her rotational nurses to organise a lawyer of her own. More worryingly, Mum had restarted her hunger strike and threatened not to eat until she saw her own children. Kim knew she was in a fragile condition and her threats were serious.

Her whistle-blowing call was the prompt to more frantic action. But once again all the professionals failed to respond to our redoubled efforts to get them to listen. The social services reacted but their cogs revolved without any urgency, so I rang the police. The local beat officer agreed to visit the next day. We heard only later that the carers experienced the full brunt of what happened next. First, Louis turned the blame on his nurses, then he turned the full power of his wrath on the policeman himself. Louis demanded it was his right to speak to the chief inspector but the beat officer stood his ground. The law stood that we had the right to visit our mother. Mum could not be kept a prisoner away from her family any more.

Monday was to be a busy day. Over the weekend our London solicitor had worked hard to find a lawyer who could represent my mother at short notice, not an easy task. Solicitors are not easily contactable at nonstandard times and it had seemed an almost unachievable task. But eventually Mr K, a housing lawyer who usually dealt with conveyancing tasks, accepted our brief to talk to Mum at four o'clock that Monday afternoon. Diana was to travel down to Cambridge to help instruct this new lawyer. So at break of day I found myself driving across the flat countryside of south

Cambridgeshire, when the mobile rang. I pulled off the road into the car park of a familiar motel. It was my brother Edward on the phone, asking me how close I was to Cambridge. His weary voice, told me there had been another development.

'Get here as soon as you can. He's trying to sell the house to the Dorchester Hotel.'

'What?' I said incredulously.

'That's what I heard from Kim. Just get there as quick as you can.' I agreed to rendezvous with him outside the local pub.

Twenty minutes later as I drew into the pub's car park he waved me down by flapping some papers in his hand. He talked hurriedly, as he explained that Kim had overheard Stepfather invite the managers of the Dorchester Hotel to the house. Next came the bombshell. I was to be left to tackle the managers on my own, as my brother had to collect our lawyer Diana from the station. The managers were due to arrive at midday. I looked at my watch. We had five minutes.

I felt alone standing outside the blue gate waiting to intercept the Dorchester Hotel people with my flimsy pieces of paper, but the adrenaline was pumping through my body. I stood watching the traffic go by. The road had been a country lane in my childhood but it now acted as a bypass for much of Cambridge. Huge trucks and a variety of cars accelerated as they went past the gate.

As I waited I heard a voice above the noise of the traffic. I turned and saw Kim, her arms waving frantically. She was at the garage gates, we ran towards each other. She was desperate to get her news out: 'You'll not be able to gain access this afternoon,' she blurted. 'Mr Stanley's hired a new bouncer. Nobody'll be allowed in the house.' She paused for breath as I stared blankly at her. 'I heard Mr Stanley tell him he shouldn't let anybody in. That means your mother's lawyer won't be allowed in.'

My mind was racing to catch up with the meaning of Kim's words.

'Come with me now,' she said. 'At least, I can get one of you in the house. He told me the garage gates are to be kept open for a few hours, so I can get you in through the garden door.'

'I can't,' I said weakly.

'Yeah, I've 'eard about them Dorchester guys,' she said, 'and the hotel managers 'ave been told to bring their own lunch!' She almost chuckled, releasing some of her tension. We decided that, after my assignation with the Dorchester staff, the best policy would be to follow her into the house and hide. Kim and I went back to our respective stations. Thoughts rushed through my head. How would I identify the men? I didn't know their names. How would they behave? Would they believe me? Maybe they would just push me aside.

As traffic filtered from the south, a gleaming bronzed Daimler eased round the corner, its powerful engine purring as it drew towards the kerbstones. Were they here?

As I tried to look in the darkened windows, the car shot off from under my nose. Had I frightened them off? Of course, they had been told to drive straight into the garage; that was why the gates were open.

With sandals flapping, I bolted up the pavement. Running like this reminded me of the old days. After some family outings Stepfather gave me piggybacks. He bounded me along pretending to be a Grand National jockey, tossing me high on his wide back. But, as he slowed and reached the courtyard gate, his right hand moved from supporting the inside of my knee to under my skirt. I learned to refuse piggybacks and one of the delights of childhood had gone for ever. I began running to compensate. Instead of allowing him to scoop me up in his arms, I ran at full velocity, enjoying the sound of the wind rushing past my ears. I ran everywhere, not only to escape his clutches, but for pure pleasure. I practised on that same stretch of pavement. When I believed I could escape from custodial eyes, I sneaked out of the garden, and pitted my prowess against the passing cars. The short section of pavement between garage and gate became my home straight in the Olympic final.

But this time I had got only halfway, when I saw that the car was only using our driveway to turn round. I ran back, feeling sheepish. The car parked facing the oncoming traffic. I moved forward to greet the driver, only to find he turned his back and ceremoniously opened the rear doors.

Two men emerged from the car. They towered over me in executive suits, with equally well-cultivated ties. I suddenly felt out of place with my glowing face, my flimsy summer dress and flip-flop sandals. As they drew near, the chauffeur continued to busy himself, reaching into the ample boot to extract the grandest arrangement of lilies with exotic foliage, followed by a resplendent platter of sandwiches on a lavish silver salver.

'I'm Mrs Stanley's daughter,' I blurted, still out of breath.

'Oh, how nice to meet you.' The taller of the two reached to shake my hand.' I'm so sorry—' But I cut him short.

'I must tell you, my mother isn't allowed to see any of her children. She's being held prisoner in her own house.'

'We've come because Mr Stanley had a proposal...We don't know...'

'You'll be offered our mother's house to buy but it's not his to sell.' I waved the flimsy papers.

The yellow tie of the elegant man gleamed in the sun as he started to reassure me he did not know why he had been called.

'But please hear me out. You can't go in the house without listening to my story. We've tried everything we can to help our mother. We love her dearly and she's being treated appallingly.' As I saw his face become concerned I relaxed a little. Maybe he was not going to be the enemy after all.

'We heard your mother is unwell and were told to bring lunch for everyone,' he said.

'He's run out of money to buy food,' I said without thinking. 'That's why.'

But we couldn't stand on the exposed pavement for long, with the chauffeur juggling the huge bouquet and sandwiches between his tiring arms.

As they assured me that our conversation would be treated as confidential, my sister and brother arrived to give further support. But now it was time for Plan B.

I felt despondent as I walked up the pavement to the shabby blue garage doors. I nervously stepped on the garden paths, past my mother's herbaceous beds filled with scented flowers. I heard the birds sing their courting songs and wished I could appreciate the delights of the month of June. Kim was waiting and gave me the all-clear signal to tiptoe into the house. I eased myself around the corner and tucked myself into the laundry. My first task was to close the door gently and pull the bolt across without alerting the bouncer, who was reputedly in the kitchen.

The laundry was a cold north-facing room with a deep freeze and washing machine. There were no chairs and the floor was dirty, cold and uninviting. I contemplated my fate.

The amiable voices of carer Georgina and nurse Pauline chattering as they pottered in the kitchen reassured me, but my legs began to ache. So when my mobile vibrated in my pocket I was delighted. It was the family checking I was safely ensconced in the house.

Suddenly, there was a loud knock on the door, and I slid behind the freezer, as stiff as its contents. There was another bash and a stranger's voice echoed through the door,

It was a man's voice telling me that I could come out of my hiding place. I made no reply. It could be a trick. He knocked again. Then his footsteps retreated and I heard the familiar noise of the kitchen door closing. After a few moments there was another knock, lighter this time. The voice was Georgina's.

'You can't stay in the laundry all afternoon. We told the new chap and he's OK with you. Come into the kitchen.'

I thought for a while, then tentatively unbolted the door. The stranger was sitting in the far corner. During the exploits of the morning, I had completely forgotten about the need for food and drink. As I looked for some familiar objects to make a cup of tea, a wave of grief came over me.

The bouncer spoke in lowered Northern tones. He told me his name was Peter and that Stepfather had hired him to control the front door for the day. He was to replace the faithful Joe who had finally seen the emptiness of Louis's promises. Peter had been told that only certain visitors would be allowed in the house. As I started to recover my composure, I become conscious that the Dorchester men were still with Stepfather in the dining room. That meant Mum must be on her own!

I grabbed Pauline to see what she thought. 'Yes, go ahead, it's a perfect opportunity,' she said. 'I'll just go and see if she's awake and tell her that you're here. Then I'll make a noise outside her room when they're all leaving, so you'll have time to leave her bedside.'

I crept up the back stairs with trepidation. It would be only the second time that I had seen her alone for over a year.

I pushed open the door. It made its familiar faint squeaks. There was Mum lying in bed looking so much smaller. Stepfather's guard chair was empty. It had taken a battering over the last months: the velvet was faded and most of its tassels had fallen off; one last golden fringe hung limply by two threads and in the middle of the seat there was a streak of encrusted stains where food had dropped.

I crept up to Mum's bed. She was sleepy but smiled her old smile as her eyes found mine. Then she looked nervously at the chair. I reassured her.

'He's downstairs with some chaps from the Dorchester, Mum,' I whispered. 'We've been doing everything we can to help you, Mum.'

'It's lovely to see you, darling, but where are the others? And when am I going to see my lawyer?' She sounded more anxious. 'I want my own lawyer. Where is he? Is he with you?'

'No, Mum. He'll be here at four as arranged. It's all fixed for four o'clock. Try not to worry.'

'Oh dear, I don't think I can wait that long. How long do I have to wait?'

I looked at my watch and could hardly bring myself to admit there were three hours to go. She was clearly tired, but stubbornly keeping herself awake.

'What's Poppy doing now?'

I wasn't sure if I should tell her. 'He's with the managers of the Dorchester Hotel,' I said.

'I am not selling the house to them!' she said in her old familiar forceful tone, less loud perhaps but just as authoritative.

I bent down and gently cuddled my mum. I was shocked that there was nothing of her. She was now so fragile. I gave her the gentlest of squeezes but she insisted I squeeze harder, just like we always did.

Then I heard the cowbell ringing. This must be the signal. As I bent to give her another kiss she anxiously held my hand.

'Don't let me down,' she whispered. 'I want to see you all.'

'Don't worry, we'll be here really soon.'

I tiptoed back down to the laundry to call my siblings on the mobile phone.

'Anything more than two hours is just too long for her to wait,' I urged.

'We're doing absolutely all we can to get there, but things are slow,' came the response. 'We've not even met the emergency lawyer yet.'

Back in the kitchen time passed slowly. The only event was the sound of Stepfather's feet on the stairs. He called for his new bouncer.

Peter returned grim-faced. He went to the back door and familiarised himself with the various bolts, chains and locks. The whole house was waiting: Mum in her bed, Stepfather in the study, the carers in their room, the bouncer in the kitchen with me hiding in a corner.

Each time the jangling bell rang above the blue gate warning us of a visitor, I ducked down under the canary-yellow cupboards that had been proudly fixed in place when I was young. First was Pam, the night nurse. She and Mum had built up a close relationship, and Pauline had sensibly called her. Pauline knew Mum would want Pam to be at her bedside when she met her new lawyer.

The next visitor was Dr F, the consultant in geriatrics. He had never responded to our letters. Peter checked that he was bona fide then undid Fort Knox to let the doctor in. Once he had been shown through, Peter perched himself on a high stool in the kitchen near an old hatchway: 'You can 'ear them talk really well. You ought to listen.' But I heard the consultant's raised voice from my position. 'Mr Stanley, I know that Mrs Stanley is poorly, she's got slight pneumonia but she's in a stable condition. If her condition is unchanged from this morning, when I examined her, she's well enough to see visitors.'

I moved closer.

'But my wife is very poorly. They'll upset her composure.' It was on occasions like this he used his lowest scary tones.

'No, I'm going to see her on my own, Mr Stanley,' I heard the consultant say quite firmly.

The tide was shifting.

As the consultant left to go up the stairs, the jangling bell rang again. Next it was the GP's turn to visit his patient. Soon after, the blue gate opened again and Peter admitted Louis's lawyer, Mr H. The bouncer showed him into the dining room, where the medical party joined him.

In another furtive mobile phone call I told my siblings what the position was. They told me Mum's lawyer was now free from his scheduled work but they were stuck in Cambridge's rush-hour traffic. I thought of Mum, frail and anxious in her lonely plight.

After the GP left Peter turned out all the downstairs lights. He double-locked the door, placed the security chain in position and pulled the bolt across. I retreated back to my hiding place, conscious that Peter could change sides at any time.

The bell jangled again, heralding the arrival of my siblings, Mr K, Mum's new lawyer and our lawyer, Diana. I strained my ears to hear what was happening at the door but dare not leave my sanctuary.

After a few minutes the doorbell rang again. This time I was braver and saw that the party were all still outside in the courtyard. My mobile vibrated. It was my brother. 'What's going on?' he asked, sounding as if I were somehow to blame.

After a few more minutes the two lawyers knocked assertively on the kitchen window. Peter opened the door on its security latch. I couldn't hear the exchange of words from my position. But I heard him replace the locks and pull the bolt across as he went to relay the two solicitors' message back to Mr Stanley and his team. After more to-ing and fro-ing, Mr H came to talk over the intruder chain. There were more delays but eventually he allowed Mum's new legal adviser into the house. I looked at my watch. It was six o'clock. Poor Mum! I hoped that Pam had been able to keep her calm. But she still had to wait another half an hour. Mum's lawyer was not led straight upstairs but shown into the dining room, another delaying tactic.

My siblings and Diana were still out in the courtyard. They pulled up some dusty courtroom chairs and I spoke to them through a gap in the window. They asked for some coffee. But there was no milk in the fridge. 'There's no money for things like that,' Georgina whispered.

There was little point getting angry, so the group outside started to sing, 'Why are we waiting?' and even attempted to play charades to relieve the tension.

At two o'clock that afternoon Mum had told me that two hours was too long to wait. It was now six hours later and she had still not seen us. Did she think we had all abandoned her?

Finally, I heard Mr K go upstairs with the consultant and I

joined the group in the courtyard, but I was not there long, as Mr K soon returned looking years older. He was ashen from the experience and sputtered, 'I didn't know the Dickensian world still existed.' His meeting with Mum had lasted less than 15 minutes. He could obviously not tell us everything but he confirmed that Mum had been too exhausted to really talk. But, more crucially, he reported that there was a conflict of interest between Stepfather and Mum. They both needed their own lawyers.

Pam came down and spoke to us through the window. She told us she had tried to reassure Mum that we would be allowed to see her in the next few days.

Lawyer K had arranged to go back and see Mum in two days' time. He never did go back. Louis had organised the medicals to declare that she was 'mentally unfit' and she could not be involved in any more decisions.

CHAPTER 9

THE WATER LILY

The police had done their work and now Stepfather could not stop us visiting. It was strange to be allowed back in the house, but it was an even stranger experience to receive smiles from our mother's carers. At last they knew the full story. We had organised an emergency fund for our mother's care. If and when the nursing agency pulled out, our monies would swing into action. The agency now realised the error of their ways and agreed with us that Louis Stanley should not know we were funding his nurses. Out of the woodwork the original faithful nurses reappeared. We were warned Mum's health was not good, but far more worrying was Stepfather's new actions. He was now determined Mum should be fed through a tube, as she was starting to lose her swallow reflex.

The other problem was that, now Mum had been declared 'mentally unfit', a lawyers' meeting was needed to arrange who should have power of attorney over her affairs. I agreed to attend the first-half hour of the meeting but I wished I hadn't, because I had to face the crooked accountant, Mr L, the money-grabbing property developer, John C, and the ineffective, biased lawyer, Mr H. Stepfather wanted his 'friend', the property developer and lawyer Mr H, to have power of attorney over my mother's affairs. I left the meeting to dash back to go through the blue gate once again as the GP, who had previously hidden away from us, was going to talk to us about Mum's health.

However, the doctor had come earlier than he told us he would, and by the time I arrived the nurses were rubbing their hands with anguish. Mum had already got a tube down her nose. She had apparently agreed to the procedure so that she could receive fluids. At first I was encouraged because the GP was at last talking directly to us, but he did not listen to our protests that Mum had explicitly told us she did not want medical intervention. All he could say was that he had already agreed with Mr Stanley that Mrs Stanley would be given the minimum amount of food down the tube in her nose. He justified this by telling us it was not pleasant to die hungry. He told us a dietician would be coming to the house later to explain the situation. When she arrived Stepfather once again took charge. The GP was pulled into his study. When he emerged the doctor almost whispered his instructions. He directed the nurses to gradually increase Mum's feed to 2,000 calories a day. Behind me I heard a loud rustle of papers and turned to find the petite dietician anxiously shaking her head. Her face and tapping pencil told me she was appalled. I tried to argue but the GP directed that this was normal practice. I wept.

Loyal weekend nurse Carol had heard my protests. She was also anxious about the effect of so much liquid food on my mother's failing body. She whispered that she would try to water the prescribed amount of food down. Had I fought for this long for Mum to be treated in this atrocious manner?

In a daze I walked around the house and in my confusion I bumped into the plump Georgina. She had been on a hunt to find me. In my anguish I had forgotten about the lawyers' meeting, which had continued after I left. The rotund carer poked a pad of paper under my nose. 'Quick,' she said, 'Mr L has returned. He's talking to Mr Stanley in his study. You must listen.' She thrust a pencil into my hand. It took me time to register what she had meant, so strange was it to have my mother's carers talking to me.

I understood later from Diana that Mr L had been instructed to return to the Old Mill House to serve a severance order on Stepfather. He was not to have joint tenancy of the house any more. I had missed this part of the two men's discussion but I gathered myself together in time to hear Mr L, Mum's so-called 'trusted' accountant, explain how the rest of the meeting had gone. Mr L had agreed to our proposal to allow Mr H and Mr C to have power of attorney over our mother's affairs, but only if we could buy the garden from our mother.

But then came the corrupt Mr L's punchline: 'I only agreed to the children's terms so we could get the power of attorney. I'll change the agreement first thing on Monday morning.' His words made me stand bolt upright. I couldn't believe what I was hearing. The man was a complete crook. As soon as the coast was clear, I charged out into the garden, the only good place to get a phone signal. I rang Diana. Her silence told me she was as shocked as I was at such deceit. She immediately rang Stepfather's firm of solicitors. Even they were aghast that Mr L had proposed such treachery.

Our darling mother was now fading fast. Her tubed feeding started to cause violent diarrhoea. As the nurses struggled in their task they sent me out to buy new sheets as they were frequently changing the heavily soiled linen. I heard the nurses talking among themselves about the wisdom of their orders to continue to pump my mother full of the liquid food. Only adrenaline kept me going. There seemed to be nothing we could do. It was not even Monday and that was when my mother's intake of food was going to be increased again.

The local vicar, the Reverend Ambrose, had visited a number of times and on each visit we had told him of our plight and asked him to intervene. He did seem to want to understand and made silly placatory comments.

Then, on Saturday afternoon, Doreen, one of the new nurses, who seemed much harsher than others, approached me. She said to us bluntly, 'Here's the name of a specialist. She acts as a mediator in families where there's strife over medical treatments.' Why had she not given us this name sooner? The mediating doctor quickly responded to our call for help. But then we hit another huddle. As Mum was being nursed in her own home we had to wait for a weekday for her to be able to formally swing into action. Monday morning would be too late.

I went back to Mum's bedside. It was obvious that my mother had started to reject Stepfather. She wouldn't hold his hand. I wandered around the house feeling utterly desolate. Again I pleaded with the reverend, but he made no response.

Our decision to seek a second opinion worked against us, for Carol, fearing backlash from her colleague Doreen, now felt unable to continue to water the food down. By five o'clock on the Sunday Carol was close to breaking point herself. By six she was distraught, she came downstairs sobbing to find us where we had hidden, unable to watch our mother suffer.

'I can't take it any more. I've tried to call her GP but he's refused to help as he's off duty. I'll have to resort to call the duty doctor.' As we stood waiting in the evening gloom Carol narrated how Stepfather had abused his position with the GP. Over the last months he had rang him frequently. On one single day he rang seventy times.

As soon as the emergency doctor arrived the nurses took him aside and briefed him of the situation. When he came down after seeing my mother, he looked traumatised. He wished we had called him earlier. He had given my mother a high dose of diamorphine. It was all he could do. Finally, Mum was at peace.

What was I to do now? It was ten o'clock at night. I tossed up whether I should stay or not. I sank into Mum's chair in the kitchen and stared at the kitchen clock's pendulum ticking back and forth. Reverend Ambrose, who had attended Mum's final minutes, joined me. Over a glass of brandy, I felt he needed to know our position. I told him that the medical profession had not recognised the scale of the problem and that we had gained access only through contacting the police. We must have been sitting there a long time deep into the night. As we sat there Nurse Doreen came down the step into the kitchen and told us Mr Stanley had asked her to stay the night. He wanted to sleep in the same room as Mum. It seemed odd to me but I was so drained that my mind was not functioning properly.

After being banished for so long, I was surprised when Georgina offered me her bed. I had got used to being rejected. I did not sleep but I lay on the divan in Janet's old room. As I grieved I looked up at the birds circling the rose in the centre of the ceiling.

At dawn I walked in the garden. It was a beautiful June morning. Memories filled every corner. I felt it was time for me to return to my children, but the care staff pleaded with me not to leave. How unfamiliar that was!

Louis ate his breakfast beside my mother's body as if nothing had happened the night before. Later in the morning, Doreen asked if I wanted to say my goodbyes. I was able to hug her body without Stepfather standing over me. As this would be my last sight of her I felt that I should not turn my back on her. So I slowly walked backwards towards the door looking at her finally at peace.

The undertaker came through the blue gate but before he bent his head to escape the lowest wisteria branch I was out in the yard warning him he might have a difficult assignment. When the vicar arrived a few minutes later I heard the two of them walk slowly up the back stairs. The stairs creaked but not with any familiar pattern. I realised I knew each family member's tread on the ancient wooden boards. I busied myself with looking at some of the old family cards on the dresser that Mum had placed there 18 months previously.

It was not long before I heard more footsteps and an ashen Ambrose appeared. He wanted me to join the funeral conference. 'You've got to come if you want to be involved in your mother's funeral. At the moment you have no role.' I didn't like the sound of this. I wanted to go home to my family.

'Where're you meeting?' I asked.

'I'm afraid we're in your mother's bedroom.' He paused. 'B-b-eside your mother's body,' he stammered nervously. 'You'll have to come. Mr Stanley is being im-m-m-possible.'

The flight of steps seemed much higher that day and the landing seemed interminable.

I could hear Stepfather saying in his firmest voice, 'The funeral must be on Friday with the burial later in the day in Sutton Coldfield.' It was a monumental demand. Then he dropped his voice to his low scary tones and addressed the quivering undertaker. 'I'm quite sure you can drop all your commitments on Friday and carry out my and Mrs Stanley's last wishes.'

Mr Painter, the undertaker, looked worried but patiently questioned the logistics. Would they be able to get to Sutton Coldfield cemetery before closing time on Friday afternoon if the funeral service was held in the morning in Cambridgeshire?

As they spoke I allowed myself some thought, why did Stepfather want to hold a service as early as Friday? I wouldn't be able to get my children back home by then. When I protested that Mum would have liked her grandchildren to attend he indicated I should leave. Until then I had resisted looking at my mother's body. It did not seem right to be leaving her like this.

I went back into the garden and waited to hear if any further plans had been discussed.

Before I left the house, the shaken Mr Painter told me that Stepfather had refused to let Mum's body go to their premises, so the undertakers were forced to bring their embalming equipment to her. Afterwards, Mr Painter became concerned that the warm weather would cause health-and-safety problems with my Mum's body. He explained that the room was to be kept well ventilated. I heard later that Stepfather did the opposite: he turned up the heating and closed the windows.

With Friday being the day of the funeral I had only two days to get Rupert and Tom home from their far-flung places. I was able to contact Rupert, who was in a youth hostel in Brazil as part of his gap year, but Tom was on a university trip in isolated Kenya, so I had to dragoon my African friends to use their local acquaintances to ferry the startled boy from his lodgings to their home and on to the airport. It was an enormous relief when I collected them from Heathrow.

I was torn as to what to do for the best. Stepfather must be in distress, so I called him to offer my support and any help he might want with the catering for the wake.

'I don't want help in any shape or form,' he snapped. 'And I don't care if I never see you ever again. In fact, I would like that.'

I was speechless. I decided that was it. That was the end. There was no need to play games any more.

Then the arrangements were changed again. It had been impossible to organise both the service and burial in two disparate places on one day. The funeral was still to be on the Friday but the burial was moved to Monday.

By Friday Painter was a shadow of his former self and when we arrived at Trumpington church I glanced at the vicar. There was something about his bespectacled eyes that told me my outpourings to him had fallen on deaf ears. The funeral was profoundly upsetting because I felt like a stranger. Two of the addresses came from men Mum had hardly known. One was from Alan Frame, reputed to be an ex-editor of the *Daily Express*. I couldn't understand why he was there. The other was from a manager at the Dorchester Hotel. The two speeches were more like eulogies for Louis than for my mother. The third address was to be delivered by Ambrose, who had asked me to write up my special memories for him to read out. He included none of our special recollections.

The wake was equally distressing. Out of the blue, without caring who heard, Stepfather shouted at my brother, who was innocently chatting to a cousin. Insisting he had no place at the party he pointed his stout finger at him and insisted he leave. Without protest Thomas left the room and walked out to the shady courtyard alone. Minutes later the doorbell rang. The undertaker wanted to bring back my mother's coffin. She had returned through the blue gate once again. The wake had hardly started but this signalled to me it was time for me to finally leave my childhood house. I knew I had to build up strength to get though the weekend before Mum's burial on Monday.

I organised that we would sleep at my mother's childhood home, which is now a luxury hotel the night before Mum's burial. The next morning some of my cousins visited us. We walked around the gardens comparing memories. The moat water sparkled even though the day was dull. Around the edges grew imposing bull rushes already turned brown. But it was the floating leathery lily pads that drew me closer to the water just like in my childhood. In the brighter part of the moat the lily flowers were open displaying their pink stamens. Even though they were growing away from the bank I suddenly felt the need to pick one. It seemed to be part of the trial to manoeuvre myself into a position to grab one of the more imposing flowers as I teetered on the brink of the deep waters.

After lunch on this dull July day, I drove on past the lych gate of the graveyard, down the hill and into the wide-open space of the newer cemetery. The family grave with the angel on top was full, so Mum desperately wanted to be buried near her elder brother in the adjoining cemetery. It did not have the oppressive yews, and overgrown cypresses and junipers of the graveyard. Instead there was a feeling of space. Its gravestones were almost regular in size with no unusual shapes or statues, I saw a knot of people huddled together in the far corner, so I parked the car and reached for my raincoat. My heart slowed, I had finally arrived at this poignant moment. There were times in my childhood when I had rehearsed how devastated I would feel if my mother died, my life devoid of any purpose. The yellow beam of the neon streetlight used to fall across my bed at a diagonal angle. Most nights I used this awkward light to look at my latest comic book or maybe play with my teddy, it was always far too soon to go to sleep. The same streetlights shone on early, misty mornings as I waved goodbye as they drove off into another world – the world of Formula One motor racing. As the car turned left at the junction, I had a final glimpse of Mum with her arm fully stretched out of the car window, waving as high and energetically as she could.

At the burial I recognised the distant knot of people as my cousins. After all the trouble our side of the family had caused them it was remarkable they were out in force. Pam, her trusty night-time nurse, was also there at the graveside. 'I'm so pleased that your mother got at least this wish,' she said. 'She'd lie awake in the early hours of the morning, talking about the family grave and its trumpeting angel. She wanted to be buried with her family.' We shed tears together. We talked in quiet tones as we waited for the hearse to arrive. I was tense but looking forward to recovering from the last two years of pain. I told myself that once the burial was over, things could never be so bad again. There were lots of unresolved problems but none could be so emotionally draining as the last few months. What was I going to do about Stepfather? He had told me, 'I don't care if I never see you ever again.' Had he meant it? Was this my way out? What were we going to do with his debts? I felt drained – sapped of all emotions and feelings.

Where was the cortège? Why were they not here? The light was getting worse, the drizzle was heavier, and, even though it was midsummer, it was a grim day. A battered old Vauxhall pulled up and the cemetery keeper emerged with the message that the cortège was stuck in a motorway traffic jam.

A motorway jam! How ironic! I hadn't really given much thought to the mechanics of having a service in one town and a burial in another. Mum's body had been roaring along, in the back of a black hearse on the M1 to her chosen final resting place. She would not have liked the image. The picture of the black hearse with the oak casket driving at top speed to reach the cemetery before closing time was not a happy one.

'How irreverent!' my mother would have said. I thought of her final wishes. Well, at least she would be buried where she wanted, even if the journey would not have been to her liking.

The hearse finally arrived and the usually unflappable undertaker was full of apologies. The Daimler followed and I could not help but wonder who the person was with Stepfather. For in the driving seat was a woman. Was she another new nurse? It was hard to tell. But once again she had been chosen for her looks. She was relatively young with bright auburn hair. I looked closely at her freckled face and I expected her eyes to be green in colour, but she was not going to catch my eye. I watched almost mesmerised as she went around to the back of the car and got out a wheelchair. Stepfather was to sit in a wheelchair? What trick was this? We all just watched; nobody spoke.

The ceremony of interment took only a few minutes but it seemed an eternity. Somehow we four children found ourselves at the far end of the deep grave, arms interlinked, giving each other the security we all needed. We were there with heads bent, perhaps bent lower than in normal circumstances because none of us wanted to see him at the other end of the grave. A cruel thought came into my mind.

Reverend Ambrose was officiating with the pallbearers lacing the burial ties through the coffin's handles. I held my water lily close, suddenly realising I did not know the burial-service wording well enough to know when to let it go. Everything but the hole was blocked out from my senses – no noise, no smell, no feelings. I was wrapped up in my world with the four of us arm in arm, as the coffin was lowered. I looked and then looked again. Surely the gold plate had the wrong date. I was jerked out of my dreaming. Mum was born on 16 June, not the 18th. I felt like shouting out, She can't be buried with the wrong date! Why had he done this?

I heard the words of the burial service as the vicar spoke them, but all I could think of was, When should I send in my floral contribution? Halfway through his words I could wait no longer and I threw in the glossy water lily. I was startled: it made the most awful thud as it hit the oak coffin. It was not what I had expected at all. I thought it would float romantically down and land on it like a petal in the wind. It shocked me that I had ruined the peace of the service with the dull thud of the weight of the lily.

It was time to then throw in our sods of earth. The earth was very red – I had no idea that Sutton Coldfield had a brightly coloured soil – so different from the light brown of Cambridge chalk. The soil was cold, much colder and less crumbly than I had expected; I let it fall through my fingers. Then came the turn of my children to do this and I noticed how upset they all were. I asked Stepfather to join us for a cup of tea and bravely gave him a peck on the cheek. Then he was gone. I would never see him again. He had refused my olive branch after the burial, but I had done my bit. I need not try any more. The man had surrounded himself with vultures and the professionals had all found it easier to turn a blind eye than take action.

The duty doctor who had witnessed Mum's treatment admitted that it had been the worst case he had attended.

CHAPTER 10

WHO WAS WHO?

It took me weeks to recover but eventually I found the energy to start reading again. Asquith's correspondence with Venetia Stanley had begun to fascinate me and I sent for more books on the period. While I waited for them to arrive I went back to selected chapters of the biography of the Asquith family written by Colin Clifford, which retold the story of the death of Asquith's daughter Violet's boyfriend in 1909. Clifford believed that this was the time when Asquith probably first met Venetia. Asquith was Chancellor of the Exchequer and his amusement at the time was to latch onto his older children's social groups. Venetia was part of Violet's group of friends. I had the first inkling that Venetia was audacious in this period when I read that she obtained a banned drug, Veronal, to give to her grieving friend Violet.

Violet's boyfriend Archie Gordon had been fatally injured in a car accident and taken to Winchester Hospital. His friends collected at his bedside but had been told he would not survive his terrible injuries. Violet, who was 22, agreed to be engaged to him as he lay dying. The couple spent his last hours, which turned into days, romantically talking of their future together.

Venetia stayed with her best friend Violet throughout this traumatic time. So did H. H. Asquith. He even missed a Cabinet meeting he had been asked to chair. It felt strange reading about the Winchester Hospital just down the road from my house. I looked at the hotchpotch of buildings in a new light and imagined the scenario inside the private surgical ward with Violet's and Archie's relatives huddled outside. I wondered if, while waiting outside for Archie to die, Asquith and Venetia got to know each other rather well. Certainly Clifford claimed that Asquith began to feel 'a particular admiration for Venetia' during these traumatic times.

So, if this event was in 1909, it is not impossible to suppose they could have been sleeping together in 1911 or well before. I found further evidence that Venetia had been invited to dine at Downing Street when just a young teenager and had joined the Asquiths on family holidays. Then I found a vital date. In 1907, according to Clifford, Venetia accompanied her friend Violet and both her parents on a holiday to Switzerland when Margot was sent there to recover from her unsuccessful pregnancies.

As I researched, I hypothesised as to what might have happened in January 1912 if Venetia had been pregnant with Asquith's baby. How did they hide the pregnancy? Where did she give birth? When did they find the suitable 'mother'? Did this surrogate know she was caring for the son of Venetia Stanley? Did she know his father was H. H. Asquith? I asked myself if I now knew more than Louis ever did. But I was sure of one thing: my mother knew nothing of her husband's roots.

I put myself in the position of Venetia's parents, Lord and Lady Sheffield. They must have been dumbfounded when they were told their daughter of 24 was pregnant and the father was the Prime Minister of Great Britain. I imagined the endless secret discussions they would have had. What were they to do?

While I was reading, I glanced at the Stanley family tree. It took me a few seconds to realise its full significance to my investigations. But there it was; one of Venetia's older brothers was called Oliver. I remembered when we were children the one time when Louis boasted of having an Uncle Oliver. At the time he seemed quite upset we were not impressed. So his boast about his 'Uncle Oliver' (see Chapter 1) had been true after all. I quickly turned the pages in the text to find any information I could on Oliver Stanley. We, as children, must have really stressed out Stepfather that day, I reflected. Surely he would not have divulged this without thinking about the consequences. This intriguing nugget of information inspired me to think up new lines of enquiries.

Over the coming months I became used to receiving copies of birth, death and marriage certificates through the post. Some of the documents were enlightening while others only assisted in the task of eliminating names. Home Granny's death certificate was one of the first I ordered.

The document told me that Mary Ann Applegate died in May 1963. But because she died before 1970 her death certificate did not record her birthdate or her maiden name. However, it did state she had been 'the widow of a cotton executive'. Of course it would, I told myself: Louis would have given the registrar these details and he would have wanted this fact recorded. There was still much work to be done. And I still had that unpleasant feeling of snooping every time I had a Stanley document in my hand. Was Louis about to appear from behind my shoulder?

I wished that the 1911 census had been on hand but, as it was now only 2003, I would have to wait eight years for it to become available. If I had that census maybe I would know where all the vital players were living in the year Venetia was pregnant. I imagined the panic of Lord and Lady Sheffield when they realised they had to find a surrogate mother for their daughter's child.

But I had the 1901 census and it became a vital document. First, I had to find where Louis's so-called mother, Mary Ann Applegate, stayed on census night 1901. Assuming the information on her gravestone was correct she would have been either 33 or 34. However, I was warned it is notoriously difficult to track women through their declared age on census night as they often lied and tellers, believing this to be the least important detail, often failed to write women's ages correctly. So my search included a much wider age allowance than the predicted. Luckily for me there were only ten possible females in the census with the name Mary Applegate who were aged between 27 and 47.

The census included middle initials for some of the individuals but, again, I was told I could not rely on this detail. So I included all the Marys, whatever their declared middle initial. I was able to rule out two immediately because they were past childbearing age. I ferreted again and four more Mary Applegates fell off my list, as they were Applegates by marriage, not by birth.

So now there were only four possibles. I slowly picked away at the list and eliminated another Applegate for none of her details matched: her father had been a dairyman, her second initial was J, she lived in Islington and she claimed to be only 27.

I was now concentrating on three possible women. Each had 'A' as her middle initial and they had all been Applegates at birth. Luckily one of them I could rule out straightaway, as her birth certificate had been easy to obtain. She had been Mary Alfreda, and she was probably too old and had been born in Ely.

The most likely Mary A. Applegate was 33. This was the right age according to the wording on the gravestone. She was also single and a parlour maid. In the data she was recorded as living in Odsall in Nottingham. Her birthplace was recorded as a town in Norfolk. As I had difficulty tracking down her birth certificate, I began to think she must be the right Applegate. Had she purposefully hidden her tracks?

The last Mary Ann on my list had been born at 22 Union Street in Carlisle, which did not seem to fit in with anything I knew. The town was not near Liverpool and I could not recall Stepfather ever having connections with this place. However, her birth certificate arrived without trouble. She had been named after her own mother – Mary – whose maiden name was Holmes. The surname did not jog any memories, but, then, why should it? Her birthday had been 11 October, so this fitted in with my supposition that Home Granny's birthday had been in the autumn. But there was one worrying detail that did not make sense. She had been born in the year 1870. If the gravestone writing were to be believed she should have been born in 1867 or 1868. This would make her 44 in 1912. Old for a first-time mother, I thought. Even 35 was considered dangerously old to give birth in those days.

Alfred, the father of this Mary Ann, had been a cotton warper. This detail made me a little more hopeful. At least there was some sort of connection with the cotton trade. A cotton warper didn't sound much of a job. Had he been a labourer? I turned my attention to the box to see who had registered the birth. There was no signature, just a small cross. So was this 'grandmother' of the 'Great Louis T' illiterate? Surely this could not be the right family. I must have the wrong Applegate. This Mary Applegate was the wrong age, and why was one parent illiterate? I needed to seek professional help.

My genealogy expert decided that the only way to be sure the Mary from Carlisle was my Applegate was to rule out the parlour maid. But he also failed to find her birth certificate. So now the only way to find my Mary Ann was by elimination. We needed to check when each of them had died. So we trawled through all the heavy boards in Myddleton Street record office to find the Mary Ann Applegates who had died before 1963, which was when my Home Granny passed away. This strategy led us to the definitive answer. The parlour maid from Odstall in Nottinghamshire had died in a workhouse in 1924. From these details we traced her birth certificate, which recorded her birth year as 1859! So this Mary Ann led us a merry dance because in 1901 she had pretended she was ten years younger than she really was!

This left me with the Applegate who had an illiterate mother and had been born in Carlisle in 1870. Now I could look at the 1901 census details with new eyes. Previously, I had found a Mary Ann Applegate of the right age who was born in Carlisle but she was living in somewhere called St-Anne's-on-the-Sea. She was recorded as a sick nurse.

I remembered Mum's justification of why Stepfather had been such a fussy eater and acted so spoilt. He had been this 'much-longed-for baby', as he had arrived after years of his mother's attempts to have a child. She always waved her arms and said, 'What a thrill it must have been.'

As I recalled the story my mind moved into overdrive. I could see the tale from a different angle. Maybe the Stanleys or the even the Asquiths were well aware that the illegitimate son's 'replacement' mother might be seen as elderly for a first-time mother. I was still confused as, according to her gravestone, she was 44 in 1912 while, according to the census, she would be 42. Did they create this longed-for-baby yarn for Mary Ann to tell to her neighbours? Would this satisfy inquisitive eyes and ears?

As I mulled over the dates I remembered another significant moment at home: Mum asking Stepfather if Home Granny was not exaggerating her age. The old lady had been keen to reach the age of one hundred. Maybe she had thought she was two years older than she really was.

The earlier census of 1891 suggested that a Mary Ann had been living in Bollington in an administrative area of Lancaster. There was no other possible Mary Ann, so I had to accept half-heartedly that this was the right woman, but I was not happy. I couldn't see the connection. Why was this woman, living in a place I had never heard of, recorded in the district of Lancaster, and why had she worked as a lowly cotton-cop winder? Nothing seemed to fit.

And then, suddenly, the memory of a trip to Hoylake came flooding back. We finally arrived at the furthest point of the Wirral. First, Stepfather pointed out a famous golf clubhouse, then, a little further down the road, he crowed that on the roundabout there had once stood a grand hotel called the Stanley. He instructed Mum to turn left into a wide-open straight road with huge houses overlooking the links of Royal Liverpool Golf Club.

'Drive slower,' he commanded. 'We lived along here on the right.' He almost whispered this. Mum sighed. She was irritated. Traffic had been heavy on the Wirral peninsular. But he took no notice. As she drove slowly past, he focused on each house. Then he pronounced, 'No, not that one. No, not that one. Yes! It was *that* one.'

'Are you sure?' my mother responded, which made him change his mind.

'No, it's not that one.' We passed another house. 'Yes, it was that one. We used to go in that door. That was the drawing room and the servant would go through that side door.' He was not acting like his normal self.

'You told me last time it was that house there,' said Mum, pointing to a different one. Her voice was a pitch higher than usual. The wipers worked overtime to clear the windscreen. 'Don't you remember we talked of the entrance and the driveway and how your mother walked under the arch?'

Suddenly, their conversation awoke my interest, not because Stepfather was confused but because I could hear warning bells of an imminent row. I would have to mind my backside. Stepfather had become flustered and he mumbled something I could not catch.

At the end of the road he told Mum to park the car so that we could view the sodden deserted beach. Then he asked her to drive up and down a few side roads, all of which led down to the sea. The atmosphere was frosty. I sat on the uncomfortable back seat wondering. Why had my mother been short with him? Whenever she was angry with him, it never worked out. He always won. If she was not careful he would be demanding that she drive us both somewhere else, miles away, and I was thoroughly fed up with being cooped up in the back of the car.

Now it struck me that maybe I could find out the name of the road we had driven up and down and maybe do another search to see if 'Mrs Stanley' or 'MaryAnn Applegate' was in the local electoral rolls.

As there was so much to find out about Louis's real mother, Miss Venetia Stanley, I put the census information to one side. I went back to my research on the early part of the twentieth century and I was encouraged by suggestions that Venetia became decadent when she was older. This lent support to my idea that she had been capable as a young girl of a sexual affair with Asquith.

When Venetia was newly wed, Violet stopped being friendly, so Venetia turned to Diana Manners for companionship. Diana's approach to life was carefree, and she had a devil-may-care attitude. As time progressed Venetia became wilder and soon her life became 'devoid of any purpose with drugs, sexual promiscuity and experimentation high on the list of her preferred activities'. (Levine)

As she sounded so much like Stepfather, I became hungry for more details of her life. I was going to have to rake through all the literature about this woman.

Meanwhile, I discovered that Asquith and Venetia went on holiday to Scilly together and Asquith's memoirs suggest it was on this holiday in January 1912 (they arrived at their holiday destination on 12 January) that he began to fall in love with her. If this date was correct, it fitted in with my theory, because this was just two weeks after the birth of Louis. I read that the Prime Minister and his Cabinet minister Edwin Montagu arrived in Scilly first and they were joined later by Violet with Venetia.

Had this holiday been Venetia's compensation for going through with the pregnancy and for giving away their baby? Or had it been a time to take stock of events and plan? The dates were logical and in Scilly she would have had Violet's valuable support. I was becoming convinced that Violet must have known about the birth of the baby. How could she not have suspected that her best friend was having an affair with her father? I was sure I was onto something big. I had to research the holiday further.

Connections between the Asquith family and Louis cropped up often in my reading. When I spotted Winchester College in the literature I was intrigued. All Asquith's sons had been educated at the school and this titbit made me vividly remember the one time Louis had made reference to his schooling.

He, my mother and I were sitting in the Old Mill House garden on a perfect June day. Somehow the conversation had drifted to my own schooldays and how much I had hated my boarding school. Mum admitted that she had also hated being sent away from home. Then she waved her hand in the direction of Stepfather, who had his eyes closed behind the *Sunday Express*. 'Poppy, you know, went to boarding school,' she said. 'He went to Winchester College and he hated it as well.'

At the time I nearly fell off my chair with surprise. By then I had lived in Winchester for three years, yet Stepfather had never mentioned anything about his schooling. 'Really?' I blurted.

'Yes,' he murmured. He used his faint little-boy voice while hunching his shoulders in an uncharacteristic manner.

Mum was enjoying herself teasing him. 'But he was so unhappy he was allowed to leave. His mother completely spoilt him.'

I was fascinated.

'Is it true?' I asked, 'Didn't you stay?'

'I lasted a couple of terms. I was unhappy.'

How I wished I had asked more questions on that summer's day.

Winchester College's archive department has kept records of boys who attended in the early twentieth century but the librarian told me his name was not listed. When I told her Louis Stanley may have attended for only two terms the archivist did not rule out the possibility of his attendance, as the school kept records only for those who stayed for longer periods. I suspected that Mary Ann had sent Louis to the College and perhaps the Asquith relatives had helped to fund the cost, so he could be educated at the same school as his half-brothers. Maybe he had left because the other boys at school guessed his roots. Had this caused him to be bullied? The plot thickened.

On some days I was sure I knew that Louis was Miss Stanley's illegitimate child but at other times doubts crept into my mind and I had little confidence in my story. Did this flibbertigibbet of a woman, I asked myself, just happen to have the same surname as stepfather? Maybe it was just a coincidence. On the other hand I found nothing to suggest I was wrong.

It interested me to read that the Asquiths and Stanleys (Lord and Lady Sheffield) had been friends over many years. Asquith often met them at luncheon or dinner parties and he was often invited to stay at one of their two country houses. Asquith must have been hugely impressed. His own lifestyle had been much more modest. He had been Britain's first middle-class premier but, I had read, he had been unhappy about this. Even though he was a radical, he has been accused of being a social climber.

Alderley Hall had been the Stanley family's home for generations and they could trace their ancestral roots back to the Normans. The Stanleys were big landowners in Cheshire and the Wirral peninsular. They also owned a London residence, a large country house in Anglesey called Penrhos and a townhouse in Chester. I wondered if Stepfather knew about this house when we went for shopping trips in the Oulton Park area.

Venetia was the youngest of seven and had been very spoilt. She was a prankster. During her teens and twenties she had been allowed to amass a menagerie of pets. How did Asquith or other visitors such as the nervous Edwin Montagu put up with her pets? Her dogs barked and made thorough nuisances of themselves at hustings and she had a monkey that clung to curtain rails and dropped on unsuspecting guests. She also had a pet bear that chased children, terrifying the nanny and the kitchen staff. Another time Venetia turned a solemn Christening ceremony into a farce by playing a number of pranks. She finished her tricks in the church by shouting in a loud voice in the ceremony about 'drowning the little gorilla'.

Strangely, I found myself reading books I had thought were irrelevant to my search, only to find they were of great pertinence. First, I found Gertrude Bell. That early-twentieth-century intellectual powerhouse was a cousin of Venetia's, this time through her mother's side of the family. Venetia's maternal grandfather was the wealthy industrialist Lothian Bell.

Venetia came from a family of politicians. Her ancestor, the second Lord Stanley, was known as Sir Benjamin Backbite because of his slanderous tongue, just like the scandalmonger in Sheridan's *School for Scandal*. Her father, Lyulph, the fourth Baron Stanley (1839–1925), had been an MP but chose to fight for most of his life against the influence of the church in the local education systems.

Her eldest uncle, Henry Edward Stanley (1827–1903), who became deaf and unpopular, also wanted to become an MP but was discouraged from doing so by his family, so he went abroad and became a brilliant linguist. He changed religion to become a Muslim. Later he entered the House of Lords and among his interests was the future of the State of India. Nancy Mitford wrote that Henry's brother had once said of him 'he will have quite a Noah's ark of wives by the time he is done'. This turned out to have elements of truth it, as he married a Spanish Roman Catholic in Constantinople wearing Turkish dress. He told no member of his family for seven years, revealing the saga only when his marriage turned out to be bigamous. When the family finally did meet his wife she was not trusted or well liked. The story hit the gossip pages of the press at the time.

It was this uncle who inherited Penrhos, the Welsh house. He lived there only occasionally, for a scandal occurred in 1897 centring on the birth of an illegitimate son, estranging him from the local people. 'Stanley had always had a penchant for falling in love with unsuitable women,' wrote Muriel Chamberlain in the *Dictionary of National Biography*. Muriel, in an email, told me that Henry was suspected of having an illegitimate child with a servant girl at the house. As Henry had no legitimate children it was his death, in 1903, that allowed Lyulph, Venetia's father, to inherit both Alderley Hall and Penrhos.

Venetia's eldest brother Arthur also became a Liberal MP and he was the Stanley MP whom I had looked up all those years ago. It was Arthur's daughter who became a Lubbock by marriage. That surname provoked vivid childhood memories.

The Stanley family were known to be unconventional and nonconformist and ahead of the times in their candour and worldliness. They were certainly an eccentric brood. Lady Stanley, Venetia's grandmother, was formidable and had the habit of turning away from a conversation on one side to loudly remark to her neighbour on the other that 'fools are so fatiguing'. She certainly was intellectual as she went on to become one of the founders of Girton College in Cambridge.

The marriage between Lyulph, the Cheshire aristocrat, and his wife Maisie made for an interesting reflection on the social positions of families in those days. When Lyulph declared his love for Maisie, his own mother regarded herself as very broad-minded and allowed him to marry this girl from trade. (This particular tradesman's exceptional wealth probably helped his cause!)

While reading about those highly challenging lunches at Alderley Hall I found that Asquith was one of the few visitors who enjoyed these testing events, while Bertrand Russell hated them. Bertrand Russell! Wasn't there a picture of him with Louis in Stepfather's study? This was one of the names Louis used to boast about repeatedly when I was a child. How did Bertrand Russell get invited to these lunches? Then I got the answer. Bertrand was Venetia's cousin! If my theory was correct it meant that Louis and Russell were cousins once removed.

I had read that the Asquith family frequently visited the Stanleys' summerhouse when Venetia was young. Photographs of Venetia lying on the Penrhos beach with Asquith and her older sister, Sylvia, fascinated me. There was another memorable image of the young Winston Churchill, spade in hand, standing beside the young Venetia. So when I had time on my hands I decided to visit Holyhead on the tiny Holy Island off Anglesey. I was intrigued because one summer when we were children on holiday in North Wales Stepfather had made my mother drive us to the tip of island. It had seemed like a wasted day for us all.

I knew the house had not survived and the local tourist office informed me that what was left of the Stanleys' estate was now a local nature reserve called Penrhos Coastal Park.

Even though it was August the weather was appalling when I arrived in Holyhead, so I donned my wet-weather gear and started to walk the coastal path around the headland. I noted that the Stanleys' coffers must have been swelled by their tollhouse, which was on the London-to-Holyhead road. As I walked I recognised the rocky foreshore. It had not changed in shape from its depiction in an old photograph that had previously fascinated me. I did not expect to find anything else, but luck once again came my way, for I found a friendly local out with her dog who wanted to show me the remnants of the old house itself. I stood transfixed. I had finally tracked down a tangible asset that had once been in the hands of the Stanley family.

I found myself ringing the front doorbell of a stranger's house. The elderly lady lived in the old dairy once attached to Penrhos. As I sat in her sitting room I noted there was no need for pictures because the walls were covered with tiles depicting blue dairymaids and azure cows on a shiny white background. As I sat in the dry and warm room recovering from the buffeting winds blowing off the rough seas, I imagined family members and perhaps even Asquith visiting the dairy and being given the best cream.

As we ate crumpets I was shown photographs of the house and learned that the family held a huge party to celebrate the arrival of the train. Travel to Penrhos was easy for Venetia and her family, as there was a direct route to Manchester and then on to London.

As I read more about the early twentieth century, I decided to consult a copy of *Who's Who*, as I had started to remember more of the past. Once, when I was in my thirties, Stepfather sat slouched in 'his' low armchair. By then the pink and white chintz material was beginning to get grimy and the armrests where Stepfather placed his huge hands were ragged. It must have been a spring evening. My mother had lit the fire but the curtains were not drawn and it was still light outside. The room was quiet except for the occasional flick of some papers. Stepfather was fiddling with a flimsy, torn, printed scrap between finger and thumb. My children were busy studying how to play with their new toys.

His eyes continued to stare at the fire as he broke the silence.

'The publishers of *Who's Who* have asked me to enter my details,' he said. His eyes, still on the flames, flicked the paper one more time.

I continued to flip through my mother's magazines as I sat beside her on the sofa. Here we go again, I thought, steeling myself for a series of boasts.

'Jackie Stewart was only invited last year and men like Reg Parnell and Tony Rudd have never been invited,' he went on. Mum was anxiously tapping her armrest with the tips of her fingers.

Lack of response was only going to goad him further, so I mumbled, 'Oh that's good,' hoping that the grandchildren might divert the conversation. No such luck. So when the silence became unbearable I asked, 'What will you put?'

'Oh, just what I normally put,' he said airily. 'It's hard to cut it down sufficiently to fit in their tiny boxes.'

Now I had to find his entry. In the library copies I could find no reference to him. I looked at various years and in various

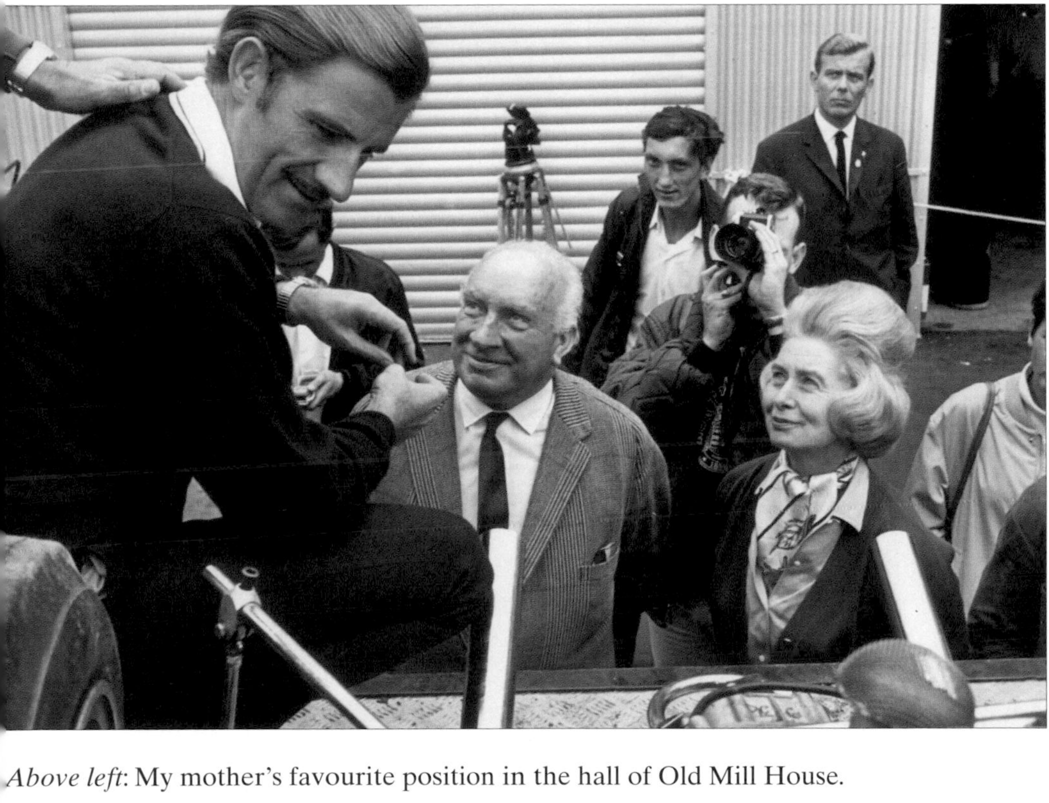

Above left: My mother's favourite position in the hall of Old Mill House.

Above right: I had been riding for the first time. Stepfather had recently entered my life.

Below: Graham Hill with his winning BRM. He had just been on a lap of honour around the racetrack. Stepfather and my mother look on.

Above left: My mother in the pits beside BRM's chief mechanic. He was sending a coded message to the driver. The metal board with its manually changed numbers was the only way of communicating between the pits and the cockpit.

Above right: The courtyard that Mum transformed into a haven of peace. The blue gate leads out to the busy road.

Below: Old Mill House and its terrace. We sat here and had tea on a summer's day.

Above: New Hall, the home of my maternal grandmother. My grandfather, who died many years before I was born, bought the house when my mother was young.

Below left: In 1915 Venetia was to marry this man, Edwin Montagu. He was Asquith's close friend and served in his cabinet. He was later to become Secretary of State for India. *© Getty Images*

Below right: Violet was Venetia's best friend during their teenage years. Violet was a keen Liberal. Later in life she became well known under her married name Violet Bonham Carter. She and her father had a special relationship. *© Mary Evans Picture Library*

Above left: This photograph of Asquith (*left*) loomed out of the darkness out me as I searched on the Internet. I provide a photo of Louis at a similar age (*right*).

© *Mary Evans Picture Library*

Below: Stepfather, Louis Stanley, posing with the famous classicist and intellectual Gilbert Murray.

My mother and father on their wedding day. I knew nothing about their marriage until I started researching.

H.H. Asquith, Prime Minister (1908–1916) with his second wife Margot whom he married in 1894.
© Mary Evans Picture Library

Above: Snap taken in 1909 on the beach at Venetia Stanely's summer home, Penrhos. Those lying on the rocks are: (left to right) Sylvia, Venetia's elder sister, Venetia Stanley, Violet Asquith, H.H Asquith, Edwin Montagu and Maurice Bonham Carter. Venetia was about 21 years old.

© *Anthony Pitt-Rivers*

Below: My mother at the wheel of the family car. She always did all the driving.

AN INTERESTING BRIDE-TO-BE

Who is Changing her Faith as well as her Name.

Dorothy Hickling

THE HON. VENETIA STANLEY

The youngest daughter of Lord Sheffield, whose engagement to the Hon. Edwin Montagu, M.P., second son of the late Lord Swaythling, was recently announced, as well as the fact that the bride-to-be is adopting the Jewish faith of her fiancé. Her father, who is an intimate friend of Mr. Asquith, was vice-chairman of the old London School Board, and was M.P. for Oldham in the Liberal interest, 1880-5. Her mother is the daughter of Sir Lowthian Bell. Lord Sheffield has country seats at Alderley Park, Chelford, Crewe, and Penrhôs, Holyhead, and a town residence in Portland Place. Mr. Montagu is now Financial Secretary to the Treasury

The piece from Tatler on Venetia Stanley's engagement. © *Mary Evans Picture Library* different kinds of reference texts, but his name never appeared. So I decided to leave the search until another day.

However by sheer coincidence, a distant friend, Michael, rang me to give support, having heard that I was in an emotional state. He knew little of the difficulties I was experiencing but he knew my family name had been Stanley.

'Oh, your father was a high achiever, wasn't he?' he said at one point.

'What do you mean?' I replied guardedly, flinching internally, as I always did if anybody called that man my father. I regretted once again that even as an adult I conformed to the family lie. 'How do you know?' I continued.

'Oh, somewhere I have old copies of *Debrett's People of Today*. I must have read about him in that.'

'What! Which? When?'

Michael was startled by my reaction but willingly posted me a photocopy of the 1989 entry in *Debrett's People of Today*.

When it arrived I slit open the envelope and my eyes devoured the text. With the first sweep I saw my name. *My* name! Anger seethed through me. I shouted at the piece of paper, 'I am not your child!' I looked again at the entry. My date of birth was the wrong year! What had he been thinking of? I read the details more slowly and began to realise it was not just that we were all down as his children, but *all* our birthdates were the wrong years. I calmed myself. The entry was a pack of untruths:

> Louis Thomas Stanley, son of Louis Stanley of Stanley House, Stanley Road, Hoylake and of Mary Ann (née) Appleby. Born 6 Jan 1912. Educated [no school mentioned] Emanuel College Cambridge (MA). Married on 25 May 1955 Helen Jean Beech daughter of Sir Alfred Owen of New Hall Sutton Coldfield. 2 sons T. A born 1957, E J born 1961, 2 daughters C J. born 1959, R M. born 1963. Career: Economist, Director General: International Grand Prix Medical Services, Chairman and Joint

Managing Director of BRM, Chairman of Siffert Council, Honorary Secretary and Treasurer of Grand Prix Drivers Association, Trustee of Jim Clark Foundation, Member of The Royal Institute of International Affairs. Author of over 70 titles including *Cambridge: City of Dreams*, *Germany After the War*, and *People, Places and Pleasures*.

Had he felt he had to lie to compete with other entries? I tried to go through his submission logically and unpick his untruths.

First he had tried to raise the status of his home background. I had never heard him talk of 'Stanley House'. Had the road near the Royal Liverpool Golf Club ever been called Stanley Road? Then I spotted the alteration to his 'mother's' maiden name. Why Appleby? Why had he not entered her real surname, Applegate? I was in shock.

Stepfather had written out 'Louis Thomas Stanley' as his own father and he exaggerated my maternal grandfather's achievements. He had given him a knighthood. For his career he had entered, 'Economist...Member of The Royal Institute of International Affairs.' The word 'economist' rang bells in my head.

More than once Mum, as she sat at her desk exasperated with the huge bills she was expected to pay, would mutter, 'He says he was an economist but he has no idea about money. I don't understand him.' She appeared stressed and had put down her biro on the tabletop strewn with invoices, blue-headed notepaper with white raised print, open chequebook and thick envelopes.

We looked up the meaning of the word 'economist'. Now I looked it up again in a substantial dictionary. 'Economics is often closely equated with political economy. Politicians are often economists because they discuss and predict future development in their own or other countries.'

Had Louis wanted to follow in his father's footsteps? Had he wanted to be a budding politician prior to the war? Had he ever put himself forward to be adopted by any constituency? Had he been disenfranchised from following in his father's footsteps? He claimed in *Debrett's* to be a member of The Royal Institute of International Affairs. I checked more of his work, where he claimed he was a 'founder' member of the club. Why did he become a member of that prestigious club? It seemed so out of line with what I, as a child, had known about him.

In the entry he claimed that his marriage to my mother had been on 25 May 1955. So if that was true I could now order their marriage certificate. 'Author of over 70 titles'. I looked at his list of published works. Was that an exaggeration? My eyes lit on *Germany After the War*, a title he had slipped in between two of his more familiar works.

Stepfather had never crowed about this volume. I was sure it had not been positioned on his heavily weighted study shelves. I was puzzled. The title did not even sound like his normal genre. I looked again at what he had entered for his educational record. Other celebrities had all identified which school they had attended but Louis had not, so perhaps he really had been educated at home. Why had he not boasted about it? Surely, in those days, having a home tutor or governess was something to be proud of. I recalled that Louis had been a talented piano player and when we asked where he learned the skill he had told us he had been privately educated in his home. I had never really believed him. His university entry reminded me that I needed to pry into his college life as well.

I decided this entry in *Debrett's* was a web of lies. I even questioned the accuracy of the date of his birth. I had a duplicate of his birth certificate in my office, but what could I believe?

I wondered what publishers and readers thought of his writing ability. The books I remembered most were his reviews of the Grand Prix year, packed with his black-and-white photographs and with relatively little text. Each spring, motor-racing personalities approached. They would say to Mum, while looking at Stepfather, 'I've just had a look at Mr Stanley's latest yearly publication. Had to make sure there were no disrespectful pictures of me this year!' Louis had thought it great fun to photograph those on the circuit in embarrassing situations.

I told myself that I should skim through some of his books. Perhaps the golf ones might give me a clue about his early life. The title *Germany After the War* began to fascinate me. I started to write a long list of book requests at my local library. Why had he written about the after-effects of war in Germany in 1944? I wasn't sure I could cope with another fat tome on unrelated topics, but I went ahead and ordered it. Maybe it would tell me what Louis did in the war. It might solve those childhood questions. Now I could no longer fight for my mother, I needed to face the past.

The more I read, the more names that I had previously forgotten cropped up in the historical texts. Not only was Bertrand Russell a cousin of the Stanleys, so were the Mitford family. Louis always seemed to record his detailed knowledge of the sisters, especially Diana. But there were more names and they reminded me of those photographs on Louis's study wall. Why did Louis know these famous people? Did he socialise with them or were they something to do with his work? What was his job in those days?

When I finally found an extended family tree of the Stanleys I could hardly believe my eyes as I spotted three unusual surnames: Lascelles, Evans Gordon and Goodenough; all had been bandied about in my childhood for one reason or another by Stepfather. Now I had found they were either relatives of Venetia or had married into the family.

But there was one name that excited me more than all the others: Bonham Carter. Asquith's eldest daughter, Violet, had married Maurice Bonham Carter, who had been one of Asquith's parliamentary private secretaries. Of course! Why had I been so stupid? Violet Bonham Carter was Louis's half sister. No wonder he had not liked my making fun of her surname. I would have to divert my attentions to finding out more about her. But I also realised there must have been huge ructions in the Asquith family when the letters were first found. They had created a great deal of gossip. But, luckily for them and the Liberal Party, the historians of the time, although amused by the intimate relationships revealed, were much more interested in the political manoeuvring that Asquith's letters had exposed. The mystery was becoming deeper.

If Stepfather had lived in Hoylake, the most likely public school he would have attended would have been Birkenhead School. Their records showed he had attended from September 1926, when he would have been 14, to December 1927. Only four terms! Perhaps his unsuccessful schooling at Winchester College had been before Birkenhead. Maybe others had guessed his illegitimacy and he had been bullied at both schools. It was common to attack boys' legitimacy in public schools at that time. I realised that, although he took a great deal of interest in sport, he never told stories of playing in a rugby or cricket team. He talked only of golf, a solitary game, one he could have easily played if he had a governess.

What had life been like for him at his two secondary schools? Had we, his stepchildren, reminded him of the taunts that were thrown at him in his childhood? Without realising it, had we cracked the edges of his protective shell? As we became older, had we asked more threatening questions than those he might have been asked in the school playground? I wondered.

It was time to visit the Wirral. As I neared, I soon recognised the flat countryside and the traffic-filled trunk roads leading to Birkenhead and Liverpool. Louis always knew his way about when we were up in Merseyside.

Stiff from the long journey, I got out of the car in Liscard and walked the length of Aylesbury Road. It was a quiet street with a line of terraced redbrick houses sloping down towards a disused battery. From the map, number 37 was at the elbow of the road, but I had not appreciated how close it was to the sea. At Liscard Battery the road widened into a walkway beside miles of sand.

I envisaged Home Granny pushing her pram along this

promenade every afternoon with Mamie helping to look after her new baby 'brother'. It dawned on me that, if Louis had not been Venetia's child, and as there was no evidence of any father, Mary Ann would have been an ordinary unmarried mother. I wondered how she would have fared in those times. But I dismissed this idea.

As I looked across the waters I guessed number 37 would have had attractive views of the mushrooming Liverpool. I wondered if the house's situation had triggered stepfather's hobby of watching estuary birds. I needed to know where he had lived after Aylesbury Road, Liscard. What age was he when he moved to Hoylake so that he could go to school at Birkenhead High?

As I walked back up the incline I came across a small park and a memorial garden. There was a café. I drank a milky cup of Tetley and rummaged through their local-history leaflets. In 1912 the whole area had been a thriving holiday resort. New Brighton, the next town along the seafront, had as its slogan 'Brighter holidays at Britain's brighter resort, with eight miles of lovely Cheshire coast'. The burgeoning town in those days attracted the new wealth from the other side of the water. Cotton was making Liverpool prosperous. I needed to learn more about the cotton trade. It was coming up far too often in my research to ignore it.

That same day I just had time to drive west to Hoylake to find Stanley Road. I suspected that Stanley House had been a figment of Louis's imagination, for I had found nothing about it from my research and it had never been mentioned in my childhood; but I needed to check with the locals. They proved to be very obliging and the estate agents confirmed that Stanley House never existed. The local librarian, however, came up with a gem of information: most of the land around Hoylake and a whole swathe of the Wirral had originally been owned by the Stanleys! Yes, Venetia's family had even owned the Royal Liverpool Golf Club and the Stanley Hotel. This piece of news kept me thinking all the way home. Had the Stanley family provided free housing for their illegitimate family member?

I discovered that the unusual surname Applegate is derived from a location, perhaps a Viking-controlled area of Yorkshire or Cumberland; or perhaps the name simply came from a residence by an apple orchard. But tracing the identity and former lifestyle of my crucial witness, Mary Ann Applegate, was becoming more and more crucial to my investigation. I wanted to unpeel her mask. Why had Louis given her surname as Appleby, not Applegate, in *Debrett's*? There must be some reason why he had made this deliberate error.

I was clutching at straws but I decided to ask some questions about the town of Carlisle. The Northern social historians gave me hope that I had the right woman, for they told me that Carlisle had been an important milling town with close commercial links with Liverpool. Carlisle's workforce had migrated either down from Glasgow or up from Liverpool. They also told me Alfred's job as a warper, in the vast burgeoning industry of the late nineteenth century, had been a more skilled one than I had realised. Mary Ann's mother may have been illiterate, but that was not at all unusual for women in those days.

At times all my ferreting seemed a silly and pointless search. However, the more I researched, the more questions came into my head. I could not let go. The hunt for Louis's roots drove me on. It was part of my grieving for a lost childhood.

CHAPTER 11

WHO, WHEN AND WHY?

I knew my research had to be covert but I also felt the need to enquire into what I saw as dangerous territory. I wanted to know if the Liberal Party's headquarters had any unpublished records concerning Asquith's private life. This proved to be time-consuming, as they seemed to hold no centralised system for record keeping. The National Liberal Club told me the Liberal Party's papers for my period in history had been moved to Bristol University. They were sure there was a bundle of papers that could be of relevance to me. When I contacted Bristol I came across my first dead lead, as both the archivist and his assistant would give nothing away. I tried again but they were not going to divulge. I even exposed myself by asking if Louis Stanley had ever stood for selection to the Liberal Party, but all they were willing to say was that the war period for the Liberals and Liberal Nationalists was ill documented. I had no alternative but to accept this situation.

I imagined how each person in this story might have reacted to

Venetia's pregnancy in 1911. What had gone on behind the closed doors? How might the brains of the second decade of the twentieth century have been thinking?

First I imagined the thoughts of the elderly Prime Minister, who was leading the country at a crucial time in our history. How did he feel when he found his mistress was pregnant? What did he do when she told him? Did he tell his wife? What about his daughter, who was the same age as Venetia? Did he tell her? Did his sons know? Did he tell any political friends? Asquith probably never contemplated paying Venetia off because he wrote the vast bulk of the letters to her after Louis was born.

And the pregnant Venetia? What thoughts went through her head? When did she know she was carrying Asquith's baby? Had she told her best friend Violet? How had she felt about giving up her baby? Had she been involved in selecting his adoptive parent? Why had she continued to see Asquith after the birth? Might she not have refused to see him any more? When did she tell her parents, Lord and Lady Sheffield? Had they been very angry? Or did they think they had to be careful because the father was the Prime Minister? But Lord Sheffield and Asquith were both Liberals and old drinking friends; had they had 'a quiet word together' and worked out what to do?

Then there was the Prime Minister's wife, Margot. Did she know? What did the other six Asquith children make of the relationship? How would they have responded to their father's having a young girlfriend? Had any of Asquith's colleagues suspected he was having an affair with a young woman? How would they have responded to the news that she was with child? They must have been worried a political scandal might erupt. What about his political enemies? Did they know?

What about Venetia's future husband? Was he involved at all? Had he known when he married her that she had already been a mother?

I kept asking myself how early Asquith might have started

flirting with Venetia. I had to prove that a birth in January 1912 was possible.

Why had HH felt the need to be part of his children's social group rather than his wife's? I needed to know what kind of woman Margot had been. I found the answer when I discovered that most observers had not written kindly of her. Margot was a habitual complainer and often appeared unhappy. Politicians laughed at her verbal errors. On one famous occasion she blurted out, 'The whole Asquith family overvalue brains. I'm a little tired of brains: they are apt to go to the head.'

I later read that by 1914 'she had reached the full bloom of her eccentricity' and she looked like 'a painted skeleton, hawk faced with a waspish tongue'. But with her immense wealth Margot had granted Asquith a higher social position and her entertaining made her a lion in London society. I then found four crucial pieces of information about Asquith's second wife.

Margot had been a serious flirt. When Asquith's first wife, Helen, was still alive, Margot and he were already secretly meeting at friends' dinner parties, as his wife did not like large social occasions. They were also 'writing long letters' to each other before Helen's demise.

However, when Asquith did propose to Margot she dithered and worried about taking on him and his children. It was an unlikely match and friends on both sides of the relationship did not support the engagement. Both Randolph Churchill and Lord Rosebery warned Asquith that Margot was far too interested in hunting and absorbed with her horses for a happy marriage. Maybe they also suspected her desire to be involved in clandestine politics, because it was not long before she was known as 'the power behind the throne'.

Much later, Asquith, in a dejected mood, reported to his daughter that Margot caused him more trouble than his parliamentary Opposition. Asquith often woke to find leader articles in the *Morning Post* gloating over some throwaway line that Margot had innocently made.

It also amused me that Oscar Wilde had also flirted with Margot: he had sent her poetry, and dedicated his short story 'The Star-Child' to her.

The fourth piece of news was even more interesting: one of the reasons Margot had became so spiky in middle age had been that three of her five pregnancies had ended in disaster. 'Margot had what would now be called a nervous breakdown.' I needed to know what date she had suffered this.

I was amused to read that Asquith's daughter-in-law, Cynthia, gossiped in her memoirs about the time she was told of Venetia's change of commitment. Bluey, a family friend, had conspiratorially relayed the rumour of the engagement to her. Cynthia must have been suspicious because she asked about her father-in-law's emotional health. Bluey replied, 'He is [so] absolutely heartbroken that it is stymieing all public troubles.' I could hardly believe what I was reading when I spotted more of Cynthia's revealing words on the next line: 'If truth be known it is really the cause of the coalition.' Had Louis's parents' splitting up caused a coalition government in wartime? This was big news. The next rumour that Cynthia heard was that Venetia was to marry a wealthy Jew. So had Louis's mother married for money?

I thought of all the times Stepfather had disliked our suitors, whatever their background. There was always some excuse for not accepting them and he refused to encourage the relationship. Their appearance was rough, they had uncut fingernails, or 'they're marrying for money' or 'to improve themselves', he would pronounce. Had this been his scheme? Had his plan come unstuck because although, my mother had been wealthy on paper, she never had the money available? When the family company was at its height the tax was so high under Prime Minister Harold Wilson that the shares were never floated on the open market. Later, when taxes eased, the company was greatly affected by the failing car industry and the greater part of it was shut down. Had Louis been deeply disappointed?

Looking back on my research into Stepfather's roots, I now realise that I was anxious because I was unpicking the seal of Stepfather's closely guarded box of secrets. If I lifted the protective lid too far, I might let out a damaging genie, which would cause further havoc in my life. At that time I felt so lonely. I had a huge need to confide. I chose my cousin David, who had helped us so much in his attempts to aid his aunt.

After I outlined my case to him, I received a surprise. All he said was, 'I wouldn't be at all surprised. I'm sure you're right.'

David would have seen another side to Stepfather, being ten years older than I. But all the same I was dumbfounded. 'Why do you say that?'

'He treated us all with disdain,' said David. 'We were inconsequential to him; in fact everybody was a serf to him. He behaved like a spoilt prig, just like how I imagine an illegitimate prime minister's son would behave.'

We chatted more. David gave me some crucial information. He explained that he had been told by his father, Uncle Alfred, that when Stepfather married my mother they made a pact never to talk about their past lives. Louis had justified this by saying that the past would be difficult for my mother. But I realised it was a perfect excuse for Stepfather not to talk about his earlier life. David thought that Mum first met Louis at the Whim Coffeehouse in Cambridge, but further tittle-tattle about our stepfather had been taboo in his own family. Although David did remember gossip about our granny's dislike of her possible new son-in-law, he even thought that she might have asked a detective to look into his affairs. He was sure there was talk of his being penniless when he met my mother, but he could remember no more.

As I ferreted deeper, I began to hear things I did not want to know. My stepfather was well known for more unpleasant antics in my hometown. At the time he met my mother he lurked in the Blue Boar hotel in Trinity Street and was called 'the dirtiest young man in Cambridge'.

I just had to make myself time to read the history books. Nothing seemed to add up.

It was a slow process to understand life in the early twentieth century. Everything I discovered had to be analysed and sorted. There was certainly sufficient evidence to suggest Louis Stanley was the product of a high-profile political love affair.

When another political scandal hit the modern media world I looked at the Asquith affair from a different perspective. Nowadays, packs of reporters and photographers sniff out scandals but in the early twentieth century the press had less power and they did not sensationalise as they do now. The Opposition was more reserved in its adversaries' private affairs. Arthur Balfour, leader of the Opposition, had always been a close friend of Margot. Even when Asquith was Prime Minister the families played golf together in Scotland. They were such good friends that Balfour even taught HH how to ride a bicycle. Rather different from today's politics I thought.

But as I read more about Asquith an icy shiver shot down my back, for I discovered that his characteristics were very like Stepfather's. To anybody else the particulars might have appeared minor but to me they were beacons.

Louis had inherited HH's style of speaking: 'cool, courageous, intellectually alert, well informed, sure of himself… with a striking command of apt and incisive language'. Louis had always enjoyed public speaking without recourse to notes. Had he been coached for this role or was he a natural?

It was reported that at the end of each working day Asquith had been like a coiled spring unloading, who launched into his evening entertainments with a boyish enthusiasm. Asquith loved intellectual pursuits, preferably in the company of easygoing clever women.

Their constitution was also identical. Asquith described his own as 'to be equally compounded of iron and leather'. Others report that he not only had more mental strength than the norm, but could also enjoy a series of late nights without any ill effect. However, the most crucial similarity in their makeup was that HH had no sympathy for those who could not keep up with him. I thought of all the times Louis had derogatorily used the term 'wimp' for all those who could not match his boundless energy.

Louis had a brilliant memory but it did not match that of Asquith. HH could absorb thousands of facts. For instance, when he was challenged to a quiz about horseracing the challenger thought he would romp home because he knew that Asquith hated anything to do with horses. However, with skills of pure assimilation from talk among Margot's friends he was a walking encyclopedia of pedigree and form. When confronted for a further wager he undertook to name the Derby winner in any requested year. To rub salt into his opponents' wounds he reeled off the winner's sire and dam.

The minutiae of literature fascinated Asquith. In the modern world he would have been a brilliant quiz compiler. Venetia's background made her well suited to Asquith's quizzing. This reminded me that Louis Stanley had been asked to set the questions on Cambridge University for the quiz programme *Mastermind* and the poor contestant who had chosen this speciality had not answered one of the questions correctly.

The two men were so similar I found it spooky. Asquith loved going on motorcar rides. Mum had spent every winter, Saturday and Sunday, taking her husband for 'a ride' around the Suffolk countryside for hour after hour. Now I was reading that Asquith went on 'motor car rides' on Friday afternoons with Venetia. They sat beside each other behind a chauffeur who drove them to Richmond Park, Roehampton or Hampstead in Asquith's recently acquired, stylish black Napier. I imagined the couple driving through the young green leaves of the parks while HH's wife, Margot, sat at home dejected.

The other passion they shared was golf. Asquith did not live and breathe politics like other premiers – 'he could put his working life aside and loved to distract himself by playing golf'. He did not play particularly well on the fairway but made up for his lack of length by sneaky behaviour and by his skilful putting. Skill on the green had also been one of Louis's strengths.

I wondered if Asquith could have ever inspired Louis to take up the game. HH died when Louis was only 16, so was this possible? I suspected that Asquith had no contact with his illegitimate son, but I felt sure that someone, somewhere, had encouraged the young Louis to play golf. If he had been brought up with Home Granny and Auntie Mamie, who could it have been?

I researched Asquith's golf. He liked to play with Margot in Scotland at a place called Archerfield. Connections with this part of Scotland kept cropping up. Archerfield, I discovered, was near North Berwick. The house was used by Asquith for his holidays and belonged to his wife's family. Louis had told us numerous times that he had lived in Edinburgh and he knew the Forth estuary coastline well. I also read that 'golf brought the whole Asquith family together – women as well as men', and Venetia was learning to play. What could I make of this? Louis had been a prolific writer. Had he ever written about his personal life in his early books? I had to steel myself to skim through some of them. In an article he had written for the magazine *The Field* I found 12 words that were perhaps going to lead me further: 'I had been bred and brought up in an atmosphere of golf.' Who had created this 'atmosphere of golf'?

He continued, 'The game, the sight of golf clubs, golf balls and golfers were as natural to my eyes from earliest childhood, as the air I breathed.'

It sounded as if he had been living with a golf professional. Who had this man been? Then I spotted what I thought might be a Scottish connection, for he wrote, 'I swung a wee club at an age when most children play such exciting games as marbles and hopscotch. The day the club arrived was my fifth birthday.'

I looked again at the Asquith connection with the nine-hole

golf course at Archerfield. I also learned that the forerunner to the now famous amateur competition, the Walker Cup, between Great Britain and the USA, had its first match at Hoylake in 1921. So had Louis been inspired as a nine-year-old to play golf when he first saw the international players outside his house?

I went back to reading his early golf articles and in his second published book he wrote of the 'shingly shore' where he grew up and the pleasure of being pulled along behind a boat as he learnt to swim. He wrote that he played golf with 'grown-up relatives and two fisher boys who both became well-known caddies.' So perhaps his 'relative' was a caddy rather than a golf pro. I was fascinated. Who was the man whom he had lived with? Could this lead me to his roots?

Max Faulkner (in the 1950s) had written a foreword to one of Stepfather's books, which made me wonder if I could find a professional golfer who had known Louis and was still alive. Maybe they could tell me how he had learnt his golf.

The first, Norman Fox, guardedly revealed that Louis 'would be remembered as a prolific writer rather than a good writer on golf'. He was 'charming in a strange way' but 'did not suffer fools gladly. I remember him very well, although I had only seen him once or twice.' I asked why his memory of Louis Stanley had been so vivid.

'You couldn't miss him! A big, big man, he was self-imposing with a smart jacket and a shooting stick covered in labels!'

His words brought back memories of that dreaded stick he took everywhere with him. In crowds he carried it dangerously with its ever-increasing bundle of smart entry cards tied around the metal struts, then plonk his huge frame on the tiny brown seat in front of others. I thought of our outing at Aintree as Fox continued, 'He'd a Leica camera – anybody with a Leica camera could not help but be impressive! He also made a nuisance of himself because he annoyed players by photographing them when they were putting or teeing off. The great Tim Shanahan complained about his behaviour and it became big news.'

This didn't surprise me, but I was surprised when he finished off by saying: 'He was nothing better than very good amateur golfer. His skill had been in analysing players' golf swings.' So had the man in Louis's childhood house been a golf coach?

Peter Alliss remembered Louis Stanley from when he was a young lad. Stepfather had been friends with his golf-professional father, Percy. Alliss recalled that 'in some people's eyes he was a monumental snob…He had a booming voice and a superior manner.' So even in his golfing days Louis had been infamous!

One of Louis's favourite brags was his friendship with the golfer Henry Cotton. During the war the wealthy sportsman had moved into the Dorchester Penthouse and had driven around in his most elegant Bentley. Was Louis his most frequent passenger?

Stepfather writes in one of his books of travelling to the Southampton docks in 1948 to meet Ben Hogan, the non-playing USA captain of the Ryder Cup. Louis had managed to call himself the 'organiser' for the American team. Louis makes much of the story of driving back up to the Dorchester in a Bentley. Was this in the British team's car captained by Henry Cotton? Then I was reminded of another story he told. Stepfather had been sitting in the passenger seat of a Bentley when he saw that another car was likely to smash into them, so he calmly took his camera from the shelf in front of him and took a photograph of the imminent accident. Who had been driving that day? Was the story true?

As various different pieces of information hit my desk I switched from one line of research to another. I was struggling to keep pace, as I was now working on more than three fronts, and searches took more and more of my time. But I felt I should read the Asquithian letters, even though almost all had been written after Louis's birth.

Meanwhile, I found these words written by Venetia's brother Arthur (the fifth Lord Stanley), which he wrote in 1938. His words amused me, as they were propitious to the saga I was to discover about his own family:

> The craving to read letters not intended for oneself and to meddle in other people's private business is one which is more widely spread than many of us would care to admit. It is, further, a craving which may be the means of causing infinite trouble in domestic lives.

From the Asquithian letters I immediately got the feeling that Asquith could be a superficial man at times and I could not understand how historians were so sure they were not love letters.

It was clear that HH wanted to show off his high status to his girlfriend. On 17 May 1914 he wrote to Venetia while he was staying with the King and Queen at the Royal Pavilion of Aldershot Camp. He pointed out to her the grand headed notepaper. Later that year when war in Europe was looming he wrote on Buckingham Palace notepaper, 'This is a souvenir. It is not likely that anything will be written to anybody from the same precise address for a long time to come.'

Even more shocking was his letter written on 31 March 1915 during some of the worst atrocities of war. Asquith wrote, 'I must write you the first letter on War Office papers.' Asquith also told Venetia that he kept her letters tucked under his pillow! Was this prime-ministerial behaviour?

Most of the other letters had little relevance to me but I became aware that the unpublished ones were held at the Bodleian Library in Oxford. I wondered what I could unravel by visiting this famous library. I was sure that any evidence of a pregnancy would have been removed, but could there be a hint somewhere? I was now more attuned to detective work and felt I was on a personal mission.

Certainly many of the unpublished letters were of a more loving nature than those that had been published in the Brocks' book. My first breakthrough in the library catalogue was to discover that there were letters dated as early as 1907! Communication continued until 1910, but the library held only three letters for 1911. All were written in either September or October. Why were there so few? If there were more, what had happened to them?

I found Asquith's handwriting difficult to read, but I include here samples of his intimate words. They were written in March 1914:

> Beloved, you do not need to be told what you are to me!

> I hope you enjoyed Saturday and Sunday as much as I did. I thought we had a heavenly time.

> I spent the most delicious hours with you yesterday evening and am looking forward to tomorrow afternoon, you will let me know where to come for you [he divulged political information]…all this is very secret…

> I hope you are having a good day my darling and not forgetting me who loves you so much.

Then I found a letter catalogued for 1914. It had an unusual format, as it was in pencil and undated. Asquith had jotted, 'Writing this in a cabinet meeting.' I was bowled over, for my initial search on the Web had been right. How could he do this? I asked myself. I was shocked by his letters. As Britain edged towards war, he wrote on 7 July 1914, 'Do say when I can come and see you…I love you such a lot.' In later letters he repeated, 'I must see you.'

Then on 5 August, the day Britain declared war on Germany, he found time to write,

> I am afraid I shall have to send you, my darling, a skimpy letter today. It is now 6.00 and I had literally not had a moment to myself, as you will see when I give you a rough record of my day. But first I must thank you for your letters of this morning.

> You say you want to see me. *How much* do you suppose I want to see you? All the same I think you are quite right to remain at Penrhos until Friday night. We shouldn't see anything of one another if you come up earlier in the day. I still try to cherish a hope that I may go with you…

As I searched the catalogue I noticed that stored in the Modern Letters room there were three Asquith writing pads. On the back of one battered blue folder, scratched in faded gold pen, he had written, 'My last letter to Venetia'! I also found two personal notes that fascinated me. One was a scribbled note with no date: 'What happened? I am eager to know?' The other read, 'Thank you so *very* much.'

While thinking, I shifted my attention back to Mary Ann. Did I have to accept the two census entries that I had in my possession for 1891 and 1901? A possible Applegate of the right approximate age had been living in St-Anne's-on-the-Sea in 1901 and Bollington in 1891. Neither place gave me much hope; neither meant anything to me. I even wondered if the village on the sea existed still.

Could I find evidence of the woman's movements after 1901 by finding her in an electoral roll? I was not very hopeful, as women did not get the vote till 1918, and only then if they were house owners and over thirty. That idea came to nothing. As I was to discover, there are no national electoral registers. I had to know the town in which she had been living in order to find her name.

The Bollington woman did not seem likely to be a homeowner, as she had started out in life as a cotton-cop winder. But I encouraged myself by posing the possibility she might have money in the form of a trust from taking on the baby.

As I started to think about electoral rolls I thought of Auntie Mamie. I knew so little about her. She was the 'adopted sister' of Stepfather and that was all I knew. I remembered how much she annoyed my mother and how she liked to stroke my hair, but I could not imagine that she would be relevant to my story.

At the time of Mamie's passing away, death certificates also included the birthdate of the deceased person. The documentation declared she was born in Wallasey and gave her date of birth as 23 May 1900, which, as predicted, showed she was 12 years older than Louis. The details fitted with Louis's story of his parents taking the baby from the local hospital. Mamie's forenames were given as Mary Eliza. This did not surprise me, as I could recall Stepfather telling my mother his adopted sister's name was changed to Mamie, as both 'mother' and 'daughter' had the same forenames.

Since adoption in the early twentieth century was not a formal process and there were no courts and no legal paperwork involved, Auntie's death certificate did not help me discover the surname she was born with. All I could surmise was that she had probably changed her surname twice, once for the adoption and the second when Mary Ann changed her own name from Applegate to Stanley. This proved a real stumbling block because, if I did not know her birth surname, I would not find her on the 1901 census or on any electoral record. But I could not rule her out completely. I had to turn over every stone to see what minutiae lay beneath.

As I had Auntie Mamie's supposed birthdate and birthplace, a helpful archivist in Birkenhead helped me search for her records. But we had to agree there was no female with the forenames 'Mary Eliza', whatever surname, born in Wallasey in the whole of 1900. In some ways this was not unexpected and suggested that Louis's story of her adoption had again been true. Perhaps her birth had never been recorded. Or had she been born in another part of the country? There were too many imponderables for me to follow this line of research. Thinking about Mamie made me again wonder why the Stanleys of Alderley Hall had chosen Mary Ann Applegate to be the surrogate mother for Stepfather. Had she already been an unmarried mother with Mamie when she agreed to take Stepfather in? When did they change their names? Why did Mary Ann Applegate change her surname to Stanley, and how did she do it? Did she have to change her details to gain access to the trust that would have been set up for Louis?

I learned that in England under common law your legal name is the one by which you are generally known, so anybody can change their name, at any time. There are no records of what people's previous names were even if they did it officially by deed poll. So a person can hide for ever under an assumed name and the search for Auntie Mamie's roots was all but impossible. However, it did explain how easily Mary Applegate could have assumed the title of Mrs Mary Stanley. Home Granny had no need to be legally identified: she never claimed any pension and she never showed any interest in going abroad, so had no need for a passport.

Had Venetia insisted that Louis and his adoptive mother take on her surname? If so, why? Was there money or pride involved?

Looking back on childhood with a more mature mind, I realised the age difference between brother and sister had been big. It would have needed some sort of explanation by Mrs Stanley when she met new acquaintances. As siblings they could never have shared childhood games together. In normal families Mamie might have acted the bossy older sister but when I knew her she had always been subservient to Stepfather. In character, intellect and looks, they were so different that the adoption story of Mamie seemed likely to be true. So this strange character was never likely to lead me to Stepfather's roots.

I was in for another big surprise when I made a call to the Emmanuel College office. Louis had lied to us about his university degree.

Louis Thomas Stanley had obtained only a pass degree in 1945 and the subject was not English. He had read theology. I could not fathom this out. He was meant to be such 'an authority' on the University of Cambridge, yet he had only a pass degree. As a child I had wondered why he didn't have dons as friends but, as there were so many people 'we don't talk to', I never thought much about it.

Now I wondered about his special university 'postbox'. When he had given up cycling Mum had often driven him in the evenings to Emmanuel to collect his post. Why had he still had it twenty or more years after graduating? I recalled another story. By coincidence two of my cousins had studied at his old college. John told me that after a visit to the Old Mill House my mother had driven him back to the college gate, with Louis in the passenger seat. The college porter had spotted Stepfather lounging in the front seat. As my cousin went into the hall the porter started to tell him a horrid story about Louis but when he realised that he might be a relative, he refused to say any more. What had he been going to say?

As I delved further in Levine's book on Edwin Montagu I found a startling paragraph where she quoted Angela Lambert in *Unquiet Souls*:

> Asquith had not the temperament for unconsummated love – certainly not Platonic love…as women soon found out. To be left alone with him was to invite immediate and bold approaches, admittedly playful to begin with, for hand holding, touching, fondling and kissing. He was simply an importunate lecher…if he found no resistance to his advances – or even active encouragement – he would take the relationship to its fullest conclusion.

This put this great statesman in a different light!

I thought of the sepia photographs of this gentlemanly frock-coated politician sporting a smart top hat as he left Number Ten. He looked so noble, so intellectual. But had he been a lecherous old man? Certainly his probable illegitimate youngest son was. I thought of the nurse who had dropped her pants for the ninety-year old man who had squandered so much but failed in his duty to care for my mother.

Levine believed the friendship of the two girls provided camouflage for Asquith's interest in Venetia and allowed the early relationship to go virtually unremarked.

The American Levine quoted from a letter Asquith had written in November 1914 to Venetia about those earlier years: 'Do you remember the night afterwards when Bluey led us astray through the wilds of Lancashire and we arrived near midnight at Gawthorpe…what fun we had…how little any of us foresaw of the future – least of all I, my darling' (3 November 1914).

Interestingly, according to Brock the date of when they were led astray was 5 December 1910! And this letter had hidden meanings. It makes clear that Asquith had taken Venetia canvassing with him, as Violet's friend, in both general elections of 1910. There was one in January and another that spanned the months of November and December. The south Manchester area was extremely important to the Liberals: they were seriously wooing the working-class vote. At the time there were worries that if the Liberals did not make fundamental reforms there would be serious rebellions. Two elections in one year with the area round Stockport being so important would have given the couple plenty the opportunity to have private times together. Further letters written in the following years provided me with scenes that fuelled my imagination:

'You will come to the garden party and if it is fine we might slip away…' In July 1914 Margot had invited more than 1,600 guests to her party, so escaping together would have been easy.

Later that year Asquith wrote, 'Take a solitary walk tomorrow beloved to our dear little hollow and think of me and our heavenly hour there…' And when he reminisces in 1915 I can visualise the lovers together: 'What delicious hours those are to look back upon when we read things together in your little room at Alderley! Those damn dogs too! How I hated them, and yet somehow they fitted into the picture…'

Additional letters reveal that Venetia went on family holidays with the Asquiths as early as 1908 or stayed with Violet at Archerfield.

Even more evidence came in when I learned the Asquith children were often farmed out to the Stanleys' house when Margot was ill or grieving for her lost babies.

I still felt it was of great importance to know if Louis's 'birthday', of 6 January 1912, fitted with the existing historical paperwork. The additional letters written in 1912 but not printed in the Brocks' book had not helped, and now I found a letter with a date that worried me. Published in Violet's early diary, *Lantern Slides*, there was a letter from Violet to Venetia dated 7 December 1911. The topic was my concern: 'I think *Friday* would be the best day for hunting especially as the meet's so near.' This made me anxious. Had Venetia planned to go hunting? Surely Venetia was not riding in a hunt when she was so advanced in her pregnancy. But maybe she wanted to lose the baby. Did this disprove my theory? From the diary of the Prime Minister's daughter I needed to analyse the movements of the two friends in more detail.

Violet is on holiday in Bavaria on 17 August 1911; she stays there at least for another three days, returning via Munich. By 5 September she is back in Britain and stays at her father's holiday house in Scotland. Unusually, Venetia is not mentioned until the 25th of that month, when Violet writes to her from Archerfield sympathising with her about an illness.

'My Darling – I am *miserable* about your plight – and feel terribly "done" by Fate at not having you here.'

What was this illness? Was this an excuse to hide away at a crucial time?

Violet remains at Archerfield for at least another month (20 October or later), still begging Venetia to reply to her letters. In another letter Venetia appears not to be at Alderley but at her country house, Penrhos, in Wales. Did Violet know her friend was pregnant? I find more details when Violet's future husband, Maurice Bonham Carter, reports that he finds Venetia depressed on 14 November. Her excuse for her depressed state was that it was near the anniversary of a brother's death (but this was three years before). Why was she so unhappy?

The next published exchange of letters between the two female friends was on 19 and 21 November. Venetia has returned to Alderley and returns information about a by-election. But, more worryingly, she talks of being out and about in London and going to clubs. This worries me but then I recover from my fears because in Levine's book I discover the nature of Venetia's September indisposition. In her letter to Edwin on 26 September 1911 she writes of suffering from jaundice!

> I am getting very bored by being ill, and require as much sympathy, and as much condolences as any one you can think of. I've been in bed solidly ever since I last wrote to you, about 10 days, which is very long. Specially as I haven't been really ill at all, only ridiculous and hideous with jaundice. It's such an absurd disease, no one feels the slightest anxiety unless a turn for the worse should land one in the grave. At last I am nearly well tho'...Nothing happens here, the house is deserted.

Now a disease such as jaundice would make a good excuse for being unable to travel and to refuse visitors if you wanted to disguise a pregnancy. I wonder who told Venetia to say this. It reminded me that Stepfather always claimed he had jaundice as a baby. It was his excuse for not eating pork joints when we were children. Delving deeper, I was confused and knew I had to find and read the interchange of letters for myself, as I became convinced that Louis's birth was cloaked in mystery. It made me afraid. Had I discovered a bigger secret than I had previously imagined? This was not just a family mystery. It involved the political world. I was fearful of asking direct questions, as this might give people the opportunity to cover any remaining tracks. The logical side of me wondered who could be upset if I exposed the truth. After all, HH's having a 'love child' one hundred years ago was not major news. However, it was the clandestine nature of the story that made me think there had been some sort of cover-up. Clearly, Louis himself never wanted anybody to know. He would have been devastated if he had been exposed as illegitimate.

I was now deeply intrigued in the many mysteries concerning my Stepfather's roots. I went over what I already knew: Louis had a paperwork father and his adoptive mother's maiden name was Applegate; she had been born in Carlisle; his probable father, Premier Asquith, wrote letters to a girl whose surname was Stanley; he had met her as early as 1907; there were family likenesses between 'father' and 'son', both in looks and character, with some surprising 'coincidences'.

I had a unique perspective on the web fabricated by the three families. Only I could see the back of the exquisite cloth where the Asquithian and Stanley plotters had stitched in the family of Applegates. From the material's reverse I was untying the clumsy knots that two families and their advisers had knitted and bound. Had they fully protected the story, or could an inquisitive stepchild break through their cover?

Naomi Levine's book continued to provide me with shocks and machinations and I received the biggest surprise of all when I read, 'Lord Beaverbrook became increasingly attractive to Venetia.'

My mind shot back to childhood memories. Beaverbrook had been one of those names Stepfather bragged about and I had wanted to make fun of it, but after the Bonham Carter episode I never risked it. Stepfather never used his first name, Max, or his surname, Aitken, or his title: he just called him Beaverbrook. My brain was addled now that this name had been coupled with Venetia Stanley's. As my mind was in torment I struggled to make sense of this new piece of information to add to my growing puzzle.

I had harboured doubts before that Venetia was Louis's biological mother, but I was now certain. My body froze to the chair as I read the next lines. I felt that, if I moved, the words on the page might disappear.

Levine's book said, 'There is some suggestion that Mrs Edwin Montagu did more than flirt with Lord Beaverbrook...in 1919 Venetia was not only dining with Aitken, accepting his gifts and financial advice, she was sleeping with him.'

So Venetia had been unfaithful to Mr Montagu! But the question that gradually matured in my brain was a big one. Had Louis met Lord Beaverbrook through his birth mother?' When had he first met his birth mother? And did he know Venetia was his parent?

I needed to know when Venetia was sleeping with Beaverbrook and whether this man had treated Louis as her son. If so, it was not surprising that Stepfather often mentioned this powerful man's name. I needed to recall all I could about Beaverbrook. But, as I did so, it was not childhood memories that flooded my brain: it was the words of Pauline, Mum's faithful nurse. I heard her confiding voice in my head. Louis had said to the nurse as my mother lay dying, 'I got my first job on the *Daily Express* as a photographer.'

Of course! Lord Beaverbrook had owned the *Express*! Had Venetia asked Beaverbrook to give Louis his first job? Was this convincing evidence that Louis must have seen his mother when he was growing up? He would probably have known he was not Mary Ann Applegate's child.

My jigsaw puzzle had become more complicated, and another thought troubled me: why had other historians not delved into this Liberal hero's unsavoury liking for a young woman or 'little harem' of women? Many historians seemed convinced that the Asquith–Stanley affair had been unconsummated. Why were they so sure? And how did they know this? But then I found more interesting material. When Venetia was married to Edwin she gave birth to a daughter called Judith. What did this say about rumours of an unconsummated marriage, which I was to read of in Levine's book (see below)? My mind was working fast again. Had Venetia told Judith that she had a half-brother? Had she told her daughter about her affair with Asquith?

Asquith knew that his lover kept his letters, but it didn't seem to worry him. I speculated whether Venetia had kept HH's letters in a bundle and tied them up with a red ribbon, as I had seen in the movies. Or was she so obsessed with power and status that she hoped they might make fascinating reading in years to come? Maybe she had even thought of making money out of them (I did find later that Venetia had sold to Beaverbrook, after the war, a memo written by Churchill). There was so much to consider.

As both HH and Miss Stanley seemed to enjoy risk taking, maybe the gamble of an unplanned pregnancy fuelled the affair. They made an odd couple. Also, why had they continued the relationship after the birth? I found it surprising that Venetia had been happy to do this. Again, what had his Cabinet members thought of Asquith's behaviour? Had they devoted time to covering up his sexual exploits? To me, these two intelligent people with their vast age difference appeared both selfish and egotistical. I thought of other male politicians over the last two centuries who have seemed almost to enjoy the high stakes of risk taking in their personal relationships. Do alpha males need to gamble with their careers? Charles Dilke and Charles Parnell both ruined their chances of becoming top-notch politicians in the nineteenth century, while the so-called 'angelic' Gladstone wantonly took risks 'talking to' prostitutes. Nye Bevan, Anthony Eden, John Profumo, Hugh Gaitskell and Bob Boothby all took risks; and, more recently, so did John Major.

Lloyd George is perhaps the most infamous philanderer of the lot. As I thought of the scandals surrounding this Liberal Welsh MP, I realised Frances Stevenson, his secretary and lover, would have been almost as young as Venetia when she first met him. Lloyd George first met Frances Stevenson in 1910 and from 1913 she was his mistress. Had Lloyd George, Chancellor of the Exchequer of the time, copied Asquith by taking a girlfriend? (At that time Lloyd

George and Asquith were the best of friends with the comradeship confirmed with their two children, Megan and Anthony – known as Puffin – running in and out of each other's homes.) So Britain had two leading Liberal statesmen emotionally charged over women young enough to be their daughters. It was at this time that Britain entered the war with Germany.

I thought of the famous Lloyd George saying, 'The greater the man, the greater the weakness', not forgetting that it was he who paid £20,000 to stop his own adultery case going to court.

The higher the risk, the more these male politicians seemed to like it. Stepfather was the same. I applied some amateur psychology to the situation. If Asquith's character was anything like his son's, then he would have loved the hunt, the secrecy and the audacity of a relationship with a girl half his age. Perhaps the need for subterfuge and the desire to write letters in Cabinet meetings was a call for attention. Certainly, some historians believe that HH was a man crying out for emotional support. The historian George Dangerfield records that Asquith actually wept in the House of Commons when he had to plead with the miners to go back to work. Some observers have even applied the Phaeton Theory to Asquith, which suggests that clever orphaned boys who have lost their fathers develop intense ambition and are unable to form stable personal relationships. (Asquith lost his father when very young and had been brought up as if he were an orphan.)

But before I could develop my conjectures I was to read another startling sentence from Levine's book:

> The marriage of Venetia to Edwin Montagu was not a success and in some quarters there was gossip that the marriage had not been consummated…Montagu remained obsessed with love for her and had to endure the anguish of sexual rejection from her until his death in 1924.

Why had she sexually rejected her husband, this clever Cabinet minister? It did not make sense. Venetia had left Asquith for Montagu. If she had been sleeping with HH, why did she not sleep with her husband? Who had known about their strange relationship? How did Edwin Montagu become such good friends with the future Prime Minister?

I needed to know more about the quiet, self-loathing Edwin Montagu.

Edwin's family arrived in Britain during the era when Jews were being persecuted in Europe. They then embarked on a series of name changes to fulfil their wish to become 'the most English of Englishmen'. But life was not easy for Edwin as a young man. He had an austere father who had no patience with his sickly son. As he grew older he was to suffer even greater problems with his father, who was a strict disciplinarian in Jewish Orthodoxy. Edwin rebelled against his father's religious demands. They quarrelled and his father retaliated by leaving his son 'cruelly' short of money (in those days parents' allowances were often sons' only income). Importantly for my story, his father's last will and testament forbade Edwin's inheriting if he should marry a non-Jew.

Asquith went to hear an excellent speech made by Edwin at Cambridge University Debating Hall while he was still a student at Trinity College. That initial meeting was Montagu's political making, because soon afterwards he became Cambridgeshire's Liberal MP in 1906 and was later to become the youngest member of Asquith's Cabinet and one of his most trusted advisers. When first appointed as Under Secretary of State for India, Edwin excelled in his speech on the Indian budget and this was reported as 'nothing short of brilliant'. The political friendship became deeper as the two keen reformers worked on paving the way for the introduction of the old-age pension.

Naomi Levine claims Venetia had engineered a classic love

triangle and had outmanoeuvred both these brilliant politicians. I had my doubts. Asquith had power and status but was elderly and married, while Montagu was younger and single, with potential for a startling political career. (Lord Rosebery had also spotted his ability and he became this earlier Prime Minister's protégé.) Significantly, he also had possible wealth once his father died. Montagu's downside was his ill health, his Jewish religion and his physical ugliness.

Why did the attractive, sexy, intelligent Venetia marry him? Was Levine right when she stated that Venetia was attracted by power, money and status in 1915? Had she waited to see Edwin rise up the political ladder? Or did the fact that Edwin was to inherit a fortune as his father had recently died have anything to do with her change of mind?

Edwin's first experience of meeting Miss Stanley was telling. He detested her. At their second meeting he was fearful of her but by the third he was spellbound. The attraction did not make sense, however. Edwin Montagu, as a government minister, must have known that Venetia and Asquith were at least 'good friends' during that time.

At this junction it is important to revisit how unattractive Edwin was to women. Violet wrote,

> His physical repulsiveness to me is such that I would lightly leap from the top storey of Queen Anne's mansions or the Eiffel Tower itself to avoid the slightest contact...the thought of any other erotic amenities with him is enough to freeze one's blood.

Venetia's wedding plans had caused a huge scandal and gossipy announcements appeared in the press, which were cutting for that period in history. On 28 July 1915 *Tatler* had a picture of Venetia with the caption 'An interesting bride to be who is changing her faith as well as her name'. *Vanity Fair* reported on 'Mrs Edwin Montagu, who, as of course you would have heard, has become a

Jewess. I call that devotion, don't you, but I am told Alderley Stanleys rather go in for variety in the way of religion.'

Up until this point I had not appreciated the early bond between Asquith and Edwin. It was as early as 1906 that Asquith appointed Montagu his parliamentary private secretary; he held this position for another three years. This early political union must surely have meant there were no secrets between the two.

Violet's words confirm the friendship: 'Montagu had practically lived in our house for many years...'

Had Asquith confided about Venetia's pregnancy? Was Montagu entrusted with the financial arrangements and the 'placement' of the baby?

Another geographical discovery came my way. St Andrews, the home of golf, was the headquarters of East Fife, Asquith's parliamentary constituency. Now I knew why Louis had treated this town like his second home.

While I was thinking, the phone rang. It was the librarian. 'Your pamphlet on Germany in 1944 has arrived,' she said.

'Pamphlet? Are you sure? I'm expecting a book called *Germany After the War* by L. T. Stanley.'

CHAPTER 12

VITAL CONNECTIONS

Weariness overwhelmed me and I was not looking forward to reading the book. I had imagined it would be eight hundred pages with small typescript, with a battered dusty cover. In the centrefold there might be a few faded pictures of tanks and bombed housing.

The librarian's voice jerked my thoughts back. 'It's called *Germany After the War*, but it's not just by Lewis Stanley,' she said. 'There's a list of authors jointly credited.' I grinned – her pronunciation error would have jarred with him. 'But it was published in May 1944, and had something to do with the proposals of the Liberal Party.'

A nervous energy filled my body. There were flurries of snow falling as I rushed out of my house, but I was determined to get to the library, whatever the elements threw at me. The librarian handed me a thin, floppy, transparent file. Surely she had ordered the wrong title. I stood in the draughty doorway of the temporary building, as the odd snowflake, brought in from the street, landed on my jacket. I fingered the plastic packet. It really was a leaflet. Just as she had said, there were several authors.

Why had my stepfather claimed this 24-page pamphlet, bound with a staple, as one of his achievements?

The flurry of snowflakes turned to blizzard conditions and I was in a daze. All I wanted to do was to get home and compose myself so that I could calmly digest this new surprise. But calmness was too much to ask of my exhausted brain and the subtitle pulsated from the kitchen table: 'Proposals of a Liberal Party Committee under the Chairmanship of the Earl of Perth'. I shivered, and not from the cold. The air around me felt eerie, for I knew the unkempt pages in my grasp included some vital clues to my stepfather's past life. I felt the strands in the web of deceit that others had engineered for him were breaking. As my tea cooled I was struck by a wave of anxiety. Would I ever find out why Louis was fraternising with the Liberals in 1944? However much I believed he was Asquith's son, I had not anticipated confirmation as strong as this.

My self-doubt was there again – always impinging on my thinking. Maybe his name was not in this booklet; maybe the librarian had made a mistake. I used my scanning skills on the tight dense text and illuminating words leapt from the pages. A physical weakness came over me. How was I ever going to find the strength to prepare for my own family's Christmas?

The chairman of the Liberal committee was the Rt Hon. Earl of Perth, secretary general to the League of Nations, 1919–33, British ambassador to Italy, 1933–39, 'Formerly known as Sir Eric Drummond'.

This was no ordinary Liberal: he had been a dignitary. I was sure Louis had never boasted about the Earl of Perth. But maybe Drummond sounded familiar. I wasn't sure. The association 'League of Nations' had rung loudly in my head. As I took gulps of my stewed tea I asked myself why these words meant so much to me.

The second author on the list was Sir Philip Gibbs, 'Author

and Journalist who had been a War Correspondent with the British Armies'. He had been one of five official reporters in the First World War. There seemed no obvious connection between Louis and Philip Gibbs (I later found he had worked on the *Daily Express*.)

However there were plenty of possible connections with the next man on the list: Sir Percy Harris MP, deputy leader of the Liberal Party and Liberal Chief Whip. Deputy Liberal leader in 1944. I was dumbfounded. Had Louis collaborated with all these eminent men? Had they known he was the illegitimate son of a previous Liberal prime minister? What had Stepfather contributed? And why?

The next contributor was Sir Andrew McFadyean, who was joint treasurer of the Liberal Party. Another leading Liberal! McFadyean had been secretary to the British Delegation on the Reparation Commission, 1920–22. This information meant nothing to me but I stored it carefully in my memory bank.

The fifth on the list was Professor Gilbert Murray, who was chairman of the League of Nations Union. Those familiar three words again, 'League of Nations'. Why did they revive childhood memories? Murray was also professor of Greek studies at Oxford. Had his photograph been on Stepfather's study wall? Or had I recently seen his name in one of the books that I had been reading? I was not sure.

I persevered with the list of authors. The next was Sir Walford Selby. He was principal private secretary to the Secretary of State for Foreign Affairs, Envoy Extraordinary and Minister Plenipotentiary. There were no immediately obvious connections with him. I read to the bottom of the page and there was stepfather's name.

'Louis T. Stanley, Emanuel College, Cambridge. Educationalist, with extensive knowledge of European Youth organisations. He has made a close study of the problems of educational reconstruction in Germany.'

What? Educationalist! European youth! I was staggered. He certainly had lived another life. The only time he ever made reference to education was when I was studying to become a teacher. I was chatting in the kitchen with my mother when something he said made me ask, 'Are you saying you were a teacher?'

'Well, yes, sort of. I studied education here at Cambridge,' he replied in his little-boy voice. Before my mother returned from answering the doorbell he continued in the same voice, 'I didn't like it.'

My mother returned full of news and I was too flummoxed to continue. How I wished I had not missed that opportunity to quiz him.

Had he taught? Why had he never talked about it? I couldn't imagine him in the classroom. In this document he called himself an educationalist but where and what had he taught? Had Stepfather ever actually qualified as a teacher? The Education Institute in Cambridge had no records of his studying or producing a paper but, like, so many of my other unproductive searches, their records were incomplete. Anyway, in those days the qualification was not compulsory. So I was none the wiser.

I checked again the date of publication of *Germany After the War*. It was 1944. But there was another far more important mystery. The Emmanuel College record office had told me he had started his theology degree course in 1942 but he had not been awarded his BA until June 1945. If he had been a 32-year-old undergraduate at Cambridge in 1942, how had he become an 'educationalist, with extensive knowledge of European Youth organisations' by 1944? Had his dissertation been on the 'problems of educational reconstruction in Germany'? I checked with the university library. They stored no academic papers written by Louis Stanley. Had his studies been before he went to university? If so when and where?

The pamphlet and the Liberal names now fuelled and fanned the flames of my conjectures. I had to find out more about these wartime Liberals. How had Louis got his name on this document? Who had invited him to be on the panel? And why?

The first supposition that leapt to my mind was that Louis had tried to follow in his father's footsteps and become a politician but maybe his father's party had not thought it prudent to include him. Maybe Louis even used the threat of exposing his roots to get his own way. Or had Asquith asked these younger politicians to look after his son? I was never going to find the answer. Those who knew the truth would be dead by now.

However, I still had plenty of unsolved problems about Germany and Stepfather. He was no linguist and had no basic knowledge of any foreign language as far as I knew. He certainly never talked about the German education system.

There seemed much more enticing suppositions to follow than Louis's first wife, a scenario I had entertained before (see Chapter 2), but, since I was ordering other material, anyway, I asked for his marriage certificate to be delivered. I found that he married Kate on 28 August 1942 in the Cambridge register office. This must have been just days before he started his studies. If he had been planning to study theology, why had he married in a register office? Maybe her family had not approved the match. There was an age difference of eight years. Louis's address was Flat 9, Maitland House, in Barton Road, Cambridge. This was where I had remembered Home Granny and Auntie Mamie living before they took over the downstairs wing of our house.

Louis's wartime work was worrying me and so I rang the alumni office at Emmanuel again. I wanted to imagine what student life in wartime had been like for the newly married couple. Had Louis escaped the draft by marrying Kate and becoming a student? The jolly college archivist who at first seemed so out of keeping for a record office replied in her upbeat voice, 'Each student was issued with a certificate to say they were exempt from conscription.' After a pause, she added, 'But they all had to do some kind of military training, the Home Guard or the fire service.'

I dug deeper. 'Could a married student have lived on the campus?' I asked.

The jolly voice changed to a more serious tone. The answer was a very definite no. 'I think you have your facts wrong,' she said. 'We didn't accept married students in the war years. During those traumatic times the college had very few students, and those who attended were all on emergency degrees.'

The plot got thicker.

As I thought about how Louis must have lied to the university authorities, the archivist's words were still flowing through my mind: 'The students studied those subjects that were essential to the war effort.' I pulled myself together to ask a further question. 'Didn't they study theology?' I reminded her of Stepfather's records.

'You've stumped me, for our arts students only studied for a year.' She paused. 'Maybe two, for exceptional cases.'

Her words had baffled me. How could Stepfather have taken three years to end up with a pass degree in theology in wartime? Maybe he really had wanted to go into the Church after his degree. He had always enjoyed talking about religious matters and he knew so many eminent clerics. So I rang all the ordination colleges in Cambridge but I was beginning to get used to the fact that his name never came up on any records.

I felt more confident that I was getting the upper hand. Louis could not control me any more I was enjoying delving into his previous life. I motivated myself by repeating, 'You can't hide your secrets from me. I'll uncover all that has been so carefully concealed.' And every time I discovered something new I declared, 'There, I've exposed the real you – I'm slowly stripping each layer of your protective shell away!' But I was also beginning to be deeply critical of all that I read. The politicians and so-called aristocrats of the day had acted so scandalously I wanted to expose their lies and discover how they had tried to cover their tracks. I was as keen to expose them, as I was to strip Louis naked.

My research energy was given a boost when a friendly historian told me that a 2003 article in *Family Tree* magazine claimed that Edward Grey, Asquith's Foreign Secretary from 1905 to 1916, had a love child in 1894. In this year Asquith was Home Secretary and Grey was already working in the Foreign Office. The historian was fascinated because the politician had devised what he called 'the perfect cover for his illicit fatherhood'. The married Edward Grey had got a girl into trouble but as he was a budding politician he devised a plan to cover up his involvement. He asked his brother Charles to marry the girl. This brother agreed to this trickery, as he had planned to leave the country and travel around Africa. Charles and the pregnant girl had a 'wedding' in a church so there would be no paperwork to support this. Apparently there were many clerics at the time willing to provide this kind of unrecorded 'wedding'. The young woman was sent to Germany to have her child but left soon after leaving the baby in the care of two local women. They later received money to fund her education and upbringing. Fascinated, I wondered if Asquith had known about his political friend's antics, as this story has only recently been discovered by a grandchild of the 'German' baby.

Furthermore, I found evidence that other Asquithian letters had been conveniently 'lost' in 1912. This time it was his correspondence with the King. In March 1912 Britain was facing a dire situation: a million coal miners were threatening to go on strike and pressing letters were sent back and forth between King George V and his Prime Minister. It is interesting that in the period when the coal workers actually put down their tools the correspondence between the two powerful leaders is missing both from stores in the Bodleian and at Windsor Castle. The correspondence between the two men has been so systematically pruned that there are very few letters for the entire first year of the King's reign.

I was finding more personal details about the Asquiths and read they had bought a house for their relaxation in an Oxfordshire village. Why was the name Sutton Courtenay familiar to me (see Chapter 6)? Was my memory playing tricks? As the village was not far from where I lived and I remembered it was where Asquith was buried, I decided to visit. It had been raining all day and I was in need of a walk. I found Asquith's grave in the ancient churchyard. I then thought it would be fun to find The Wharf, Asquith's weekend home.

I was directed to a house situated close to a bend on the northwest side of the main village road. As I looked at the surprisingly small frontage I remembered that it was here that Margot reigned supreme. At weekends the couple had an endless stream of visitors who reported that their sitting room was dense with smoke from HH's cigars and her Turkish cigarettes.

I had time to kill before my next appointment and I noticed there was a gloomy path in the shadows of the bend. It went between two brick walls. I got to the first turn in the path and as soon as I heard the rushing water I knew I had been to this place before.

When I reached the picturesque bridge I remembered more. Louis never chose to walk, but that day he got out of the car and took us for a riverside stroll. The others had walked on but I stayed to play in this little wooded corner of tranquillity. When I ran to catch them up they must have been standing opposite the Wharf's riverside garden.

So Louis had discovered the Wharf before I had. Had he been researching, just as I was? I shivered. It was an eerie experience to feel I might be following in his earlier secretive footsteps.

I looked for clues in my memories of Louis's attitude to politicians. Louis disliked Roy Jenkins intensely. Whenever he appeared in an interview on TV Louis could not resist making disparaging remarks about him. So I was amused to see that Jenkins had written a biography of Asquith (*Asquith*, 1964). He turned out to be a great admirer of the Liberal Prime Minister, for he wrote, 'The issues he confronted were momentous yet he remained calm, unruffled and dignified. Even more importantly he survived them.' Jenkins also admired Asquith's ability to hold an 'easy authority' over the Cabinet, which at that time was full of brilliant men. But it was Jenkins's Introduction to his biography that fascinated me, as I learned that the discovery of the letters from Asquith to Venetia must have caused huge family ructions. Jenkins asserts that Violet Bonham Carter, Asquith's daughter and Venetia's old friend, suffered a considerable shock when she learned of the letters' existence. Once she composed herself, Violet desperately tried to persuade Jenkins that the letters should not be used in the biography of her father. In Jenkins's book he describes how he challenged Violet about her father's affair: 'In deference to Violet Bonham Carter I made certain excisions from my original text. She did not exactly exercise censorship, although the copyright of the letters lay with the Asquith heirs and not of course with me.'

As I probed, Jenkins's words grew in magnitude. What had Violet been trying to hide? Was it something more than the extent of Asquith's infatuation with her best friend that she had tried to conceal?

Violet particularly appealed to Jenkins not to use the letters in relation to 'his description of the formation of the coalition'. She argued that the letters would give an unfair impression of her father's 'state of mind'. Had Jenkins guessed that Violet was covering something up?

From Jenkins's book I learned it was Judith, Venetia's daughter, who after her mother's death discovered the Asquithian love letters. She started the editing process but she herself died young, leaving the unfinished task to her American publishing husband, Milton Gendel. He decided he could not publish the letters himself, so Gendel handed them over to the Asquith family. First, they were given to Violet's son Mark Bonham Carter, who worked for a publisher. That familiar surname again, Bonham Carter, I said to myself.

I went back to the Introduction of the biography and found

that Mark, being young and probably ignorant of his grandfather's affair, passed the letters without closely reading them to his friend Roy Jenkins. This action could have been disastrous for the Asquith family, as they were desperately trying to preserve their father's reputation.

He went on to describe how he and Violet had argued a great deal 'but in the majority of cases she generously gave way to me. In a few I gave way to her.' I was sure Jenkins had done some serious sleuthing. As a friend of the family, what had he allowed to slip through his net?

It dawned on me that the Jenkins's biography had gone through three editions, but I had been reading only the second, published in 1986. It was essential that I peruse the final edition of Asquith's biography, as it had been published after Violet Bonham Carter's death.

In this edition he had changed his wording to, 'Asquith had a great Prime Ministerial infatuation and epistolary romance (and maybe more) with a then, young woman, called Venetia Stanley.'

Jenkins was also more upfront in this edition about the furore the letters had caused in the family. He and Mark Bonham Carter realised 'that a time would come when they had to show Violet his manuscript' and admit he had in his possession a stash of letters written by her father. He wrote that 'we rather fumbled telling her about the cache…The romance with her father was therefore a natural and profound shock for which I did not fully allow at the time.'

Jenkins admitted that, after Violet had read his manuscript, 'the atmosphere was distinctly fraught', but it was at their first meeting that Violet made a remarkable gaffe. Jenkins remarks that she had 'not the slightest idea of any special relationship between her revered father and Miss Stanley until seeing my draft'. Jenkins, rather than accuse her of lying or of being in denial, called her comment 'implausible'. He was clearly amused by Violet's further remark, claiming, 'It cannot be true, Venetia was so plain'! Jenkins commented that Violet's remark had 'a ring of spontaneity' about it and her impulsiveness added to 'the conviction of her denial'.

Jenkins had probably not dared to write more because Mark Bonham Carter was his publisher and he was Asquith's grandson. Mark's father, Maurice, had been another of Asquith's parliamentary private secretaries in 1911. Surely he, the future son-in-law, had known about the pregnancy.

I diverted my attention and found rich rewards. Mark Bonham Carter had worked for a publisher called Collins. That name made my knees tremble – Collins had been the name of the man Stepfather had always mentioned on Thursdays; they had often 'lunched' together.

Had Jenkins suspected that Violet's passionate reaction was because she feared the letters might expose her father's sexual relationship with Venetia? Had she worried that the correspondence might reveal the existence of Louis? I wondered if Roy Jenkins had ever challenged Louis? Could this be the reason Louis so detested him? Had Jenkins always suspected? If only Roy Jenkins were still alive.

I reflected back to when the letters were first found. The publication of them must have been a tricky time for Louis.

While I matched up my research at the Bodleian with Roy Jenkins's work, I discovered another intriguing fact. Judith's own daughter, Anna Gendel, has given more Asquithian letters to the library but there is a date before which they must not be released – the year is 2015. This is one hundred years after the formation of the First World War coalition. The year Venetia told Asquith she was leaving him to marry Edwin. This disclosure made me wonder what other secrets are hidden away.

Asquith himself was not completely honest in his *Moments of Memory: Recollections and Impressions*, which he wrote in old age. When he started he had little material, so he asked his lady friends to lend him the correspondence he had once sent them. Clever Venetia, having been Lord Beaverbrook's lover, was ready for the request and gave him a typed copy, which she called 'the extracts from Mr A's letters leaving out any sentimentalities' (Brock). Of course it was expedient for Asquith in these memoirs to pretend he did not fall in love with Venetia until the spring of 1912.

I reflected more on Venetia's family. Judith's own daughter, Anna Gendel, would be Louis's half-niece. Had they ever been in contact?

While my children were listening to Agatha Christie mysteries on the car stereo I had my own real detective story on my hands. I was prying into history and untying the strings of a web of deceit that had deeply affected my family. I feared I was entering mysterious waters, but I went back to scavenging. Where and what else could I scour for more information?

Why had Venetia left the doting Asquith to marry a man of a different faith? The Prime Minister had clearly needed Venetia's company. So why had she wanted to leave this arrangement? Maybe at 28, having known him since her early teens, Venetia felt she could no longer cope with Asquith. Perhaps she thought no other man would marry her or perhaps she was pregnant again. Or perhaps, with so many eligible young men being killed in action, marriage was her insurance.

These were all possible reasons to leave HH but why choose to marry the lonely and pockmarked Edwin Montagu, whose face, Katherine Asquith is said to have exclaimed, resembled a tennis court. This man's large ungainly body and slightly twisted mouth had not proved at all successful with the ladies, and, although his mother had increasingly put more pressure on Edwin to find a Jewish girl to marry, he failed miserably to do so. Edwin was a bundle of moods, rarely appearing happy, and was to become devoured by hypochondria.

For someone so lacking in self-confidence it amazed me how Edwin ever attracted the confident, wayward Venetia. The relationship did not add up. It threw up another question. Why had this man been prepared to accept a marriage with Venetia Stanley on her strident terms?

Further thoughts flashed through my mind. Had Venetia ever told her husband about her earlier pregnancy and the birth of Louis? I even found myself wondering if Louis had ever met his stepfather. Surely it was unlikely that Venetia had confided to her husband about a baby born out of wedlock whose father had been his best friend, but, alternatively, had the Premier confided with his close ally about the illegitimate pregnancy? The latter seemed more likely.

I had to remind myself that few observers outside the inner circle even knew that Asquith had a consistent female friend before the Brocks published *H. H. Asquith: Letters to Venetia Stanley*. It was this publication that unleashed the rash of speculation in 1982. I tried to think back to that year. Was Stepfather any more difficult or angry at that time? It must have been an anxious time for him. Reviewers of the text enjoyed writing a series of discussions as to the nature of Asquith's relationship with Miss Stanley.

Kenneth Lindsay, in the *Contemporary Review 1983*, was perhaps the most brutal and called Venetia 'a heartless political adventuress, who settled down happily with a Montagu fortune and together with the rest of her kind, helped to make for a third party in British politics; whether or not this has been a good thing for British politics and for Britain is still open to question.'

A. J. P. Taylor, the famed TV historian, claimed that he had gone along with the Brocks' judgement – that there was no sexual contact – until he did his own research and came upon a letter ending, 'You know how I long to . . .' Taylor believed there was only one interpretation of that letter.

In July 1914 Asquith himself calculated that, since the first week in December, he had written no fewer than 170 letters to Venetia. Some argue that her feelings for him in his make-believe world were almost irrelevant to Asquith. They suggest he needed someone to relax with, someone who would listen without argument and who could provide adoration and comfort. I wondered how much emotional strain and pressure writing such long letters had caused Asquith. I was not sure I agreed with Jenkins's claim: 'This vast epistolary output would have been an impossible additional burden for most people, but for Asquith they were both a solace and a relaxation. They no more interfered with his duties than Lloyd George's hymn singing and Churchill's late night conversations.'

Whatever the strain it is clear that HH was reckless with his posted words. In several of the letters Asquith warned Venetia that the information he divulged to her was 'secret', 'very secret' or 'only for your own eyes'.

Asquith even put his letters in the ordinary post. Philip Ziegler, the author, has called this 'a terrifying indifference to the rules on national security' (*Standard*, 1982). Our premier, Ziegler argues, passed on information that 'could have done real damage to the country if it had fallen in the wrong hands: a secret trip by Kitchener [or] the despatch of submarines to the Baltic'. Other commentators were equally damning, while Levine called his lack of security the act of 'a deranged mind'. Asquith was more concerned that there might be rumours: 'I hate even the possibility of gossip about us' (20 July 1914). He was particularly concerned about Venetia's own family: 'I am rather alarmed at the family curiosity about the contents of my letters and I am sure you were judicious in what you read them [and didn't read]' (4 August 1914).

The politician Enoch Powell pointed out that Asquith never showed, in any of these domestic letters, that he had a 'vision' or 'an exalted aspiration' for the country. His life was just 'a succession of parties, drives, golf and bridge'. Ziegler was even more hard-hitting: 'A man of 60 who becomes besotted with a woman of 25 is usually the object of pity or derision. When the man is the Prime Minister of a nation at war…the matter verges on a national scandal.'

Ted Morgan (when writing on the life of the young Winston Churchill,) describes how 'a messenger came into the Cabinet room with a letter from Venetia and he would read it in great concentration and then settle down to reply at length, ringing for a messenger, who would then take the reply for dispatch. Other members...were dismayed at the time he spent on his personal correspondence during meetings over which he had been presiding, lost in his private thoughts, while grave wartime matters were being discussed.'

This was amazing!

It is worth reiterating that it was as early as 1905, when Venetia would have been 16 or 17 years old, that HH started to join in with his older children's social activities. It was in this period he got his reputation for being 'an importunate lecher' and Asquith started to form his 'little harem'. Certainly he shocked the sedate Edwin Montagu when he found Asquith 'playing musical chairs with a posse of girls'.

Levine was the one historian fascinated as to whether they did or did not sleep together. 'If he was like this – is it likely he kept his friendship with Venetia platonic?' she asked. She reminded her readers that, after twenty years of marriage and five pregnancies, Margot had withdrawn into herself and concluded, '...the nature of the prime minister, his reputations as an importunate lecher, his need to touch, and to be with women, Margot's illness and subsequent disinterest in sex...strongly suggest that the affair had a strong sexual component, even if actual consummation may not have taken place.'

This comment made me think about Margot's emotional state. How had she coped with being the spurned wife? How had she dealt with Venetia, who was so frequently invited to the Wharf or their Scottish holiday home, Archerfield? At first it seems that Margot just accepted Venetia as another of Asquith's 'little harem', but slowly it dawned on her that their relationship was different. Venetia was not the only recipient of letters from Asquith. Viola

Tree, an actress and favoured friend, had received a number of letters (at a time when perhaps Venetia was out of action due to pregnancy) in 1911. But Asquith got into trouble with his wife for writing letters many years earlier.

In 1898 Margot grew suspicious over letters to a young unmarried woman called Mouche Duncombe. Asquith tried to calm his wife's fears with the words, 'You surely know that nobody can or will ever take your place, or any part or inch of it, in my heart and life' (Clifford, *The Asquiths*). Asquith was to repeat sending these kinds of placatory letters to his wife over the next few years. Significantly for my story, he was to send these conciliatory words to his anxious wife when he steamed away in January 1912 to holiday with Venetia in Sicily: 'I love you always wherever I am, and you know well that no one ever does or ever could take your place.'

I became most interested in a discussion published in the letters section of The Times Literary Supplement between a correspondent called Forbes (17 December 1982) and one called Nicholas Walter (4 January 1983). These two men, with different opinions, wrote about the possible consummation and discussed whether Venetia did sleep with Asquith. Much of the debate revolved around a footnote in the Brocks' book. Here he refers to a comment made by the future Lady Diana Cooper (née Manners) and recorded by the author Philip Ziegler (Diana Cooper. A biography 1981).

The story goes that Cooper had been lying in bed soon after Venetia's engagement was announced, recovering from a broken leg, when Asquith visited her. HH had told Diana how distressed he was with Venetia's desertion. He then told her how much he had always liked her. The next day a letter arrived for Diana prominently marked 'Personal', with the instruction that any reply should be similarly labelled. Diana, who was no moral angel, was daunted by the letter's contents. The letter convinced Diana that Venetia had been Asquith's mistress, because, although the message had been obscurely expressed, he seemed to be offering Diana the vacant role. That evening she consulted with her future husband, Duff Cooper, who went into a rage about the obscured suggestions and helped her compose a suitable reply. Diana was anxious not to upset her friend HH, but she was sure from the tone of his letter that her duties would include 'the physical'. Duff supports this story in his diary for the year 1915; he writes that Diana was 'quite certain that Venetia was Asquith's mistress' (Levine).

Let us return to the *TLS*'s discussions about whether Venetia was or wasn't Asquith's mistress. I read that one of the two correspondents, Forbes, dismissed the above story and called Diana's talk 'second hand gossip', but the letter in January 1983 from Nicholas Walter took my interest. Walter claimed his father, William Grey Walter, was one of Venetia's lovers in her later years.

I decided I needed to find the *TLS* for that date and see for myself what Walter Jr. had written. Eventually I found the relevant archived page:

> I must question his [Forbes's] confident denial that the relationship between H. H. Asquith and Venetia Stanley seventy years ago was physically consummated. My father W. Grey Walter, who was one of Venetia Montagu's young lovers fifty years ago (he makes a brief appearance as such in Virginia Woolf's diary for July 21 1934 and I inherited the Cartier cigarette case he was given for services rendered) told me in the 1970s that she told him in the 1930s that Asquith had indeed been her lover in the full sense in the 1910s.

This letter led me to research William Walter, and I found he had indeed been a young lover of the lady in question. He had been born in 1910 and was 23 years younger than Venetia. Unfortunately, Nicholas, the journalist son of William, has since died, so no further details can be acquired. However, the Cartier cigarette case 'for services rendered' got me thinking. If only I had started this research earlier I might have received more first-hand information.

A useful document came to my attention. It was a booklet designed to help family historians search for an illegitimate ancestor, and it told me that in common law, where men and women were living together but not married, the couple declared their child *filius nullius*, meaning no one's child. The baby had no right to carry the surname of either of its parents. In modern Britain, documentary proof of age and birthplace is essential, but in days gone past many parents never registered a birth. There was no penalty for not registering a birth until 1875. The vast majority of people never needed a birth certificate and many adults (especially females) were illiterate. As late as 1874, only two-thirds of legitimate births in Liverpool were recorded, so it is safe to assume that very few illegitimate ones were ever registered at that period. The booklet also told me that wealthy girls didn't register an illegitimate birth. 'For an upper-class unmarried girl to become pregnant was always a matter of deep shame.' The upper class concealed the truth by being sent away on 'extended holidays', deciding only later who should take on the baby. The thought came to me that I had read that Venetia had taken a long holiday abroad. Which year had that been? I found the answer: she was away from July to August 1911. So maybe...

The booklet made me think more flexibly and postulate that Louis's birthdate was wrong, as it was conveniently recorded exactly six weeks after the supposed birth on 16 February 1912. Was this because 'they' wanted to cloud the date? I had already recorded a problem with the dates on the letters in Violet's diary, so had the birth of Louis been earlier? Had the Stanley parents alone dealt with all the details? Did Venetia demand to be in charge? Asquith must have wanted some say in the matter. He had his career and his party to protect and could not afford the scandal to become public. If the baby was frail, or perhaps 'the Stanleys' were undecided as to who should care for him, had 'they' waited 'for instructions' from Asquith and Venetia, who were on holiday together in Sicily just days before the birth was registered? It all appeared to be very expedient.

I told myself I had to be flexible concerning Stepfather's actual birthdate and not become fixated by memories of his birthday. Why believe this was correct when the rest of the details on the birth certificate were probably fabricated? How much earlier could the birth have been? By law you can delay recording a birth for up to six weeks but in this case the law is irrelevant. Louis could have been hidden away for far longer before being registered. The baby could have been secreted in any of the large houses owned by the Stanleys. Was Louis perhaps born in the Stanleys' summer home Penrhos on Anglesey or in Ireland? Penrhos was conveniently close to the crossing port.

I thought about Mum's comment when she saw the photo of Louis as the Edwardian baby in the pot-bellied pram. She had joked that 'the great Louis T started as an exceptional baby. So big for a nine-month-old, really exceptional for an exceptional man.' My mother had brought up four babies. She knew this one was not nine months old. I now started to work on the premise that Louis's date of birth could have been before 6 January and I found two Asquithian letters that gave me further pause for thought.

On the eve of Venetia's birthday in August 1914 Asquith wrote, 'It will be twenty-seven years tomorrow since you opened your eyes on this sinful world, and it is not yet quite three since I made my great discovery of the *real* you.' To what was he referring?

In the other letter he wrote, 'I sometimes wonder, looking back, whether you would rather that I had *not* made it and that things had continued between us as they were in the early days of Venetiad.'

I wondered if Asquith was obliquely referring to her anxiety of giving up a child when he continued in this vein: 'I believe – indeed I know you have told me, and you never lie – that it (my success) has made a difference to the interests & pleasures perhaps also at times to the anxieties in your life.'

I gave some thought to the position of Venetia. How would a young woman cope with the advances of an older man with a powerful position? Had Venetia as a girl offered resistance to the Prime Minister's advances or had she flirted? Men in positions of power and influence are often sexually attractive and Asquith in his sixties was said to be still a handsome, virile-looking man. One can perhaps compare how Venetia felt when one reads about the young Diana Manners. For she found the advances of the Prime Minister 'very flattering' and when in hospital 'he came to delight me and swell me with pride before the nursing staff'.

Angela Lambert's work also helped me. She was another writer who queried the sexual nature of the relationship. She interviewed in February 1984 the clever and devious Diana about Asquith and Venetia's possible sexual relations. Diana said she was convinced 'some sexual contact must have taken place'. I wondered why Diana had couched her words like this, as it was she who had initially spread the gossip that Venetia was 'painfully deflowered by Edwin' (Forbes, *TLS*, 17 December 1982) when she knew that no intercourse had taken place in the Montagu marriage.

Had the gregarious Diana tried to divert attention away from what she certainly knew to be true? Diana was a woman famous for telling different people different stories at different times. Another thought struck me. Maybe she kept quiet because she had intimate knowledge that there was a product of the union – a young male who had the surname Stanley who did not want to be exposed as illegitimate.

I was beginning to discover the Asquith family seemed almost unnaturally keen to cover up Asquith's need for 'other' women.

Nicola Beauman, Cynthia Asquith's biographer, wrote, '…among his family the subject of his lecherous hanky panky was almost taboo…and his sexual predilections…were thought by Cynthia to be so unmentionable that she violently inked over all references in her diary.' A more revolting aspect was that, rather than talk about sex, Asquith liked to stuff a lady's finger in his mouth and suck it when out motoring with her. Duff Cooper reported, presumably from Diana's experiences, that the worst part of this, for ladies, was that he made no verbal comments afterwards, so the embarrassed woman felt they could not rebuff him. At other times, Beauman reported, that bemused ladies used all their art to fend the groping man off them without giving offence.

I was annoyed that Ted Morgan in *Young Churchill* used 'a confidential source' to claim that Venetia was repelled by Asquith's 'drooling high thigh stroking advances' and that for the 63-year-old Asquith, physical fulfilment was less important than the emotional comfort. Who was this mystery person?

However, the most condemning quote of all was from another member of the harem, Ottoline Morrell. She gossiped to Lytton Strachey that Asquith 'would take a lady's hand, as she sat beside him on the sofa, and make her feel his erected instrument under his trousers' (quoted in *The Asquiths* Clifford).

Ugh! Like father, like son.

Ottoline Morrell was not a name I knew, but when I investigated further I found she was a famous socialite who held glorious weekend parties for her literary friends. The Asquiths' country home, The Wharf, was not far away. These literary giants often wrote about their time at Garsington Hall, and Huxley, in his novel *Crome Yellow*, portrays Asquith as 'an old man feebly toddling across the lawn after any pretty girl'.

The biography of the young Ottoline – *Ottoline Morell: Life on the Grand Scale*, by Miranda Seymour – helped my thinking. In 1899 Asquith's unhealthy approach had so terrified the young naïve Ottoline that she fell mentally unwell. The story goes that she had sought advice from the practising lawyer on her future education when things went terribly wrong. Up until that moment she had thought of Asquith 'as a friendly informal tutor in the paternal mould. It never entered her head to think of him as a lover...but something happened'. Seymour claims that nobody knows what occurred that day but the poor girl was so distressed by the event she gave up her university place and fled to Cornwall. Two months later she was being treated for a nervous collapse. Seymour suggests that the prescribed treatment, of the 'sun of Italy and Germany' was an excuse to get away from the clutches of Asquith.

In Seymour's book I found further links with Stepfather's circle of acquaintances. Venetia's cousin, the philosopher Bertrand Russell, the man Stepfather had so often talked of, had been one of Ottoline's long-term lovers.

But let us return to Edwin Montagu, the man Venetia married. On more reading, I realised that the close personal friendship of Asquith and Montagu must be important to my story. Edwin frequently stayed at The Wharf and called at Number Ten almost every night. Intriguingly, Asquith rewarded him with a healthy promotion just four months before his engagement to Venetia. My thinking expanded. Edwin was a friend of both Venetia and HH around the time of Louis's birth.

It absorbed me that Montagu was one of the few surnames that were mentioned in the historical texts that did not remind me of my childhood. I could not remember Stepfather ever mentioning the name, though this is not surprising given that he had died when Louis was only 12, but in my research I found two possible connections to stepfather: Montagu Sr had made his fortune in Liverpool (in silver bullion) and Edwin's elder brother had been called Louis. I also read that the young Edwin was sent abroad by his parents to recover from an unspecified illness. Had he, I wondered, suffered from smallpox, because observers often mentioned his unpleasant skin?

By 1911 Edwin adored Venetia, insisting on buying her something 'very special' that Christmas. His first proposal was in July 1912, just a few months after that holiday in Sicily. Venetia accepted. Her acceptance of his first proposal made Edwin 'blissfully happy'. However this was not to last, because shortly afterwards Venetia reneged on her promise. Montagu proposed again in 1913 but this time Venetia did not hesitate in her rejection. Edwin's third and final proposal was in early 1915. Venetia vacillated, finally agreeing on 19 April. This time Edwin was ecstatic: 'I have never received, I need not tell you, a letter so thrilling and delicious as yours…Its result is, that I am not the only member of the cabinet writing to you during its deliberations.'

I found it shocking that these two great statesmen, both Edwin and Asquith, were irrationally competing with each other over this hedonistic woman. They even jealously fought over their yearnings to write her letters in meetings. These were not immaterial council affairs. They both wrote in front of their Cabinet colleagues when discussing serious issues about the state of the nation. The country was at war with Germany and many were dying on the front.

I discovered that stored at Trinity College, Cambridge, were letters between Montagu and Venetia. They had been found, after Venetia died in 1948, among a huge number of boxes that contained Edwin's private papers. Lily, Edwin's 'puritanical' sister, had sorted them but, since many were seen to be of a 'sensitive nature', she had organised for them to be burnt.

I was worried that my research was becoming off-target but I thought a day or two in Cambridge might do me some good. It was a long shot, but these letters might help sort out the puzzle of why historians thought this woman had chosen not to consummate her marriage.

Scarily, I did remember there was a period when Louis regularly visited Trinity College. Was this when the letters were first deposited there? Had he gone there to read them and learn about his own history?

CHAPTER 13

WHAT ELSE COULD I SCOUR FOR INFORMATION?

I experienced a peculiar thrill the day I found a faded black-and-white image of Alderley Hall. The photograph was taken from its magnificent frontage showing an elegant porch and wide bowed French windows, but I could distinguish little else, as huge cedar trees hid the rest of its exterior. I wanted to visit the area but my work forced me to postpone the trip. However, the enforced delay reminded me of a strange wild-goose-chase car journey I experienced when I was about ten. Stepfather had acted a little out of character. He had wanted Mum to drive to a particular location in the countryside. We had been up at either the Oulton Park or Aintree racing circuit and had stayed in the Adelphi Hotel, and Louis had been lording about in his home territory. Stepfather was, however, useless at navigation outside his familiar haunts, but that day he attempted to use the AA map, for Mum had already been driving for many miles and was becoming irritated with him.

Eventually, we found the place he had been looking for. Mum was annoyed. There was nothing to see. He had brought her to a relatively small house in extensive grounds with mature trees. Why had Stepfather wanted us to come to this place of such little interest? The light was fading and we were all hungry. As we sat in the car Mum talked of the drive being too big for the house, but she was anxious to leave. She did not want another night's driving when we would arrive home after two in the morning. As we turned for home down the curving driveway I asked about the huge clumps of bright-pink, dark-red and mauve blooms. They were strange to me. Rhododendrons do not grow on Cambridge chalk.

I have vivid memories of the driveway at its T-junction exit. Rush-hour traffic was passing and we were trapped there for many minutes. It was hard to see oncoming cars in the gloom and I remember nervously looking out at the high sandy-coloured walls on both sides of me as I felt tension build between Mum and Stepfather. The field opposite with its white hooped railings was illuminated from the bright headlights of the streams of passing cars that appeared from around a bend in the road. Louis was irritated that none of them would slow to let us out. Each time there was a lull he goaded Mum to take a risk. But, each time she edged out, another vehicle appeared from around the corner and behind the high driveway walls.

Why had Louis wanted to go to this place? Was it Alderley Hall? Had he ever been allowed to visit the place as a child? I read that the contents and outbuildings went under the auctioneer's hammer in 1932 after a fire, and the grounds were sold in 1938 after the deaths of the two Stanley heirs. I wondered what Louis had known about this and how he had felt about the sale. Had he ever felt deprived of his natural inheritance?

I needed to see if the literature about the house matched up with my memories. I had to find out if acid-loving plants had grown there. In my mind it became a crucial question. The estate office of Astra Zeneca, the drug company that now occupies the land where Alderley Hall once stood, sent me a booklet about the gardens when they had been in the hands of the Stanleys. To my disappointment there was no reference to acid-loving plants, but I did learn that, according to the records of the head gardener, Herbert Asquith was a frequent guest at the Stanleys' house parties and often read the lesson in the local church. This was helpful but I dearly wanted to know whether Rhododendrons grew there.

I did not want to make the journey to Cheshire unnecessarily but as I searched more I eventually found what I was looking for. In the June 1931 edition of the *Alderley and Wilmslow Advertiser* it was reported that the grounds of Lord and Lady Sheffield's estate were full of azaleas and rhododendrons. Now I had to make time to visit what was left of the once grand estate.

As I neared the village of Nether Alderley, the typical Cheshire white metal railings, with their distinctive curved tops enclosing rich cattle pastures, quickly reminded me of my numerous journeys through the county. Then excitement grew when I spotted blocks of red sandstone. Those were the kinds of bricks I had remembered in the driveway, so different from Cambridge stones. But, as I turned into the grounds of the drug company, there were no narrow gateways as I had remembered. The campus comprised a mass of modern buildings with the Tenant's Hall and the Stanley Arms pub the only remnants of the Stanley era. I looked at the hall. Had it been the uninspiring house that my mother said was misplaced for the grandeur of the drive? As I walked around the present grounds I could not help but be impressed with its scale. Gardening articles had described the grounds as magical with a large pond and huge fountain surrounded by gently rising, grassy slopes full of flowering shrubs leading off to long rose walks, while the tea-house shrouded with wisteria opened to an Italian garden bordered by high walls and wrought-iron Adam gates. I imagined Asquith walking around the grounds with Venetia on his arm. Surely no man, whether Prime Minister or not, could fail to be impressed with the magnificent beauty of these extensive grounds.

However my task was to search the grounds for any remnant

signs of wooded stems and leathery leaves of rhododendrons. On turning a bend from one block of offices to another, I was pleased to get partial shelter from a bitter wind cutting through my thin coat, but that was not my only joy, because there in front of me were huge swathes of rhododendron bushes. I forgot the cold. I had my answer. Further confirmation came when I left the grounds huddled among the swarms of company employees. For as I drove out of the complex using a different exit I found myself on a modern version of the junction I had remembered. Now there were traffic lights to help the employees out to the main road but the exit joined the main road in a similar manner. One side of the red sandstone wall must have been demolished but there on the other side were the huge blocks of local stone that weathered by forming black smudges over its surface.

So had Louis been researching his own roots when he dragged us there? It seemed surreal that the only reason I had been party to his search was the fact that he never drove.

I still dreamed that the surname Applegate in 1901 census might appear on a teller's walk close to Alderley Hall, especially now I knew the estate had employed more than two hundred people, most of whom had worked there all their lives. But I had great trouble finding the Hall in the census and I could not work out who their neighbours were, because the Stanleys had refused to be in the Alderley Edge return. They were snobs and they did not want to be associated with the 'Cottontots' of this new town. They insisted their details be recorded as living in Chorley, so finding their true neighbours was almost impossible.

However, it finally registered with me just how close Manchester was to Venetia's home. It would be easy for her to visit Cottonopolis, as the city was called. By 1913 it was producing 65 per cent of all British cotton with wealthy Cottontots meeting every Tuesday at the new gloriously extravagant Manchester Exchange. The poorer parts of Manchester were a forest of arrogant chimneys belching black smoke.

I discovered more interesting details about Asquith's second marriage. Margot suffered years of anguish in childbirth, for she experienced five pregnancies but only two of her babies survived. During her first pregnancy she became hysterical. Margot was convinced she might die in childbirth. However, when it came to the birth it was the baby who died. But Margot suffered from the most terrible grief, becoming an insomniac and acting almost as if she were insane. After another baby died, Violet confided to Venetia that the house was filled with piercing shrieks for weeks after the baby died. Even more significant for my story was that, after the birth and subsequent death of her fifth child, her doctor insisted the couple sleep in separate rooms. The year was 1907.

As I ferreted for more letters and documents I discovered two more vital supporting pieces of information. Margot had what today might be called 'a nervous breakdown' in 1913. Had she found out that her husband had fathered an illegitimate child when three of her own babies had died? The other vital clue was even more significant, for, according to Clifford in *The Asquiths*, there are 'claims that an oath was sworn over Puffin's head' when he was born in 1902 (this was Margot and HH's last surviving child, Anthony, who directed films from the 1920s to the 1940s) between Asquith's first and second families, 'so that the affection between the two families was indefeasible'. So all the older five Asquith children had been sworn to secrecy! Why was this?

Meanwhile, I made myself read Louis's book on the history of the Dorchester Hotel. It might just throw up some tasty morsel for me. After all, he had claimed to have lived there. Surely he could not lie in this text, as the Dorchester has its own records. It was hard to read, as his words made him sound so much of a celebrity that I began to think I had got it all wrong. Had he really been part of the government or one of its advisers, as he implied? Strangely, the day I finished the book I went back to the Web and found an article on Louis. It had been written by an Austrian who claimed

Stepfather had been a 'crown adviser'. There was still a tiny bit of me that believed my Stepfather did have a prominent position. Maybe he had signed the Official Secret Act.

Louis was 80 years old when he wrote the book on the Dorchester. Had he risked revealing a little more, knowing that my mother would not read the whole text?

In the book I found two shadowy clues, for he wrote of H. H. Asquith's second marriage in a nearby church – St George's – in Park Lane. The pointer for me was Louis's written details about the witnesses. He recorded who had signed the register: a prime minister in office (Lord Rosebery), a retired prime minister (Lord Gladstone), and a prime-minister-to-be (Lord Balfour). This detail stood out from the rest of the text because it had nothing to do with the hotel. Why did he include it? Was it a fact he could no longer keep to himself? There was no other logical reason. The second clue was the inclusion of an image of himself with other photographers explaining that he and they had been at the hotel to take a picture of Prince Philip on the eve of his wedding. As a joke the royal party had insisted on reversing the situation so that they took a picture of the photographers. As I looked at the snap I recalled that Louis had been proud of this picture. Did this reveal that he had worked for the *Daily Express* as one of its photographers? Was he the cameraman for the royals? How did he get this job? Another connection was that Sir Walford Selby, a contributor to *Germany After the War*, had also worked for the *Express*. I thought back to my mother's funeral. The stranger Alan Frame had given the eulogy for my mother, and he had once been the editor of the *Daily Express*! It had meant nothing to me at the time but now it meant everything. Louis must have persuaded this younger editor that he, L. T. Stanley, had been an important employee of the newspaper.

I went back to Stepfather's book. In it he explained that the hotel was considered to be a safe place to be in the war as it had eight floors of reinforced concrete and claimed to be 'bomb proof, earthquake proof and fire proof'. He implied that in those days he had eaten many meals in the Grill Room, as it became 'a popular place to spend a wartime evening'. Louis recalled that he had been a resident in the hotel between 1944 and 1945. So had this been when he contributed to the Liberal leaflet? Had he lived a double or even a triple life? In 1944 he was meant to be studying at Cambridge and married with a young son.

Louis could not resist the temptation to brag that he had sat on a committee with Lord Beveridge, another Liberal MP and the man who would be father of the British welfare state, while he stayed at the hotel. This surprised me. Had he sat on the famous social reform committee of 1942? What qualities did Louis have to serve on this committee?

I was intrigued by his reference to Oliver Stanley in the book. I reminded myself that Oliver Stanley had been the only member of the Sheffield family to support the marriage of Venetia and Edwin, as I thought again about the extraordinary day when Stepfather had blurted out that Oliver was his uncle. Had he met his uncle when he lived in the Dorchester? Had he known he was his uncle? Had Oliver helped his illegitimate nephew over the years? He was eight years older than Venetia and thirty-three years older than Louis. He had a distinguished military career but lost a leg in the war. I found it interesting that in the 1950s he was one of the fascist Oswald Mosley's few friends. Diana, his second wife, of course was a cousin of Oliver and Venetia, having been originally one of the Mitford sisters.

Another close relation from the Earl of Derby's side of the family was also called Oliver Stanley. He may also have helped Louis, as he became a politician and was Minister of Transport in 1933. This Oliver Stanley was responsible for bringing in the 30mph speed limit, compulsory driving tests and third-party insurance. I suddenly remembered a terrible rumour that had recently been passed on to me. It was thought to be why Louis did not drive. Louis had driven into a group of army recruits who were out road training in wartime. He had scattered the troop and some of the men had been killed. He had been charged with drunken driving and been banned for life. Nobody knows how this rumour had started and whether there was any truth in it. But it would explain why he made my poor mother do all the driving.

In January 1940, the political Oliver Stanley was made Secretary of State for War. Had Louis worked for this relative? Or had his uncle found him a military job? For I could still not understand what Stepfather had been doing when he was 27 or 28. How did he avoid the draft? Maybe Oliver had given him an intelligence position or a post in a ministry. Had Louis made a mess of it and been asked to leave? Had he been 'sent away' to university after his driving fiasco to be penitent and read theology? If he had committed his horrendous driving offence while working for the government, this crime would surely have been the end to his career as a budding politician.

I went back to the archivist at Emmanuel College and obtained a complete list of all students attending in wartime. I needed the exact details this time. The finer details showed he had not sat his first exam until 1944. This was a divinity assessment, in which he achieved a 'Special Class 3' and a 'General exam (Class 2)'. But it was his third exam in 1945 that most fascinated me: 'Declared to have deemed to have passed Law'. He had not even taken an exam. Louis never got a proper degree.

I was now sceptical of everything I read. I questioned whether the 'special pass' had been organised by somebody of importance. Did he get special dispensation from the university because he had contributed to the Liberal booklet on Germany?

I remembered the special postbox at Emmanuel (see Chapter 11) and then recalled the huge fuss when he wanted to join the Graduate Club, which had recently opened in an ugly concrete building overlooking the Cam. Had the club authorities tried to decline his membership?

As there were no recorded electoral roles in wartime I could find no reference to Louis and his first wife Kate living together until 1945. They were recorded as living in a block of flats called Maitland House in Barton Road. I remembered that building: sometimes Mum had left me there when I was very young to be looked after by Home Granny and strange Auntie Mamie. I had not liked it.

Although their names were in the register for the block of flats I could not understand the entries. For, although Stepfather had been married for three years, he was registered as living in number 7 with his mother and 'Auntie' Mamie while Kate was living at number 9 on her own. Then for the year 1947 none of the party were registered. In the following year, 1948, they were recorded as living as man and wife in number 9. Then, in 1949, Louis had managed to register himself twice – once with Kate and once with Mary Ann Stanley (Home Granny). She was registered in the flat until 1953 and I would have been five. What had been going on? Then all became clear.

Louis was pretending he was living apart from Kate so that the university authorities would not know he was married. Then in 1948, when Kate wanted the divorce, they pretended they were living together. In 1949, after the divorce, they lived in separate flats again. So had Stepfather always played devious tricks?

I obtained the birth certificates of Stepfather's two sons by Kate. The documents helped unravel the picture a little but there were still many perplexing questions. The registered address was Maitland House. I remembered the flats as having only two bedrooms. Had they both been living in a small flat, short of money, with a five-year-old and a baby in 1948? Yet Stepfather had told us he had lived in the Dorchester Hotel and the Caledonian Hotel in Edinburgh and driven a Bentley. Kate, I remembered, had come from a wealthy shipping family. Had her family disapproved of Louis T. Stanley and cut her off?

I looked again at his sons' birth certificates. Stepfather had entered himself as a theologian on the first. On the second document five years later he had been a theologian and an economist. So I ordered my mother's marriage certificate dated 1955. On this he had dropped his theological ambitions and entered one word: 'economist'. It was all very perplexing.

I heard distressing news from my mother's adored night nurse. Mum had confided that Louis had deceived my mother about his plans for marriage. One day she thought she was going shopping with Uncle Louis, as he was then. But without her knowing he had fixed up their wedding ceremony at the register office in Cambridge's Shire Hall. He had pulled her up the steps and her high heels had fallen off as she tripped. My mother went through with the ceremony, with two men Louis had found in the street as witnesses. So Mum had no family at her wedding. This must have been difficult for a person like my mother. She must have been in love to go through with it, but the story told me again about the power of persuasion of Louis T. Stanley. Louis had been married to Kate in the same registry nearly 13 years before. On my mother's marriage certificate Louis had upped his deceased 'father's' status. There was no reference to the cotton executive – this was too lowly. Louis had entered him as a 'gentleman'!

What part did my 'real' father play in the stories of my past? I knew so little about him. My first job was to find what records the Church had on him. I found that all the early records had been destroyed, supposedly under the Data Protection Act. However, from some letters held by the Bishop of Winchester I found that back in 1953 the Bishop of Ely had not defrocked my father and there were many letters of support for him. However, there was one from a Canon Woodward that upset me. He had written it just after the divorce proceedings between my mother and father and he claimed it attracted 'deplorable and sensational publicity'. My father, he wrote, had married a 'domineering purse proud woman' and she had found 'a man of dubious reputation who was said to run after wealthy women and had been in one or two previous matrimonial upsets'. This clergyman's view was that my father should have spoken up in the divorce proceedings because 'his greatest fault was his silence'. Another vicious letter called my mother hard and spoilt and tried to make out that she demanded a Rolls-Royce and a butler when she started at her rural rectory. Sometimes my mother had referred to 'hard two-faced unchristian Christians' when I was a child. Had she suffered their wrath?

One bright Saturday afternoon I decided to visit the village of Broughton, Oxfordshire, where my father had been vicar when he was first married to my mother. I could not find the church so I let my curiosity guide me to Broughton Castle. As I drove down a tarmac driveway I saw a fourteenth-century fortified manor house with a wide moat. It reminded me of New Hall. Surely this parish had been no ordinary first appointment, as nestling in the trees to the front of the castle was the parish church. A helpful graveyard gardener pointed to a large building behind an unkempt brick wall covered with years of growth of thick ivy tendrils. The hidden overgrown path led me to the rectory.

I gazed at the beauty of the building, and tried to imagine what life must have been like. My parents had lived here through the war and the first two of their four children were born during this time. I felt drawn to ring the rectory doorbell. I had not planned to visit but the building attracted me and I was becoming very curious. I soon found myself stepping over the threshold and being greeted by the new owners after I explained at the door my reason for visiting, It was a large vicarage and more homely than many. I felt the house was welcoming me into its two large reception rooms; one had oak panelling, a gift from the owners of the castle. It had been the first house outside London to have sash windows. The present occupants told me the house once had 11 bedrooms. The master bedroom overlooked the spacious garden, with a long sloping lawn leading down to a shadowy pond under a huge tree. The top floor of the house had been altered but there was enough space for perhaps five live-in maids. I was prying into the past again. But, unlike delving into Stepfather's past, this did not induce in me fear. I felt my mother was almost showing me the house. She had moved here as a newlywed in 1937 and lived here until 1945. The thought crossed my mind that it could have been here, rather than in Cambridge, that my dad had been caught with one of the maids, or was it in this village he had an affair with the married 'June'.

My parents were ideal candidates for the parish in those days. Lord and Lady Saye (Fiendes family) took more than an active interest in the appointment. Along with New College, Oxford, they appointed the vicar of Broughton. The crucial credentials were an intellectual graduate from the university to look after their souls while the wife was to have a flair for entertaining. Yes, my parents were suitable appointees!

The present occupants entered into my enthusiasm and started to tell me more of the rectory's history. As we imagined what life might have been like in the 1940s, the couple remembered an old newspaper cutting that had been stuck on one of the maids' cupboard doors. It had instructions on how to prepare for domestic life in wartime. It was strange to think my mother's hands must have pasted it there. I remembered one of the few times Mum had allowed herself to talk to me about past times. One of my children had asked her if she had any items he could take to school that would show what life had been like. My mother retrieved from an old cupboard a school shirt she had created out of an old pillowcase. We had marvelled at the exquisite needlework. Later that same evening as we talked she wistfully added, 'I had two little evacuees.' She did not make eye contact with any of us. She just stared at the clock's hands. I willed her to continue. 'It was the shock of the boys' arrival I remember so well. There was so much straw and chaos. They were so mischievous but I grew so fond of them.' I tried to quiz her more but the moment had gone. The subject was changed and I never heard any more.

I was directed on to the house of the Roberts family, who had bought it from the Church Commissioners after my father had left the parish. I asked her if there might be anybody still alive in the village who might remember my parents. She found a ninety-year-old woman who relayed her memories to Mrs Roberts. People, she recalled, would travel miles to visit the rectory's spectacular garden parties and in wartime the rectory was open to all. The Babers, she said, had been her saviour as she was lonely, as she had recently arrived from Ireland. She also took in evacuees but like so many in the rural community she had no bathroom, so my mother opened the rectory to them all. She recalled other events.

'Mr Bustin,' she recalled, 'was the taxi driver for the village. Then there was Basil Roberts Buchanan. He was the vicar just before Reverend Baber.' It was an emotional moment to hear confirmation of mum's caring nature. But the name 'Buchanan' raised hairs on the back of my neck. At first I was not sure why, but then it came to me. I had visited periodically over the years the church secretary my father had married after his divorce. On one occasion I admitted that I was concerned about the behaviour of my stepfather. The usually quiet unassuming lady whispered, 'Did you know that Louis used to mysteriously ring us up!'

'What?'

'We used to get nuisance calls about every six months.' Her voice was getting louder and I did not have to lean so close to her face. 'The phone would ring and we could hear someone breathing on the other end of the line. If I took the call the man would always ask to speak to Leslie. When I asked his name the plummy voice always insisted he was "Mr Buchanan".'

I was stunned by her words but she was keen to get the memory out into the open.

'Your father usually agreed to speak with him but during the course of the conversation the caller always asked after Leslie's health. We found the calls disturbing.'

They both thought they recognised the voice but dismissed as fantasy the idea that it had been Louis. For why should he want to ring his wife's first husband? However, their suspicions grew when the Mr Buchanan they had known died but the calls had continued.

So my father's wife decided that the next time the mysterious caller rang she would tell him that the Buchanan they knew was not alive. The strange caller told her quite calmly that he was the 'other' Mr Buchanan. Not from Oxford but the one who had Yorkshire connections.

I was keen to ask questions but her words kept flowing: 'After your father died, I thought the calls would stop but they didn't. But, soon after, BT introduced 1471 [to obtain the number that has just dialled you]. I then had concrete proof the nuisance calls were from Louis Stanley.'

I was stunned.

As a child I had never known where I was born. These were the dark days, which we did not talk about. But through accessing my birth certificate I discovered I was born in Hills Road in Cambridge. By chance I found that the house was up for sale, so I took the opportunity to visit. I had made no appointment but the vendor, who was watering the garden, welcomed me. As I waited for her to finish her tasks I noticed the long garden full of mature fruit trees. I imagined my mother with her gardening catalogues spread around her charting where each should grow.

The house was a solid interwar building with seven bedrooms. On the first floor there was a strange arrangement of levels, where there had originally been a back stairs to the maid's bedroom. My mind leapt to my father's misdemeanour – had it been in this house that he had committed adultery?

The friendly vendor called for my attention to show me the deeds, which she had laid out ready for any potential buyer. The document showed me that my mother had bought the house in October 1945. It was an emotional moment when I saw her signature. Her scrawling handwriting had hardly changed but it was strange to see that her bold script had penned the surname I had been born with but barely used.

I wanted to understand Venetia's extravagant lifestyle after she married Edwin, so I allowed myself to read the diaries of Duff Cooper. The series of intriguing love letters sent between Duff and Diana gave me a glimpse of life in the Coterie, and I noted they shared their social group with the Montagus. Louis had talked or written about them all. The significant ones were the Mitford family, Bertrand Russell, Clemmie Churchill, Beaverbrook, Gilbert Murray, Walter Monckton, the Aga Khan and Oliver Stanley!

Duff's future wife's free spirit had influenced and encouraged Venetia to partake in much more risqué endeavours than she had with her previous, more sensible friend, Violet. Diana even took Venetia on a tour of transvestite clubs in Berlin in the 1920s, a supremely daring adventure in those days.

As I read on, I took in a sharp gasp of breath: the words 'the Dorchester Hotel' were on the page. I sat bolt upright. Venetia's best friend had lived in that hotel! The words were gold dust to me. During the Second World War the married Diana had an extravagant lifestyle that allowed her to stay in the Dorchester. I researched more: 'The Coopers were installed in a bilious-coloured suite on the eighth floor of the Dorchester hotel the hotel was much favoured by the homeless rich. Its ultra modern wind resistant steel structure offering, in theory at least, protection.'

In her hotel room Diana held court, surrounding herself with friends. Stories of debauchery emerged with regular habitués being Oliver Stanley's wife, Maureen, and Venetia Montagu (Ziegler). Further confirmation came from the words of another contact in Ziegler's book who complained of 'That horde of hard faced tipsy women, who occupy your sitting and bedroom from 6 p.m. onwards…some harder featured and some no doubt tipsier than others.'

So no wonder Stepfather had a romantic attachment to the Dorchester Hotel. He had probably seen his mother during wartime. Was this why he had been so desperate to write about the hotel's history? There was a time when he befriended Field

Marshal Lord Bramall (Britain's Chief of the General Staff), who was at the time chairman of the hotel's board of directors. Stepfather got his way and I remember his smirk when he finally had the hotel's records in his hands. Why was he so happy?

Reading about Diana Cooper helped me more and I now understood why Louis had looked so shocked when my son Tom had excitedly told his grandmother he was going to Avon Tyrell, an outdoor adventure establishment, for his school journey. It had been the home of Baron Manners, Diana Cooper's father. Not only that, but the Manners family were close friends with the Asquiths, with two of their sons taking their honeymoons on this estate. Stepfather must have been shocked to hear a member of my family use the name Avon Tyrell. Had he lived his life permanently on edge?

Intrigued, I searched for more information about the Coopers. Suddenly the name 'Lord Furness' leapt out from another page. Could this man be Kate Furness's father? Is this how Stepfather met Kate, his first wife, at a party, at the hotel that the celebrities of the time called 'The Dorch'? My mind was working overtime. It was little wonder Stepfather had an unhealthy passion for the place.

I investigated further. Lord Furness was Kate's wealthy uncle. Her father, John, was a moneyed director of the once famous Furness Withy shipping line, but died shortly before she married Louis. Had she been grieving when they met? She was only 21. Had Louis guessed she might inherit a fortune? I imagined Stepfather fending off his fiancée's questions about his own father just as he had done with us when we were children. It was well within his abilities to impress a lady by pretending to grieve for a father he never had.

But I was also learning about the sexual morals of the times. It had worried me for some time that Venetia must have been unusual having sex with Asquith in those more puritanical days. But Duff Cooper's diaries showed me just how much sleeping around the aristocracy did in those times, with both the newly married Duff and Diana being equally promiscuous. And the writing of Nicola Beauman explained the role of married ladies: their jobs were to manage large houses and remain devoted to their husbands at the same time as 'conducting an intense love affair'.

But Venetia stood out from her social crowd. Although it was acceptable for married women to sleep around, single women did not.

It was a long shot but I decided I should make the effort to retrieve both Asquith's and Venetia Montagu's wills. Maybe there was some sort of trail in their paperwork. After HH fell from power he became a peer of the realm, so his probate papers were more difficult than normal to retrieve, but I persevered and read them. His will was simple and the money involved was small. However, Venetia's will proved far more exciting. She died twenty years after Asquith and left £116,000, a considerable amount of money for 1948. She requested the money be divided between her daughter Judith and a lawyer called Walter Louis. I guessed the advocate's surname was purely coincidental, but I stored it in my memory bank. As the will did not appear straightforward, I showed it to our lawyer, Diana, who had worked so hard on our behalf. She specialised in family law and had written wills for clients to obscure illegitimate births. Her judgement was that Walter Louis had been used as 'a front' to hide the real beneficiary or beneficiaries in Venetia's will. I had made a huge step forward. If Venetia had provided for Stepfather in 1948, then surely mother and son must have had some form of contact. So, if he had inherited money from Venetia, how had he managed to blow it all in seven years? But, of course, I knew how!

Chapter 14

What? Surely not!

My mother's grave in Sutton Coldfield needed some temporary ornaments, as it would be at least six months before the headstone could be placed. I remembered that one of our last outings, the two of us together, had been to my simple little beach hut that overlooked a pebble beach. Stepfather, with his large paunch, chose not to descend the steep flight of steps, so I was able to enjoy some rare minutes with just Mum.

I returned to the shore and selected some large, rounded pebbles and then drove north to place them around the edges of her plot to designate its borders. In the centre I planted powder-pink miniature roses and matching hollyhocks. However, when I felt the sun hot on my back I realised I had no way of keeping them watered. As I worked the red soil, I became conscious of a grieving young couple standing near a child's grave. The couple's grief put mine into perspective. Both of them were untidy in their appearance and their sunken eyes told me they lacked sleep. I struck up a conversation.

'We come every morning and stay most of the day,' the young woman told me in a typical Black Country accent. 'So don't you worry about the watering: we'll be delighted to care for your mum's grave.' I was grateful and touched by their kindness.

One month later my mobile rang while I was in Staffordshire. I had planned to visit my mother's grave on the way home.

'Are you sitting down?' It was the guarded voice of my brother. 'I've some bad news. You're not going to be upset on me, are you?'

'*You're not going to be upset on me, are you?*'

What a strange thing to say! What news could he have that would perturb me? Mum was already dead. But I didn't have time for further reflection before he continued.

'Mum's grave is all sandy. We think her body's been moved.'

'What?'

'Cousin Jean visited this morning and she says the wooden cross is still there but everything else is in a heap. Your roses and stones are missing.'

'Vandalism?' I stuttered, aghast.

'We think she's been taken to Trumpington.'

'What? How? Why?' I was thinking of Mum's hatred of the graveyard.

My brother was losing patience with my monosyllabic utterances.

'Poppy has had Mum's body removed.' His voice was abrasive as he tried to keep his emotions under control.

'Dug up? Surely you can't do that.' My brain was reliving video footage of police scenes that I had viewed in news extracts on TV.

'Yes. Reburied in Trumpington,' he said.

'But she hated that place!' I countered.

'I know,' came the tired voice, 'but that's what's probably happened.'

I put the phone down. What was I to do? I had planned to visit the Sutton Coldfield cemetery.

My mind was muddled and I found I was not concentrating on the road. A large truck blasted its horn at me. I was not in a fit state to drive, so I pulled into a service station and made my first call. I rang Diana.

'We're so sorry,' she said. 'We heard that your stepfather might try this but we never thought it would be possible. Exhumation of a body is usually a lengthy process and to get permission from the Home Office takes over seven years. We've no idea how your stepfather managed to do it. We heard this morning that it was carried out three days ago.'

My mind whirled. Three days ago! Stepfather certainly knew how to hurt me deep down and harshly. Why and how did he do it?

What about my planned visit to the grave at Sutton Coldfield? I was nearly at the junction to turn off the motorway. What if cousin Jean hadn't noticed the discarded pebbles? I could have found myself paying homage to an empty plot of earth for years to come. Now my mother's plot was just a hastily refilled hole, my hollyhocks flung brutally to one side.

Still sitting in my car, I rang the custodian of Mum's cemetery. She was clearly embarrassed but said that she had received instructions from Mr Stanley to leave the temporary teak cross on the plot once the remains had been removed. She conveyed her deepest regrets but told me that matters had been completely taken out of her hands.

As I left the refuge of the service station I tried to concentrate on the business of driving on the crowded road, but my mind kept reliving the news of the last ghastly hour. Diana had used the word 'exhumation'. The word sent shivers down my spine and shock was clearly taking effect. Another lorry driver flashed his lights as I dithered near the junction to Sutton Coldfield. Should I still go to the grave? As I slowed at the exit road, my brain cleared. Of course! It was not the old grave I should visit, but the new one. I knew that seeing the new pit would upset me but, as I was already tearful, I decided the best thing to do would be to confront the reburial straightaway.

I rang the vicar in Trumpington, but he told me he had a meeting that evening and wouldn't be able to see me.

'Are you telling me I can't see my mother's grave?' I felt so emotional that I had difficulty controlling my voice.

He sighed, and with a sudden change of heart agreed I could visit.

As I drove into the flat Cambridgeshire countryside, I relived the day of Mum's burial: the elegant water lilies floating on the moat and my awkward attempts to retrieve the best pink-tinted specimen. I recalled the dull echo when I had dropped the leathery flower into the deep hole. The heavy bloom had not floated like a feather, as I had hoped, and I could still hear the embarrassing thud. Yet I believed the sodden flower had made a bond linking my Mother's soul with her family home.

I recalled the coldness of the red earth on my fingertips and the seven grandchildren, each crumbling their token sod of earth over her coffin. As I thought about the meaning of eternal peace, I swerved to miss a hedgehog. The scurrying animal brought me out of my trance. But why had Stepfather wanted her interred in the very place she had not wanted to be buried? How could anybody allow this? Who had been at the lonely, cold ceremony?

The clocks had not yet gone back to winter timekeeping but the light was already murky as I reached the outskirts of Cambridge. As I drove into the vicarage driveway I realised I was weary.

The vicar came to the door with his rimless spectacles slightly awry and gave me a clerical smile. As I walked into his plum-coloured hall, with its large antique dresser and framed mirror, I allowed myself to reflect that his home was far from a typical draughty rundown rectory.

Once I was seated in his expansive lounge he started to answer my queries. 'Don't worry. Your mother would've liked it…the plot's in the new part of the churchyard. We had a field consecrated and she's in there.'

'A field?' I queried.

'Yes, she's buried near a sapling, a nice position. Do you want to go now?'

But his plan to avoid my inquisition was spoilt when his wife brought in a tray of cups. Clearly irritated, he started to pour a cup from the china teapot balanced on a stool as I continued with my questions.

'Please explain what happened. My mother was reburied without any of us present.' He stared at me. I waited for a reply. None came.

'When were you going to tell us?' I asked again. 'Did you know that Louis told the cemetery keeper of Sutton Coldfield to replace her little wooden cross in the ground after she was dug up?'

He shuffled the teacups around on the tray.

'Her final resting place meant so much to her. In her last months, she spoke of little else to her nurses. She adored her family and now she's buried one hundred miles from them. Not only that, but she's been dug up and brought to the very place she didn't want to be buried,' I said passionately.

'We don't know that,' he countered.

'What do you mean? You checked out her final wishes, didn't you?' I quizzed.

'No, but I saw the reburial licence,' he said, his face set in a stubborn mask.

I had a copy of my mother's letter in my car, so I went out into the gloom to retrieve it. I pointed to the relevant underlined word. 'I want to be buried in Sutton Coldfield not Trumpington.'

He didn't react. His eyes were fixed, staring out at the dark. The silence was poignant.

'He misled me,' he uttered at last.

'What do you mean, "misled"?' I asked.

'Your father,' he was tensely, holding the wide arm of the chair and corrected himself. 'Mr Stanley rang me and said, "I want to tell you something in confidence." I could hardly hear him – you know how he often speaks in a low voice.'

I nodded. 'He said, "I'm planning to do something and I want your reassurance you'll keep it confidential." As soon as I agreed he told me of his plans. I had no alternative but officiate. She was a parishioner and this is my parish.'

'No alternative?' My voice was high-pitched, showing my disbelief. 'Digging up bodies is not normal. Didn't you ask for advice from your superiors? Why didn't you tell us?'

Once again he was fiddling with the teapot.

'Do you want sugar in your tea?'

The conversation started to go round in circles, so in a more placatory voice I asked, 'How do you rebury bodies?'

'You don't want to know all that, my dear,' he answered.

'Tell me,' I insisted.

'Well, only certain teams of men who are allowed to exhume...Are you sure you want to hear all this?'

'Perhaps not,' I said. I had heard enough for one night.

As he eased himself to the edge of the chair, and I rose to follow him, I noticed he wore stout walking shoes and there was a flashlight tucked behind the frills of the armchair. I felt there was something rather depraved about visiting my mother's new grave with a torch. As I left the vicarage I heard the wind blow and thought of my mother out in the cold, lonely and abandoned.

When I got home I tried to behave normally but my children knew something was wrong. How was I going to tell them? I did not feel up to the job. I knew I had to maintain some sense of calm.

CHAPTER 15

MIXED FEELINGS AND MIXED RESEARCH

Exhumed!

There was no doubt the word 'exhumation' was frightening – it gnawed at me, creeping in and out of my muddled mind. If I tried to use it, I gagged.

I could not picture the true scene. The cinematic world reverberated in my head. I recalled dark chilling films, or nightmares, eerie lights shone through swirling mists in shades of grey. Ghostly diggers with lined, gaunt faces eyed each other conspiratorially, without uttering a word. Their clothes were ragged. Their hands bare. There was no reassuring pastor, no grievers.

Just men, always men, shovelling sods of earth in grim silence.

I felt I might never again be able to sleep soundly unless I found out what had really happened. So I rang the fatherly Mr Painter, the undertaker.

'I'm very sorry, very sorry,' he whispered, unable to hide his embarrassment.

'But how could this have happened?' I begged.

'We had a – a phone call from Mr Stanley,' stammered the undertaker. 'He told me of the reburial licence.' He paused. 'Last Wednesday night he demanded that my lads and I drive to Sutton Coldfield to collect your mother's remains. He didn't care what arrangements we had in our diaries. He was just like that for your mother's funeral. Do you remember?'

As if I could possibly forget.

'I tried to explain that I'd no idea how to organise a reburial. I'd never done it before. I told him we couldn't do it.' There was an expectant pause before he continued, 'But you know how persistent he is – you know we've still not been paid for your mother's funeral.' He took a deep breath. 'Before I had time to discuss the matter with my son, a man arrived on my doorstep with the reburial licence. I never knew one could get one issued so quickly after an interment.' He paused and sighed taking time to compose himself.

'My son believed Mr Stanley would go to any lengths to get the job done. We didn't want this assignment to be insensitively handled so out of respect for your mother we agreed to rebury her.'

'What about the – the digging up?' I asked, trying hard to collect myself.

'We didn't do that,' he replied. 'Specialist teams are brought in to do that. There are only three teams in the country that do exhumations,' he continued, and I shivered as he spoke. 'They work under lots of rules and regulations. Because no one should see them working they excavate in the dead of night. They have to obtain special permission to open the graveyard. By rule of law they must put the old coffin immediately into a new one with specialised machinery. Even though you mother's coffin was only two months old, they put it straight into another, bigger, casket. Our job was to take your mother's ungainly double coffin back along the motorway from Sutton Coldfield to Trumpington graveyard. That same morning Vicar Ambrose reburied her. Just Mr Stanley attended the graveside alongside a red-haired young woman. Was she a nurse?'

Realising what he had said, he continued more hesitantly, 'Yes, I suppose we were rather surprised you weren't there.'

I mumbled a reply but I don't think he was listening,

'This was the grimmest job I've ever had and I've been in the funeral business for fifty years. So much has happened in our dealings with Mr Stanley, I suppose we shouldn't have been surprised.' He paused. 'After the reburial he just ordered the young lady to drive him straight to London. He never acknowledged us or uttered a word of thanks.'

I undertook to fight the authorities: the established Church and the Home Office. In the following days and weeks I started to query the situation. If the speed of issuing the exhumation licence astonished Mr Painter, the undertaker, I knew I had to investigate the matter further.

I thought of our childhood hero, Graham Hill. I recalled his oft-repeated words, 'We would like you to do deal with this one, Mr Stanley. Only you can cut through the red tape.' It had worked in the motor-racing world, but how had stepfather swung this one?

There were battles ahead, but they took time to develop – as did my research.

I thought about Home Granny. I was convinced she must have had some contact with the young Miss Stanley or her extended family. I went back to the 1901 census and the problem of finding a Mary Ann Applegate who fitted my criteria. There was only one suitable Mary Ann but she did not seem to fit. She was two years younger than I wanted her to be and she was living in a village called St-Anne's-on-the-Sea. I looked at the details one more time. It was then pointed out to me that as her name had been entered last in the household perhaps she had not been employed as the sick nurse for the tenants but had been a paying boarder. It proved to be the tiny goad I needed to put more thought into why the woman was living in this unknown tiny village where there were no known links with Stepfather.

The details on the map hit me with a bang! There staring me in the face was the connection. St-Anne's-on-the-Sea was Lytham St Annes. In 1901 they had been two separate villages, 'Lytham' and 'St-Anne's-on-the-Sea'. The wording of the latter village had taken its name from the local parish church. Of course there was a connection with Louis. We had often visited this seaside town with its famous golf course, Royal Lytham. The map set my heart racing. Had he learned to play golf here? I was now interested in the address where Mary Applegate had been living. I wondered how close Orchard Road was to the links golf club that often staged the Open Championship.

But before I researched this I needed to work backwards and take another look at the 1891 census. Where had Home Granny lived ten years before? For, although Lytham excited me, I realised it did not help me connect her to the Stanleys of Cheshire, Stepfather's birthplace, Liscard, or his supposed childhood home of Hoylake.

Again, the only possible female in this earlier census with the right surname and age had been an Applegate living in a place called Bollington, which I had been told was in Lancashire. I looked again at the census records. Bollington was in Cheshire! I reached for the map, which proved even more exciting this time. For there was the link I hoped for. Bollington was less than ten miles from Alderley Hall. The recorded census details had seriously misled me as to its position. Even more interesting, Bollington was a cotton milling village.

At last I recognised that my search for Stepfather's roots was providing me with a certain amount of fun. I immediately wanted to know about the cotton industry in this town, especially cop winders. I thought back to the second decade of the twentieth century. If Asquith's scheming advisers had recommended that the fictitious father of my Stepfather, Louis Thomas Stanley, should be entered on the birth certificate as a senior worker in the cotton trade they must have known that Mary Ann knew about this industry. This would fit in, as Mary Ann would have to be able to talk knowledgeably about her 'husband's' work.

However it worried me that the age of the Mary Applegate in Bollington was two years adrift. The only piece of real evidence I had was her death certificate and, on that, Home Granny should have been born in 1868 or even 1867. Why did this female in each census want to make herself two years older?

I contacted the experts at Bollington museum and sent for more books, this time about the cotton industry. I questioned whether Mary Ann would have travelled to Bollington and lived with experienced cotton workers, with the schoolhouse where she boarded only yards away from the mill. The historians told me this movement of young girls was common in the late nineteenth century. So I had to believe the future 'Mrs Stanley' had started her career as a cotton-cop winder in this vast booming industry. When the cotton experts told me the Stanleys had been lords of the manor for the land around Bollington I was even more certain I had the right Applegate.

I now knew the chosen foster mother had been born in Carlisle, her mother was illiterate and her father a cotton warper. Her mother died when she was in her teens and, although she had an elder sister, she may have had to act as 'mother' to her younger brother, Fred, and the other children before her father remarried. By 21 she had followed her father into the cotton industry, moving to Bollington in Cheshire. Ten years later she was living in a town by the sea that was later to be known as Lytham St Annes. But there was no firm link to the aristocratic Stanley family.

It is a pity for my story that we do not know if or how Venetia showed her emotions in her correspondence with Asquith. Only a few of her letters remain and it is thought HH probably destroyed them. Margot reports that one evening she found Asquith depressed and lonely sitting by a burning fire tearing up old correspondence. His wife claimed the letters were to another woman, whom Asquith also wrote to, but, as Margot had always denied that Venetia had ever been important to her husband, this was probably not true, according to Margot's biographer, Daphne Bennett, in *Margot: A Life of the Countess of Oxford and Asquith*.

It is not hard to deduce from the Asquithian letters that Venetia suffered emotional traumas about leaving Asquith. Was this because she was genuinely fond of him? Or was it because she knew that Asquith had become heavily dependent on her? Certainly, by February 1915, Venetia is trying to ease herself away from the Prime Minister and her letters are less frequent. But he, sensing she is plotting to leave him, makes more demands of her.

So had Asquith's depression in wartime inadvertently pushed Venetia so far that her only recourse to escape his clutches was to become a nurse? She was not naturally a caring person. I recalled the terror of the young Ottoline Morrell, who had flown distraught from Asquith's advances. Had Venetia panicked in a similar way and was prepared to do anything to escape his increasing demands? If this was so, her plan misfired, as Venetia's nursing exploits only made Asquith more difficult. He missed her company and begrudged the time she spent in what he called her 'prison'. 'I resent more than I can say that you should spend your days doing what almost any charwoman could do. I have never in my life known a case of more shocking and wanton waste.'

Asquith found their enforced separation so painful that he intervened in her planned instruction and organised that her training base be closer to the House of Commons. 'Darling try to write me a line…tomorrow – a last line from behind your iron bars. My love, I live for you' (5 April 1915).

It was during Venetia's training to become a wartime nurse that both Edwin and Asquith competed for her attention. Each wanted to escort her back to her base.

Again it shocked me that historians of the day had tried to deny that this was not a love affair. How had Violet Bonham Carter and the eminent Brock persuaded them that this affair was nonsexual?

There were many significant wordings in the Asquithian letters. On 16 March, he uses 'Your lover' to finish his letter. Surely this could mean only one thing. Even more explicitly, he signs off with the words 'Your own devoted lover' in a letter six days later.

Why had Brock ignored these signatures? Why had the other historians failed to pick up on the language of these letters? What more will the letters stored in the Bodleian Library reveal when they are allowed to be opened in 2015?

To discover the emotional flow between the three tangled lovers, the first few months of 1915 need further scrutiny. There is no doubt that Venetia could lift Asquith's wartime spirits: 'We have never had a more heavenly day than today's – don't you agree? You said some dear and delicious things that I shan't forget and we were all through in complete understanding. What a joy that is!...Never was a man so fortunate as I.'

But Asquith's pressure on Venetia was mounting and by the end of March he was writing every day and often more than once. In those days letters arrived in London on the same day as they were posted, so there was plenty of opportunity to get a quick reply. The post in the city was so quick it could be compared to today's texting and emailing between lovers.

Asquith often tells Venetia how much he wants her but his language becomes more desperate on the seventh of that month: 'Without you, I am only half of a pair of scissors.' Venetia must have written encouraging words back because in his next letter he has become more confident again: '...in a word it has made me a new creature and it is from the thought and love of you that has rescued me.'

But his hopelessness has returned by the following day. 'Write me. It doesn't matter how short it is, before you disappear. It makes so much difference to me. I love you more than words can tell and I am always *everywhere.* Yours…'

Venetia is in a very tricky position. It is in this period that she is meeting with Edwin and they are discussing the possibility of marriage while Asquith ups his rate of letters. On 30 March Asquith wrote to Venetia four times. He had now written more than 30,000 words to Venetia. His anxiety about their relationship increases and by mid-April, he writes, 'You will tell me the full truth at once? However hard it may be to me?' He must know that Edwin is making moves towards Venetia and as his jealousy increases he begins to reveal racist feelings about his old friend. Edwin Montagu is now referred to as the Assyrian or Mr Wu while his home was the silken tent.

By deduction it can be assumed Edwin formally proposed to Venetia on 22 April, but Venetia, ever vigilant, insisted their engagement remain a secret until she could find a time to tell Asquith of her decision. But she failed miserably to do so. Instead of telling him face to face, she bottled out and wrote him a letter 13 days later. Historians view Venetia as a coward at this time because she had plenty of opportunities in the intervening period to tell him the bad news. She even failed to divulge her news when HH stayed up in Cheshire with her family, but Asquith knew something was amiss: 'I thought once or twice today for the first time…that I rather bored you and that you would have been more relieved than sorry, if someone had joined us and shared our talk.'

Venetia cannot have penned an honest reply, for Asquith's next letter shows he was much more hopeful. But Asquith's optimism does not last. Two days later he again suspects something is afoot. He writes this letter just two days before Venetia sends the fated rejection letter.

'I walked back with the Assyrian from Mansfield Street, [Venetia's London abode] and we had as always good conversation. I don't honestly believe that, at this moment, there are 2 persons in the world (of opposite sexes) from whom I could more confidently count, whatever troubles or trials I had to encounter, for whole-hearted love and devotion than you and he; of course, in quite different ways and senses.'

How had Edwin felt walking late at night with his so-called best friend knowing he had stolen his political boss's mistress?

On the Tuesday of that fateful week, instead of writing, Asquith decided to call on Venetia at her London house in Mansfield Street, but, to his utter surprise, he was refused entry. This unexpected visit must have been the catalyst for Venetia to compose her fateful words.

The following day, 11 May, she put her letter in the post. The British Prime Minister's immediate response was to write these poignant words:

'Most loved—

As you know well, *this* grieves my heart.

I couldn't bear to come and see you.

I can only pray God to bless you – and help me.'

Venetia, stuck in London with her heavy cold, was unable to flee. She was either too upset or frightened of how Asquith might react, because she never responded. Asquith found her silence unbearable: 'This is terrible. No hell could be so bad. Couldn't you send me one word? It is so unnatural. Only one word?'

In another of his anguished letters he wrote, 'Don't press me now to say anything – except that I love you – always everywhere. Your heartbroken and ever devoted.'

Michael Brock believed it was at this moment that Asquith came to the realisation that 'the divine daily confidence' was 'a humiliating sham'. Venetia was later to admit that she was appalled by her own behaviour at this time and called her own actions 'treacherous'.

I tried to put myself in Stepfather's shoes. How would one feel if one's mother and father's relationship ended in this manner? When did Louis realise that his father's romantic antics had denied him the very political position he must have hankered after?

However, Asquith had other predicaments to face. At the same time as his personal loss, a political storm was blowing its full force around the Prime Minister, and the trouble brewed because his mind was not on the state of the nation. For the next two days, rather than worry about political decisions, he tormented himself by wondering if he had the courage to visit Miss Stanley. To me he seemed weak and self-centred. Was this man prime-minister material? How could he be concentrating on the job in hand while he and Venetia were exchanging five letters in one day?

It was just four days after Asquith received Venetia's letter that the famed politician failed his fellow Liberal colleagues and agreed to a coalition with the Conservatives.

When the dust had settled Asquith writes to Venetia in June. It shows how much he was affected.

> No one – not even you, who know me so well – can ever imagine what your letter on 12th May (exactly one month ago) meant to me…Look back on the whole time we have spent together, in the most perfect and heavenly intimacy that could ever exist between man and woman…I had the best that a man had or could have. Your heart-broken and ever devoted.

The fact that Venetia found the time to write to Asquith on her wedding day got me thinking. Had Edwin and Venetia created a screen through which the historians could not see? Perhaps the marriage sham had created thick billowing smoke to disguise Asquith's affair.

Levine's theory of a love triangle does not stand up to analysis because, rather than a happy period during the run-up to their engagement, it was an excruciatingly painful month for both Edwin and Venetia, and of course Asquith himself.

Venetia is now uncomfortably the centre of a political sandwich with Edwin using her access to the Prime Minister to further his own ambitions. After a disastrous Cabinet meeting he asks, 'Why does Winston hate me so? Find out for me. I want to try and get over it' (22 March).

Venetia may agree to Edwin's political requests but she emotionally taunts him. She lunches with other men when she has previously told her fiancé she was far too busy to meet him. Edwin retaliates with anger and, unsure of her love, fails to recognise just how much Venetia is mocking him: '…it looks as if what you wanted to say was "please understand I am not in love with you".' He continues in his letter by pleading with her to be honest: 'On the other hand you won't pretend will you? I am slow of understanding and very apprehensive…' (23 March).

This was no great love match, I remind myself. Venetia has turned down Edwin's proposals at least three times and now she is vacillating again. Edwin in his frustration writes on Treasury paper that he has had enough of competing with the Prime Minister. 'Can you possibly expect me to go on being allowed to see you only when he is not free…you could not even let me know when I might see you, till you saw what he wanted' (3 April).

Once again, she stalls and replies, 'Darling what am I to do? Obviously what I ought to do would be to try & carry on as I've been doing…'

What did Venetia mean by these words? I asked myself.

She continues, 'Why can't I marry you & yet go on making him happy?...neither of you think that fun…I am so perplexed & wretched…Go on loving me & above all make me love you…'

She ends the letter with six disturbing words, which are written just four days before she agrees to become engaged: 'Darling I think I love you' (18 April).

It is not just the lack of love that Edwin is blind to, but also the consequences of Venetia's dislike of physical contact with him. When she turns away from his advances, he plaintively asks, 'Is it because you feel so little trusting that you turn your head in alarm each time I might take advantage of you?'

April is an anxious time for Margot as well. She senses there are serious issues in Asquith's life and accuses him of being secretive. On 13 April he tries to reassure his wife but his signature words 'Ever your own husband' demonstrate how differently he feels about her compared with Venetia. Margot knows her husband well and is not placated by his attempts to reassure his love. I found it ironical that three days later Margot writes to Edwin reasserting her wish that Venetia be married off!

Margot was not the only person who was worried, as both Venetia's and Edwin's families are anxious about their relationship. The Stanley family showed their apprehension with anger. Venetia, weighing up her options before her engagement, wrote, 'Isn't it a depressing thought that among our friends and relations (except perhaps my mother) there isn't one who would be otherwise than annoyed if we were to marry?'

Once her decision was announced, Venetia's 77-year-old father, Lord Sheffield, refused to talk to the engaged couple, and Lady Sheffield queried her daughter's love for her fiancé but believed the match a better proposition than Venetia's 'present position'. In another letter to Venetia's married eldest sister, Lady Sheffield appears to be pleased that Venetia is 'settled off at last and that she will not be harassed by her vagaries any more'. It appears from these letters that Venetia's deep involvement with the elderly politician had been well known within the family.

Venetia's grandmother was no less concerned: 'Venetia's future has always been rather a problem and if she is going to be really happy and settled one must shut one's eyes and swallow the ugliness of her marriage (and the bridegroom)!'

Interestingly for me, Venetia's brother, Oliver, came into the story again, as he was the only family member who stood by his sister's decision and agreed to be the intermediary to help deal with the anger of their parents.

The shockwaves continued to reverberate around all who knew Venetia. Asquith's family were deeply shocked. Violet's reaction was to send a long diatribe to the engaged couple. She was highly displeased with her childhood friend's behaviour and wrote in her diary, 'Apart from one's personal almost nervous recoil at the prospect I couldn't help regarding it as an unambitious and disappointing solution for Venetia's life.'

Even Asquith was anxious about Venetia's future happiness: 'you say…and I devotedly hope and pray that you are right, that you believe you love him enough to make sure of your happiness with him.' But, Asquith's eldest son, Raymond, being the rebel he was, rather enjoyed hearing the shockwaves echo around Venetia.

When a fiancée lets down her future partner by secretly planning to escape to France, a normal man would realise there was little potential love in the relationship, but not Edwin. He was angry but always conciliatory with his future wife.

He had other concerns about her plans to travel. These were financial. If he was to inherit his father's fortune, his fiancée had to become a Jew but with Venetia living on the wrong side of the Channel she could conveniently delay any participation in her religious classes. The religious classes were a bore for Venetia, but she was, at least, honest about her lack of faith and desire for her future husband's money.

> I shall never think of myself as a Jew any more than I think of you as one…I go through the formula required because you want it for your mother's sake…I am going to be quite honest because I think one is happier rich than poor [27 May 1915].

Edwin did not disagree with Venetia's views and had little taste for the strictures of his own inherited religion.

In earlier years Venetia had nothing but scorn for any religion. However, when she was on the horns of her dilemma in March of that year, she did take Anglican communion. This was only for the third time in her life, otherwise she was agnostic.

June 1915 proved to be a miserable month for all three entangled in the 'love triangle'. Venetia seemed the least affected.

She was despondent about the nursing she had to perform at her base in Wimereux, but this part of Boulogne was called the 'overstaffed annex of London society'. So her social life continued unabated. She often met up with various men she had known in London. Her emotional support came from her brother, Oliver, who had recently been personally helped by Asquith with his army career. He made frequent visits to see her.

But back in London Edwin was miserable. He pined for his fiancée while his mother quizzed him about the depth of Venetia's love. Edwin finally obeyed his mother's instructions and asked Venetia, just one month before their marriage, if she was not marrying to end her difficulties and unsatisfactory life. Was she pretending to be in love? Perhaps her feelings for him were all a delusion, he suggested.

While the engaged couple argued, Asquith struggled along with the new coalition. He appeared to be very depressed.

Finally after many pleading requests from Edwin, Venetia grudgingly returned to England, but again the couple argued, this time over their wedding plans. Venetia wanted a secret marriage but Edwin insisted they announce their engagement in the papers. 'We need tell no-one the actual date. In wartime no-one will be surprised.' Venetia was not worried about the quick arrangements, but she *was* concerned about gossip. And she was right. The engagement caused a great deal of tittle-tattle.

At the time of the announcement Adelaide Lubbock, Venetia's niece, was abroad but confessed to reading all the national papers in order to find out more of the story. On her arrival in England she found that her social circle was talking of little else. Like the rest of her family, Adelaide censored her aunt's ruthlessness and cold-blooded acceptance of 'the Assyrian' and cried, 'How could she become a Jew for the sake of £8,000 a year?'

Of course the person who was happy with the announcement was Margot. On 13 May, when she had first heard the news, she bumped into Cabinet member Fisher at Number 10. He was in a furious temper with Churchill over the sending of troops to the Dardanelles, but Margot's diary tells how she made Fisher waltz around the room in order 'to cheer him up'. They continued to waltz together around the room to create what Margot wrote of as 'One of the most bizarre scenes that 10 Downing Street has witnessed'. Margot's diary is not known for its accuracy so perhaps in reality it was her own sheer joy that encouraged her to dance around the room so brazenly. Just 12 months before, Margot had written, 'If only Venetia would marry – how I loathe girls who can't love but claim and collect it like a cuckoo for their own vanity.'

More problems for the engaged couple arose as the wedding day approached. The Chief Rabbi refused to marry them and other religious issues caused delays, but Edwin's family intervened. His brother devised a 'glorious new plan' and his sister Lily persuaded the moderate Rabbi Joseph from Liverpool to perform the marriage at the West London Synagogue on Monday, 26 July. Even though the country was at war, no expense was spared, with the reception being held in Edwin's brother's sumptuous house. But Venetia's father refused to attend and Asquith's daughter-in-law, Katherine, was the only member of this family to be present. The wedding caused more sensational attention in the press and I wondered how the young Louis would have felt about this press coverage when he first read about his mother's wedding.

Cynthia, who later married one of Asquith's younger sons, reported that Venetia just toyed from the beginning of their marriage with her new Cabinet minister husband. She noted that Venetia refused to go away for their honeymoon, not because of the war, but because she wanted to stay and socialise with her London friends. After only two months of marriage Venetia appeared weary and listless but she had already acquired the love of money.

Interestingly, Cynthia raised her concerns about the consummation of the marriage in October to her brother-in-law,

Raymond. In his flippant reply he told his sister-in-law that he understood that Venetia and Edwin had 'a conjugal agreement'. So what was this? What had they agreed to?

It had been the brilliant Raymond Asquith who was the first person to start Venetia's Coterie. Initially, members were to be part of learned discussions with partying, pranks and gambling all part of the added attractions. However, when he left for the Front and Diana Manners became its leader, standards declined. The wild parties now lasted all night and the shocked but delighted press avidly informed the country about the behaviour of its members. As the women's male friends died at the front, they had nothing to lose by being 'daring to the point of outrage'. They took morphine and chloroform and drank themselves silly on champagne. Worse still, the group believed that marriage was reserved for family, convenience and public occasions, while weekends away were for clandestine sex. As long as discretion was observed and rules followed, the charade continued while hostesses arranged sleeping partners as they would dinner parties. The married Montagus' London home became a haven for the Coterie's sumptuous parties and their country pad, Breccles Hall, became the ultimate escape from London and the war. Edwin had been officially accepted as 'an honourable member' but many continued to call him Mr Montagu and seemed to tease rather than fully include him. He never fitted in with their wilder antics. Who, I wondered, was Edwin's sleeping partner at these events, as women found him so unattractive?

Raymond Asquith declared that the terms of the Montagu marriage were 'to permit a wide licence, both parties to indulge in extra conjugal caprices as either may be lucky enough to conceive', adding that Venetia was 'less delicate' than other women when it came to sleeping with ugly men and that she might worry about the bed being too empty rather than too full! So had Raymond always known that his father was sleeping with Venetia?

Further confirmation about the couple's sexual life came from

Raymond's letter writing to his friend Conrad Russell. He told him it was 'a marriage of convenience' and his further words were barbed with sarcasm: '...if a man has private means and private parts (especially if they are large) he is a convenience to a woman.'

Raymond dug his knife into Venetia's back when he hinted to his friend that Venetia might have lesbian tendencies because of her notoriously bad behaviour with Diana Manners.

Raymond Asquith is well known in his own right but most of the literature I had read about him featured his teenage years. As I pondered on family ties I suddenly realised that he would have been 34 and married himself in the year Louis was born. Because of this age difference I had not fully appreciated that they were, of course, half-brothers. Unfortunately for my research, Raymond died fighting at the front in 1915. His letters had been a juicy source of information for me.

The more I examined the historical texts the more I disliked Venetia Stanley. Texts describe her as a clever conversationalist and Sir Harold Acton, skilled in the art of repartee himself, considered her to be one of the wittiest and best conversationalists of her day. Arnold Bennett reported she had a 'darting tongue' with a snide sting. Certainly that description sounded like the barbed wit of Stepfather.

Everybody agreed that Venetia was indifferent to convention. She was 'a free spirit with a sense of sin' and one 'who lived for fun'. She was described as a hedonist who had no qualms about enjoying the life of the privileged. That sounded familiar!

As a young girl, Venetia was a tomboy who 'permitted herself in the morning of her youth no recourse to her femininity...[She] rode like an Amazon and walked the high walls of Alderley with the casual strides of a boy'. But as an adult she became 'a beguiling mistress of beauty, candour and seductiveness', while Ziegler claimed 'she had the reputation of rendering even the most virile man impotent'. Certainly there were times when Asquith experienced her frosty demeanour. Once he compared his relationship with her to the skill of rock climbing. 'Mount Venetia', as he called her, was covered with a surface of ice.

Venetia seems to have lacked empathy. Soon after writing her fateful words to Asquith she wrote to Edwin in June saying, '...it must have shown him, more clearly than anything else I've ever written, how little I really cared for him.' Was Venetia always so brutal? Had she really hated Asquith? Had she been ensnared by his power? Or was she playing games with her future husband's emotions?

Naomi Levine believed Venetia was exciting, forceful and politically sophisticated and 'no ordinary woman'. Few others, Levine believes, could have handled a relationship with a prime minister 35 years older than herself. No ordinary woman would have converted to Judaism to marry on the terms she negotiated with Montagu.

To complete the similarity between mother and son, I find that when Venetia turned 30 she developed a liberated approach to sexual experimentation and by the time she was 35 she was regarded as promiscuous.

CHAPTER 16

HOW FAR COULD A COTTON-COP WINDER RISE UP THE SOCIAL LADDER?

I was grieving, but the pain pushed me to become a ferreting bloodhound. Details of where stepfather and his adoptive mother, my Home Granny, lived when he was a small boy still intrigued me. It made sense to me that the Asquithian advisers had recommended registering Liscard as Louis Stanley's hometown because of the rapid development of new housing across the Wirral. The rampant cotton trade was causing an overspill on the peninsular from the mushrooming city of Liverpool. Liscard was growing so fast it had already become fused with Wallasey and other neighbouring villages. Hoylake, being further away, was reserved as a holiday resort of special merit with a growing residential area for Liverpool's merchants and professional men.

I contacted the archivist at Birkenhead School again. This time I obtained two priceless pieces of information: Louis Stanley's home address had been 1 Hoyle Road, Hoylake; and Somerville in Poulton had been his preparatory school. At last, I had a tangible address. Hoyle Road was close to Stanley Road, the street where he once pretended to my mother he had lived as a child. One end of Hoyle Road was on the seafront. It all made sense. On my childhood visits to Hoylake, after the full viewing length of Stanley Road, Louis had purposefully asked Mum to drive up and down the local streets. Stepfather pretended he wanted to see the sea but it was not this at all: he wanted to go past the house that he had lived in as a teenager. The address was a real breakthrough, for now I could search the electoral rolls for Hoyle Road.

But first I tried my luck with Somerville School. It had closed down and no useful records survived, but it had served the Poulton community, which was one of the villages swallowed up by Liscard. So that narrowed down my search for Stepfather's previous abode. Everything seemed to be dropping into place and it was not long before I determined where Mary Ann Stanley had registered to vote. In 1918 she lived in Rake Lane; Louis would have been six, with his preparatory school close by. Then, when Louis was between 11 and 14, she moved to Seabank Road, again in the Liscard area.

I envisaged his life when he was 12: walking to preparatory school, satchel on his back, while his 'sister' Mamie would be going to work, as she was 22. Then in 1926 when Louis was 14 the family moved to Hoyle Road. Did they move so Louis could travel to Birkenhead School on the local train? Which suggests, if he had schooled at Winchester College, and I suspect his story was true, it was before this date.

So now I knew of his whereabouts as a child, but it did not solve the problem of his birthplace. Aylesbury Road, Liscard, where Louis's birth certificate claimed he had been born, was split into two electoral wards. However, to give strength to my argument only the numbers under 31 had been recorded for the year 1912. So did this mean he could not have been born in number 37 on 6 January?

I returned to the Wirral libraries and checked the local maps for 1912. Would they confirm whether 37 Aylesbury Road had been completed in early January 1912 or not? Here, I had one of my few pieces of bad luck: the corner of the early, large-scale map of the area had been torn, so I still could not prove when it had been built. So I decided to knock on the door of number 37 and ask if the current resident knew if there were any deeds for the house in existence. There were none. But the owner confirmed she had been told the house had been built in late 1912. That seemed to clinch it. If it hadn't been built until late 1912 Louis could not have been born in that house as early as January.

But there was more research to be done in Hoylake before I could return home. I had written to the owners of 1 Hoyle Road but had no reply, so I knocked on their door. They were out, so I decided to walk on the nearby beach. It seemed surreal. As I loitered enjoying the brisk wind pushing from behind I thought of Mum. She had rarely been in a good mood when we came to Hoylake. She used to blame the traffic, but had other things annoyed her? Was she just fed up with his directing her on what to her must have seemed like aimless circular routes?

Then I remembered that Louis used to walk across the road to play the 17th hole when he was a member at the Royal Liverpool Golf Club; at least that's what he told us. I imagined the boards of the club littered with the name L. T. Stanley, so I decided to visit the clubhouse hoping the residents of number 1 might return if I dallied long enough. But his name was not on the honour boards and the club archivist told me there was no record of his ever being a member. This was odd. If Louis had played to a good standard his name must be recorded on the boards of other local clubs, so I visited the other numerous links courses. The story was the same: his name never appeared. But the unusual name of D'Arcy Hart did. This name had cropped up in my reading and now I was spotting the name in the local directories, which I was studying.

When I investigated further I found that Walter Louis D'Arcy Hart was the same person as 'Walter Louis', the solicitor named by Venetia in her will. He had married one of Edwin's sisters. I recalled that 'Walter Louis' was in charge of the distribution of Venetia's funds at her death. This brother-in-law of Edwin's was a lawyer who specialised in setting up trust funds. Of course! There must have been a trust fund set up for Louis. This D'Arcy Hart must have been in charge of his money and he had a house within walking distance of Hoyle Road. More fertile research was still to come.

I returned to Hoyle Road late that Saturday afternoon to find that the owners had returned. The family, although surprised, welcomed me into their solid, mock-Tudor, Edwardian, semidetached house. It had a particularly substantial staircase. I looked at the handrail, imagining Louis charging down as a tall lean teenager ready to grab his clubs.

The residents took me into the kitchen, where they were preparing tea while listening to *Sports Report*. I was in luck. They had recently moved in and had the deeds of the house readily available, so in the warmth from the cooking we laid them out on the table. The Stanleys had lived in the house for 16 years, moving out in 1941, when Louis was 29. Most intriguingly, there had been a mortgage on the property. The mortgagee was 'Mary Stanley', whose 'husband' was entered as a 'Cotton Agent'. At last I had printed evidence of the family. But, crucially, the father's name did not appear on the form. My eyes searched for the names of the guarantors for Mary Stanley. The first was Hilda Mary Bailey, who then passed the role on to Margaret Lydia Key in 1935. As I analysed the small print I felt that same eerie feeling creeping slowly along my backbone as if Stepfather were going to pounce on me. But I now had the upper hand; I was digging up his very roots. The room turned from very hot to freezing when I spotted Louis's signature. He had signed the change-of-mortgagee form in 1935. It was an immature version of his signature, but easily recognisable.

Where had Mary Ann Stanley found the money to live in this substantial semi if she had no husband? Was it not Louis's trust fund that raised her status from the lowest position in the cotton industry to the ownership of this grand house? Had she acted throughout all those long years that she was married? Had Louis had to pretend that 'Dad' was permanently abroad? I wondered about Hilda Bailey, the guarantor. Had she known Walter Louis D'Arcy Hart? Stranger still, Hilda Bailey had lived in a grand house only minutes away from where I now lived. Why had this guarantor lived in Winchester? Had she been paying the mortgage for Mary Ann Stanley? The second guarantor, Margaret Lydia Key, had lived a few miles away in West Kirby. How had she fitted into the story? Why did she take on this role? Was it because Louis himself was now master of the house at the age of 23?

I did not need to travel far to find out about the Baileys. Hilda's father, Walter, had been the town clerk and a solicitor. So, had Walter Bailey been friends with Asquith, Edwin Montagu or perhaps Pa Stanley? Other likely connections were Violet Bonham Carter, who often stayed with friends in the area, and 'Bluey', her good friend Harold Baker, who became warden of Winchester College.

I had a deeper thought. The deeds showed that the house was sold just months before Louis married Kate Furness. Maybe the trust ran out when he married or when he turned thirty. Had he married in order to secure a home for his mother and sister? After all, Mary Ann had come a long way from her lowly roots, living in a large house, near the sea, in a middle-class holiday town. She would have no savings. Stepfather would have had to provide for her in her later years.

Now it was the turn of Mary Ann's parents to be investigated, so I had more serious census work to do. I felt the extended family might give me as many clues as Mary Ann herself. Could any of them have a connection with Alderley Hall? This time I moved forward in time. Mary was 11 in the1881 census and the family were still living in Union Street, Carlisle. Mary's half-sister,

Elizabeth, who was seven years older, worked as a draper, and now there were two younger brothers, Fred, four, and William, two. Alfred, Mary's father, I discovered, had first been married to a fellow cotton worker who was only 17 on their wedding day. She died of typhus fever, leaving Alfred with a baby of seven months. Two years later Alfred married Mary Ann's mother, Mary Holmes, when he was only 22.

Next I analysed the 1891 census and eventually found the relevant data collected in April that year. Alfred had moved to Hassop Street, Beswick, not far from Manchester. Why had Mary Ann's father, moved? And it appeared that he had married for the third time. What had happened to Mary Ann's mother? The answer was in the death registers: she had died in 1886.

Alfred's new wife, Jessie (sometimes known as Janet), came from Glasgow. Was she another wife who worked in the cotton industry? In 1891, Mary Ann and Elizabeth had both left home but brother Fred, now 13, was at home, and so were two new brothers, Alfred and Charles, who had been born since the 1881 census. (William, another brother, appeared to have died.)

Asquith had been MP for Glasgow in his later years. Was Jessie's connection with his constituency significant? Or was I getting too suspicious for my own sanity?

My policy of looking at maps came in useful again. I plotted the position of Beswick, an area now known as East Manchester and only 12 miles north of Venetia's home. Hassop Street was near the station that served the line from Alderley Edge. Had any of the family worked for one of the train companies? Probably, I thought, as there were many important railway lines nearby. My search was gaining momentum, and by the time of the 1901 census Alfred had moved again, not far this time, but 33 Robert Street, Newton Heath, was again close to the road to Alderley. This made me think again. Could it be the brothers or sister of Mary Ann who were involved in my story? Perhaps this was more likely than her father.

While up in the Lake District I took the opportunity to visit

Carlisle's library and talk to the local historians. What was life like for cotton warper Alfred? I asked. Warping, I was told, was a skilled job with long working hours and poor pay. Union Street, the road Mary Ann had been born in, was on the outer fringes of the city. A workhouse with the same name was nearby and it had been so despised that the road was renamed Rydal Street.

The houses in his street were terraced on a two-up-two-down principle with shared outdoor privies. As we searched for the railway lines on the old map the historian added, 'Life was so hard for cotton workers those people would have done anything to get out of it.' He of course could not hear my mind agreeing, Yes, I know: anything.

The local historian also suggested when and why the family moved. Perhaps they travelled south in 1883 when Dixons, the main cotton employer in Carlisle, went bankrupt. At that time there was an exodus of families. That year Mary Ann would have been old enough to leave school at 13.

On my way down South from Carlisle I paid a visit to Lytham St Annes. From the records, I could see that the 'St-Anne's-on-the-Sea' section of the town had been beautifully laid out with well-arranged streets and handsome villas. Orchard Road, where Mary Ann had been living in 1901, was a thriving street where small shopkeepers and skilled craftsman lived. Where number 25 once stood is a hotel car park but the road is still close to the main shopping centre. I took time to 'feel' the area and imagined Mary Ann Applegate working as a sick nurse returning to her boarding rooms. What had life been like? Why did she come here from Bollington? It seemed an unlikely decision. Had she been made redundant when the cotton trade started to decline? How long did she stay? Perhaps she had lived in the town for only a short period. Had she been in a relationship? Did she have any connections with the game of golf? Maybe some of these questions might be answered if only I had access to the 1911 census.

It crossed my mind that Stepfather might have lived in this town as a baby. As I explored a bend in the road, a large synagogue caught my eye. The Jewish faith kept popping up in my research and I was beginning to think along new lines. There were too many Jewish connections to ignore. Had Edwin anything to do with the organisation of the adoption of Stepfather? Venetia became a Jew and certainly socialised with her husband's friends as a married woman. But was the Jewish connection made earlier than 1915?

Who had been the person who once inspired Stepfather's love of golf? I recalled again Stepfather's written words: '[My] childhood house was filled with the aura of golf.' Again, I looked at his early books. There was one on lawn tennis. I had a breakthrough. It was dedicated to his mother: 'To my mother a graceful player in the day when lawn tennis was a refined late Victorian pastime.' I was annoyed with myself for not thinking that a woman could have been the keen golfer in his life!

I rang the famous Royal Lytham & St Annes Golf Club and obtained some interesting history of the course. Surprisingly, the game had been far more egalitarian in those times and half the earliest members had been women. Many townswomen provided hot pies for the players. I could imagine Mary Anne aged 31 doing this. Caddies were also a major part of the golf world, with each player hiring either a boy or girl from a caddy master and paying them two shillings and sixpence (12.5p) per day.

Starting from Alderley Edge, I drove along winding roads, enjoying the rolling green hills on the edge of the National Park, to find the town of Bollington. I wanted to see where Mary Ann had lived and worked. The local librarian told me the schoolhouses had been demolished, but there was a cotton museum in one of the three original mills. To get there I drove under an unusual brick bridge built at a thirty-degree angle to the road. Had I imagined it or had I been under this aqueduct before? I had not expected Bollington to conjure up old memories. Could Stepfather have made my mother and me visit Bollington?

I learned a little more about the cotton trade and then started to make my way back to where Alderley Hall had stood. Maybe I could find the stone gateposts with their strong, winged eagles, of which I had seen photographs. The site of the hall was just eight miles away. As I approached the entrance I spotted a garden centre and braked heavily. I loved buying plants from different places. However, I was too late to swing into their car park, so parked in the lane opposite. As I crossed the road, there in front of me were the Alderley Hall pillars in the grounds of the garden centre. They conjured no old memories but as I walked back to my car I was astounded to read 'Bollington Lane' on the grimy road sign. At last I had made the vital connection between Mary Ann Applegate, Bollington and Alderley Hall. Mary Ann Applegate had lived really close to Venetia Stanley in 1891, so there was no reason to doubt she could not have lived near in 1911.

Lord Swaythling, Edwin's father, I read, was more wealthy than I had envisaged and his merchant bank, Samuel Montagu, was considered by the City to equal that of the Rothschilds. This was mega-money and Venetia enjoyed spending his son's share. Much was spent on her appearance: she was dressed in high-fashion clothes and wore fantastically large hats to ensure she seen as a 'magnificent Jewess', according to Cynthia Asquith. Her underclothes were the most sumptuous money could buy. Edwin bedecked himself in an astrakhan coat and bought many fabulous jewels for his wife, but she just left these 'discarded on her bed' (Levine). He bought a rundown mansion in Norfolk and employed Edwin Lutyens, the expensive architect, to renovate it. Their friends, the Coopers, could not believe it when, after only two years of marriage, the couple were in debt. But it was true. By 1918 Edwin owed £60,000. Venetia had taken to gambling in Nice and Cannes and Edwin took his wife's jewellery to the pawnshop.

After Edwin's death Venetia continued in her extravagant lifestyle. She kept her passion for monkeys, entertained glamorous guests who arrived in expensive cars and flew her own De Havilland Gypsy Moth (Stephan Buczacki). Venetia Montagu's serious downfall came in January 1936. She was caught cheating at bezique and 'All London is talking about it', according to the memoirs of the author and journalist Robert Bruce Lockhart. If all London was chattering, how did Stepfather cope with this? He would have been 24.

I felt privileged to visit the ornate Wren Library in Cambridge, where the letters between the 'Monts' are stored. The letters tell of their unhappy relationship. When Secretary of State for India, Edwin wrote long loving letters back home, but Venetia hardly bothered to scribble a few lines back. Her letters showed she was both callous and cruel, giving him details of her dinner dates and her gambling exploits. She took no notice of Edwin's pleas to write more often. She did not write for months on end. When she did, her letters started with, for instance, 'Oh Darling I wrote you a frightfully good letter but have already lost it, so must write another one, a bad one.'

She taunted Edwin with her sexual exploits. She even told her husband that she was undergoing an 'Aaron's Operation' – a new operation, named after the surgeon that allows 'more compatible coital activity'. She underwent this operation twice, once in 1916 and again in 1919.

Edwin's political downfall was orchestrated, like Asquith's, by their old Liberal colleague Lloyd George. Jews were still not fully accepted into society and initially Edwin kept his head down in the Cabinet and worked exceptionally hard. He worked first with religious fervour in India for Asquith and later he worked all hours at the Paris Peace Conference for Lloyd George. But Edwin's downfall was his desire to gossip. This made him unpopular and he began to be referred to as 'Shylock, the Merchant of Venetia' (Cynthia Asquith). When the more experienced Edwin became obstreperous in cabinet meetings and when trouble arose in India, Lloyd George used a political mix-up as an excuse to make Montagu a scapegoat. He forced him to resign before a crowded House of Commons, where the Tories rose to their feet, laughed, cheered and waved their papers in derision. Surely even the hardhearted Venetia must have been moved by such harsh treatment.

This was the end of Edwin's distinguished career. He has been heralded as the 'architect of Indian self-government' and 'the best Secretary of State India ever had', but many believe he never received the credit because of Lloyd George. Montagu lost his seat in the general election two years after his forced resignation and quit politics an embittered man. He died aged only 44 in 1924. Stepfather would have been 12.

Edwin had explicitly wished for a non-Jewish funeral. But sadly his Jewish relatives overruled his last wishes and insisted on holding a Jewish memorial service for him in London. Venetia refused to go. I looked in the papers to see who had attended. Beaverbrook attended and so had Oliver Stanley! Oliver Stanley had emerged as a key player in my story.

There had been a number of references to male love in the texts and I was thinking on another front. Perhaps Edwin was a closet homosexual. Edwin's close friend (from 1909), the economist John Maynard Keynes, was homosexual and he married a Russian ballerina (Lydia Lopokova) in 'an agreement' that suited them both. Had Montagu married to cover his sexuality? Edwin fitted the stereotype of a closet gay man of the times: insecure, anxious about his failings, often in poor health, unappealing to women, and he wrote to his mother every day until he was forty. As homosexuality was illegal, marriage was a social necessity.

I found more supporting evidence. In Conrad Russell's letter to Raymond Asquith he wrote that he did not fancy sleeping with Edwin; in Raymond's reply he agreed that this thought did not take his fancy. It was a strange comment for these two young men to make but they had a number of talented homosexuals in their friendship group.

Interestingly for my research on Stepfather, I found that Tom Driberg, as known as the gossip columnist William Hickey of the *Daily Express*, also agreed to a show marriage that was never consummated. When Driberg was found cottaging, his employer Beaverbrook made sure the press never knew of the story and paid his legal fees. Driberg worked in Berlin. He had been spying on the communists for M15. Was there a connection here with the pamphlet *Germany After the War*? I was suspicious.

The month of May 1915, when Asquith floundered and formed the coalition, was an important time in British history and analysing it in more detail helped me understand the premier's state of mind.

In the months leading up to May, Asquith's letters became more and more demanding. He started to plead with Venetia. He told her he would struggle with the demands of government and leave tasks undone if she did not stand by him, and he said that if there had been a pistol around he might have shot himself.

I wondered again at the nature of this relationship. How had Venetia coped with these challenging letters? Had Stepfather inherited from his father this trait of emotional blackmail? He was certainly adroit at that game.

Venetia knew her engagement would be crushing news for Asquith, so she tried to wait for a suitable political time to tell him. Unfortunately, because she dithered, she chose one of the worst weeks to impart her news. Her letter arrived at Number Ten on the day the morning's papers carried extracts from 'Report of the Committee on Alleged German Outrages' (the Bryce Committee). This, coupled with the hatred engendered by the Zeppelin raids, the gas attacks and the sinking of the *Lusitania* meant that feelings against the Germans were at a high pitch. Anti-German rioting and looting reached serious proportions that day.

Only five days before Venetia's rejection letter landed on his desk, HH had vehemently refused any mention of working with the Tories. But after her letter arrived he started to wither politically. In the following two weeks, instead of fully concentrating on the national crisis around him he wasted time wondering whether he had the courage to call on Venetia. Quickly the political outlook became bleaker. Conscription was becoming a thorny issue and Asquith was dragging his feet. Rumours about shell shortages at the front were rife and Sir John Fisher and Winston Churchill violently disagreed in stormy Cabinet meetings. Fisher became so angry that he clandestinely fed his complaints to the press, who in turn fuelled more furores against Asquith.

From all accounts, Asquith appeared like a man in tatters in the days just after Venetia had left him. Many observers claim he was inconsolable. Descriptions include 'shattered', 'bruised and broken hearted', 'ill and distracted' and 'depressed'. Certainly, HH's colleagues were utterly astonished. Previously he had always engaged his cool deliberate manner, which over the many years of stewardship had allowed him to escape from his most serious political problems. But now his famed 'wait and see' policy disappeared overnight and he acted completely out of character.

Enoch Powell summed up the situation: 'The adored woman upon whom so much worship had been lavished and to whom the secrets of the state had been laid bare, simply crushed the relationship out of existence…as callously as one would squash a fly…it left Asquith with the stuffing knocked out…' (Levine).

Most historians have been convinced that Asquith could have ridden the political storm that surrounded him that month if he had not been so emotionally low. Bonar Law, the canny Tory leader, spotted Asquith's low spirits and suggested to him that a coalition might relieve the man of his political problems. The evidence is that Asquith listlessly agreed with little further thought. His Liberal colleagues were furious. He had made the decision on his own with Lloyd George being the only Liberal he consulted.

So, with his emotions awry, Asquith wrote this official letter to

King George V from his panelled drawing room in Downing Street on 17 May: 'After much refection and consultation today with Lloyd George and Bonar Law I have come to the conclusion, that for the successful prosecution of the war, the government must be reconstructed on a broad and non-party basis.'

Inevitably, Venetia was not far from his thoughts. From the same room on the same day, the Prime Minister wrote, 'I am on the eve of the most astounding and world-shaking decisions – such as I would never have taken without your counsel.'

Here was the British Prime Minister agreeing to a coalition because of Miss Stanley. This one action ended the last Liberal administration, and the party was left in such disarray that it never held office again. Not until 2010 has the Liberal Party held any governmental power, and it is ironic that the modern coalition formed then was between *virtually* the same two parties (the Liberals joined with the Social Democrats in the eighties, and that union eventually became the Liberal Democrats).

I reflected once again on the saga. Had Asquith really agreed to this wartime coalition because of his unbalanced state of mind? How had Stepfather felt when he learned for the first time that it was his mother's actions that had contributed to his father's decision to form the wartime coalition? At what age had he discovered this? Could the history of the Liberal Party have been different if Stepfather's mother had not sent that letter in that week?

No wonder the Asquith family and the Liberal Party have been trying to cover up the coalition story. The Prime Minister appeared from all accounts to be far more concerned about himself than his country.

Three months later, in the cold light of day, Asquith is disappointed with his own hasty decision, writing to Venetia's sister, 'I rarely go back on my original judgements. This time I feel an unusual uncertainty. Venetia who as so often and now for so long my best counsellor, was gone…' (June 1915, Clifford).

Asquith had been a popular prime minister. In peacetime he had achieved a great deal but when the war causalities mounted the public saw him as weak and unable to deliver the dynamism they wanted. Historical verdicts suggest there were two Asquiths: the urbane and conciliatory peacetime leader and the hesitant and increasingly exhausted Asquith who practised the politics of muddle and delay.

Carlo D'Este, an American historian, was highly critical: 'Britain in 1914 lacked a true wartime leader' (*Warlord: The Fighting Life of Winston Churchill from Soldier to Statesman* 1910). While Stephen Koss believed that Asquith had acted like a schoolboy allowing Venetia to reign supreme: 'Her power over Asquith, and thus indirectly over the conduct of the war, is awesome; the responsibility she carried must have been a burden to her.' From the point of view of a soldier in the trenches, Asquith's love letters would hardly have reassured them that their Premier was fully concentrating on preserving their lives!

'I fear I am in peril of breaking down...my own soul is not wholly or whole heartedly engaged in the things that appear and probably are of supreme importance' (18 February 1915).

'My own darling – I am writing in the stress and tumult of a windy and wordy controversy about munitions etc between Ll G Winston and AJB – and I daren't abstract myself more...I love you more than life' (22 March 1915).

Previously, the Asquithian letters had been important to me because they had shown the Premier's feelings for Venetia, but now I had to ask more questions. Had Asquith been unstable before his 'lodestar' deserted him? Was it only the ever-increasing troubles of the war that made him so depressed? Or had his domineering troublemaking wife made him almost mentally deranged? A number of his letters indicate that Asquith was so depressed that he was thinking of ending his own life. Was this true depression or were his ever-increasing threats his method of keeping this intelligent young woman by his side? How did Venetia cope with his threats?

Even in the earliest months of the war, Asquith displayed his frailties: 'Sometimes I am afraid that I may burden you with my preoccupation. After all this is the biggest thing we are likely to see and I shall and I must take you with me every day until it is carried through or I succumb…' (1 October 1914).

As the war progresses, his unease slowly grows. By January he admits depression; this increases and then in February he writes, 'You are truth itself, if I could doubt you I should welcome death' (19 February 1915). Four days later he is even more depressed: 'Your love is my life' (23 February). At this time he starts to use the phrase 'I love you more than life' more and more often.

In early March his mood brightens and he informs Venetia he is not feeling suicidal any more, but then his deep despair returns: 'The tragic pall of black unrelieved midnight darkness – which would spread over me if I had to go on living and working and worrying'. He tells Venetia that her company was 'the best 'restcure' and 'strength restorer and doubt killer and soul inspirer and (above all) *life giver*'.

For a man who was usually so self-reliant the beginnings of a lack of self-confidence also start to appear: 'I sometimes think that Northcliffe and his obscure crew may be right…maybe I am a fool…' And he continues with his relentless pressure on the hapless Venetia: 'I live for you…without you, life would lose all that makes it worth living.' On 2 April he writes: 'Do reassure me, love of my life. Otherwise…' and here he leaves a long line.

Asquith believes that Miss Stanley and Montagu are at this time secretly discussing plans to marry but this does not stop him bombarding Venetia with Asquithian threats. Then on the very day Venetia accepted Montagu's fourth marriage proposal, Asquith's letter, which she would have received the next day, warned her, 'You are my life' (23 April).

Were these charged emotional threats the reason why Venetia agreed to marry the pockmarked Cabinet minister in such bizarre circumstances? For the first time I started to feel sorry for Venetia. How had this aristocratic young girl coped?

Certainly Asquith was fickle, for within hours of receiving Venetia's fateful letter on 12 May he turned his attention to another woman. He went back to previous confidante Sylvia, Venetia's older sister. Once again, she became his solace. He wrote to her, 'I am in the stress of the most arduous and exacting things that you can imagine and I miss (more than I can say) what has helped and guided me so often during these three years…'

Asquith continued to be deeply upset but after those first few weeks of anger he never reproached either Venetia or Edwin. Two months later he asked Sylvia to choose two miniature silver boxes as a wedding present to the couple. On the eve of Venetia's wedding he wrote: 'Take [the] boxes with all my love and more wishes than words can frame for your complete and unbroken happiness.' Once safely married, Venetia and Edwin did agree to continue their companionship with their shared friend. At first, they found their meetings hard, but later, when Asquith no longer had a Cabinet post, he often visited 'the Monts' in their London home and stayed for long weekends at Breccles in Norfolk.

After Venetia left his side Asquith suffered more grief, for his academically talented eldest son Raymond was killed in the Battle of the Somme. He withdrew into himself and missed more and more Cabinet meetings. Edwin, who had stayed politically loyal, warned his old friend of Lloyd George's ambitions, but Asquith did not listen. So in December 1916 Lloyd George usurped Asquith and the Liberal party was split. Lloyd George continued to be vindictive and denied his former colleague any part in the Peace Conference by organising posters that read, ASQUITH NEARLY LOST YOU THE WAR. ARE YOU GOING TO LET HIM SPOIL THE PEACE?

It was a sad end for Asquith. In 1920 he lost his Fife constituency and turned again to drink for solace: 'At fifty-eight the dignity of a statesman alternated with the comic figure of a drunk' (Jenkins, *Asquith*). It was also a sad end to the Liberal Party.

The old affection for each other was obvious after Edwin died in 1924, as Venetia sent Asquith two touching letters, the first soon after her husband's death:

> I know it is not necessary to tell you how deeply he loved you and what a real and lasting grief your political separation was…Do you remember how we used to laugh at him in Sicily? Thank you for all you did for him to make his life happy.

Later she enclosed a special copy of *Hamlet*:

> My darling Mr Asquith, I've never thanked you for your divine letter, you know how dumb and inarticulate I am, but you do realise, I hope, how glad I was to get it. I hope I may see you sometime when you get back. Much love always.

For the next four years the old 'companions' continued to meet up, and in 1928, when HH had already suffered a stroke and had a semi-paralysed leg, he made one last supreme effort to visit Venetia in Norfolk. It was to be his last outing of any consequence before he died.

Venetia was a frosty individual. She was no better a mother to her daughter than she had been a wife to Edwin. Judith recalled that her mother had been so cold to her she questioned her love, according to Levine. Had giving away Louis affected Venetia? Or had she been so keen on enjoying life to the full that she cared little for her own daughter? Judith had no recollections of Edwin, as she was only 18 months when he died. But within her memories of childhood are two highly significant events for me. When Judith was eight she remembered receiving a special gift from Lord Beaverbrook. The literature on this man always records his generosity so, if he sent presents to Venetia's daughter, then it is likely he had helped her son, Louis.

But it was Judith's other childhood account that excited me. Judith at the tender age of four or five recalls H. H. Asquith visiting her mother in 1927. She recalled his tears falling as he saw her. He said, 'This, then is the child' (Levine, in conversation with Judith's daughter, Anna Gendel).

Whom had Asquith been weeping for? Could it be tears for his lost son Louis Thomas Stanley? Margot had lost three babies, each dying when they were very young. I had not thought about the effect these deaths had on HH. Through the course of these unsuccessful pregnancies his wife had changed from a vibrant woman to an anorexic spiteful dragon. Had Asquith felt the trauma of giving up his living healthy baby son? Had he been determined to be involved in his placement?

Biography writers regard Asquith as a good father. He was certainly devoted to his daughter Violet, but I wonder how true this was in regard to his legitimate sons. The three older sons who fought in the war never received one letter from their father. This deeply upset them, and Katherine, Raymond's wife, never forgave her father-in-law for failing to write when her husband was in such grim circumstances. Katherine must have known it was not from lack of time that he failed to communicate.

But let us return to Judith, Venetia's daughter. Naomi Levine was fascinated by the couple's lack of excitement and communication about the birth of their baby. Edwin told their best friends the Coopers that Venetia was at last pregnant, after seven years of marriage. But, oddly, Edwin revealed that he did not plan to stay in this country for the birth. He was going to India. Seven months later, 6 February 1923, was Judith's recorded birthdate, but Levine notices 'a strange silence' concerning the arrival of this child, in the many letters to, from and about the Montagus. The impending arrival is never mentioned, nor does anybody congratulate the parents around this date. There was nothing written about the baby's looks, her weight, her name, or even the mother's and daughter's health. Why the silence? It had intrigued Levine. It now compelled me to ask: why?

Even ten days after 6 February Edwin still mentions nothing about the birth in his letters. Was it these letters that were burnt by Edwin's sister Lily? Did the letters say too many private things? Did Venetia explicitly ask her friends not to mention the baby? Or perhaps there was another explanation: perhaps Judith was actually born on another date altogether. I was intrigued to find that Venetia travelled immediately after 6 February, just as she had after 'the birth' of Louis in 1912, when she and HH went on their holiday to Sicily. Levine provided me with more intrigue, for there had been not just gossip but also confirmation that Judith had not been the daughter of Edwin at all but that of a wealthy philanderer, Eric Dudley (Earl of Dudley). Dudley had been one of Venetia's long-term lovers in the 1920s. Edwin Montagu had apparently known that the child was not his but agreed to keep the fact secret. Judith claimed she was told of her true parentage. This seems highly likely, as she chose to be buried on Eric Dudley's son's estate. So perhaps the marriage did stay unconsummated.

I could not understand why, if there had been such wild clandestine sex, the women didn't become more frequently pregnant. However, I did discover that married women were able to pass off a lover's child as their husband's, just as Venetia had with Judith. Certainly, in those days, married women of the upper classes took risks but unmarried ladies did not. Contraception may have been available for the upper classes in 1916 or 1917, when Marie Stopes first gave hints on basic ways of avoiding pregnancy, so it was not so surprising that the Coterie members had a kind of sexual freedom in the later years of the war. But, if Venetia was sleeping with HH in 1911, things would have been very different. As she was young and presumably sexually inexperienced she might have been unlikely to know even the crudest contraception techniques that would have been available to her married colleagues. It appears that in those days the wealthy relied on concealment rather than backstreet termination. Aristocratic women used their large estates to hide their pregnancies.

The works of the Countess of Warwick (mistress to Edward VII) helped my understanding of Edwardian life. 'Our rule was, "No scandal!" Whenever there was a threat of impending trouble, pressure would be brought to bear, sometimes from the highest quarters, and almost always successfully, publicity would cause chattering tongues and as we had no intention of changing our mode of living…' (Warwick, *Discretions*).

I remembered that, once she was married, the Coterie became even more important to Venetia, and I recalled that, if legitimacy was required within the group, a code of silence was respected. This might explain their silence over the birth of Judith.

I noticed another Jewish connection as I came across the name Montifiore, an unusual surname, and I immediately connected it with the clergyman who confirmed me: Hugh Montefiore, pastor of Great St Mary's, the University Church of Cambridge. Could there possibly be any connection? I could not resist looking up his details. Yes, his family were Jewish and his father Claude had been deeply involved in the religion but his son Hugh converted to the Church of England.

I had not been religious but I agreed to become confirmed when I was about 16. I became even less keen on the idea when I found out that I had to take classes on my own at home with one of Stepfather's friends. I wanted to be outside on those long summer evenings, but I had to content myself with sitting beside Mum's heavily scented arrangement of garden flowers and wait to hear the jangle from the bell above the blue gate as Mum wanted me to answer the door. I always felt so awkward with the man. My teenage senses were nauseated by his garish and unlikely clerical uniform of a wide purple tie obscuring what I saw as an effeminate lacy shirtfront. But then, once he had come over the doorstep, I found I did not have my allotted time because, as soon as

Montefiore placed both feet over the threshold, Stepfather appeared and invited him into his study. Stepfather had never taken any interest in my upbringing but on those days he talked, sometimes for hours, to my instructor. When I mentioned to my mother that I just waited rather than be taught, she replied in a derogatory manner 'Montefiore is one of his cronies,' as if this explained it all.

But I was soon to discover another scandal. This time it was Venetia's own legitimacy that was questioned. Rumours within her own family suggested she was not the child of Lyulph Stanley but of Lady Stanley's brother-in law, George Howard, of Castle Howard fame. The family gossip tells that George Howard was unhappily married to Venetia's aunt Rosalind, so, when Venetia's mother (Maisie) and Lyulph were 'homeless', they were invited to live on Howard's large estate in West Yorkshire. It was here George and Venetia mother's had an affair. Virginia Surtees, a Stanley descendant, suggests that the paternity of Maisie's last child was a well-guarded secret, but Lyulph accepted the child with good grace. Surtees, supports her argument by claiming there was a strong resemblance between George Howard and Venetia, and that she was dark whereas all her siblings were not.

Was this why Venetia's mother had such difficulty controlling her daughter? Maybe Venetia's predilection for extramarital relations came naturally. My search into George Howard's children proved fruitful. His son, Geoffrey Howard (Venetia's probable half-brother) was a Liberal MP and another of Asquith's parliamentary private secretaries. And Mary, George Howard's eldest daughter, added the rich icing to my research that day, as she married Louis's old trusted friend Gilbert Murray.

Chapter 17

Edwin, Lily or Who?

There were so many lies in Stepfather's birth certificate that it now seems strange that I had wanted to believe his date of birth was correct. Was it because 6 January was etched into my memory as a date I had to keep free so I could support my mother and help make his birthday a fun time?

I looked again at the dates of letters and the movements of Venetia in late 1911 through to early 1912. Initially, I had been thrown by Violet's published diary. According to this, Venetia had probably been out hunting on 7 December 1911. But, as I had so much more evidence, I had not let it worry me. This paid off, as I eventually found a reference to ladies continuing to hunt while pregnant. Both Margot and her daughter-in-law Cynthia hunted during her pregnancies (Nicola Beauman, *Cynthia*).

The other letter that had foxed me was one she had written to Edwin on Christmas Eve 1911. She informed him she had travelled on a night train from Archerfield, arriving that morning at six, hardly a likely journey for somebody eight months pregnant.

What made matters worse was that Venetia rarely put a date on her correspondence.

But we do know she goes on holiday to Sicily with Montagu, Violet and Asquith in the middle of January 1912. Venetia leaves England to join them just five days after the supposed birth. I decide I must backtrack and reread Edwin's letters to her, as these do have firm dates and I might understand her movements far better.

Venetia takes an extended holiday to Garmisch in Bavaria and returns on 17 August 1911. From Edwin's letters she could well have left as early as 28 July, but certainly by 5 August Venetia reports that her three female companions are her mother, Aunt Blanche and her cousin Clementine. Violet is also on holiday in this area at this time but the two friends do not mention meeting. Venetia reports in her letters to Edwin that she was very tired at this time. Was this thanks to her pregnancy?

On 8 September Venetia visits the Asquiths at Archerfield and stays at least until the 15th. There were plentiful meals, games of chess, pouring rain and thick fog but 'far fewer guests' than normal. Why did only Edwin, Bluey, Raymond and Violet attend? Were they the ones who could be trusted?

When Venetia returns home to Alderley Hall on 16 September, we get the first reports that she is not well. Was jaundice a cover story? She had 'only just got up for lunch' and claimed, 'I don't mind being ill.' Maybe she really did have the illness. I was once again reminded of Stepfather telling us that he had been a jaundiced baby. On 4 October in Edwin's letter he mockingly described her as 'jaundiced' instead of being ill-tempered. On 26 September she writes that she is 'very bored by illness and requires as much sympathy and as many condolences as any can think of', having been in bed for ten days and had had no visitors. However, she does invite Edwin to her parents' Welsh house for 10 October, when 'others will not be there'. He does not visit until 1 November.

Venetia's letter to Violet on 11 October tells her she is still not well enough to go on a short shopping trip:

> I was very unhappy at getting ill but it made me, if possible, more wretched than I was before, at not being with you. I am afraid – the doctor for once was right about not letting me come…I'm afraid I shan't be able to, for ages.

In another undated letter Venetia writes, 'I am beginning to feel that this thing will never be over. Bung the doctor says everything is excellent and yet he won't allow the place to close. I am so absolutely well otherwise. I feel very much bored by it.'

It appears that Venetia is still indisposed on 20 October as Violet is becoming concerned that her friend does not reply to her letters.

As many of Venetia's actual letters, as opposed to the published ones, have no year mark and some no date at all; some of them may have been catalogued wrongly. But it is possible to discover that Venetia was back in circulation from mid-November and was living at her parents' address in London or staying away with her brother Oliver. So it is highly unlikely Louis was born on 6 January 1912.

The letter that had previously foxed me about going hunting with Violet, dated 7 December 1911 in Violet's diaries, *Lantern Slides*, actually has no date written on it, so it could have been catalogued wrongly. Of course if the baby was born in October these letters might well be listed correctly. Venetia could well be out hunting in December after a birth in October or November.

However, in another vital letter Venetia has written the date, 21 November 1911. Clearly the baby had arrived by then because she writes to Violet,

> I daresay I am, like Margot, tho' with 'doom doomed'. I hunted *your* hunter yesterday and I'm afraid she won't do as she gave

> me a fall and I should be terrified beyond words if it were to happen to you. Oliver and I are alone here. We play lots of chess but I'm afraid...

So I work on the premise the baby was born earlier than January 1912. Interestingly, the Stanley parents were writing to both Edwin and Asquith in mid-July 1911. They were arranging appointments. The purpose of those meetings is unclear. Were they to talk about what arrangements should be made for the unborn child? So perhaps the baby was expected even earlier. Perhaps Venetia had been sent abroad to Bavaria to have the baby and had given birth in July 1911. She had been on holiday with three trustworthy female relatives.

In my view, the most likely time was between late September, through October to early November, when Venetia was 'ill'. Jaundice is not common but mothers can pass on this illness to their babies. Premature babies are especially susceptible. So maybe Louis had been quite ill as a newborn and maybe this explains Venetia's gloominess. Perhaps she had postnatal depression. Or was she sad because she had to give her baby away? She does not sound like that sort of woman, but it's possible.

Perhaps when Louis thrives rather than dies from his illness, the two parents decide to take a holiday in Sicily to discuss what to do. They take Edwin (later Financial Secretary to the Treasury) with them to help sort out the financial details and maybe discuss finding a suitable and trustworthy foster mother. During the Sicilian holiday the three plot when and how to register the birth. Perhaps Violet was included or overheard these intense conversations.

They fix upon a cover story for Mary Ann and on his return Edwin advises her how to register the birth. Meanwhile, they find a building plot with unfinished houses in Liscard to record as the birth address, knowing there would be no neighbours to gossip. So Mary Ann goes to the registrar on 16 February and records her foster child's date of birth as the earliest legally possible date.

This holiday is significant because Margot was left crying at home. Asquith had chosen to holiday with Violet instead of her. Or perhaps Margot knew that lover Venetia was holidaying with her husband after safely delivering Louis.

As he left, Asquith had once again had to placate his wife and penned,

> Why should you think that anything you have written has 'alienated' me? It could not, even for a moment, and even tho' I thought some things you said (or suggested) a little less than just. I love you always wherever I am, and you know well that no one does or ever takes your place.

This holiday was too important not to be fully investigated, so I decided to go back to the Wren Library and find these letters for myself. I found it chilling when the curators told me that the seven letters about thc holiday and other matters referred to in Levine's title had 'gone missing'. Although the letters were in the catalogue they were no longer available.

More details of the holiday came from Violet's diary. She had been in Murren enjoying winter sports and had planned to meet Venetia at Lucerne but was delayed by an attack of tonsillitis, so kept her friend waiting for 24 hours. Once together, they travel down Italy by train together. In Rome they bathed together in a fountain and then visited Venetia's uncle, Monsignor Stanley (who had upset the family by changing religion to become a senior Roman Catholic). When they finally arrived in Sicily Edwin Montagu was there to welcome them and took them to the Villa Igeia Hotel in Palermo, which was right on the sea: '…it laps up quite audibly and visibly day and night a few yards off a marble terrace broad and cool onto which our four bedrooms open in this order: Father – sitting room – Montagu – Violet – Venetia'. Rather clever arrangement, I thought! I also noticed that Violet took her maid but Venetia did not.

The holiday was not short of high jinx, and I suspect from Violet's diaries that Venetia gave poor Edwin a hard time as the girls shamelessly teased the man who paled and felt the chill when he saw the skulls in the catacombs. The future Secretary of State for India tries to join in with their silly games but becomes the butt of all their jokes. 'We played hiding in the garden and jumping out after dark. Montagu is the best person in the world to play with. He is *so* frightened – and *so* frightening,' Violet recorded on 21 January (*Lantern Slides*).

Violet gives us a flavour of the intimacy of the holiday: 'You would laugh if you saw us rumbling off in our grotesque landau-Father-Venice – Montagu and I, every tooth in our heads rattling – over the most mountainous and flinty roads, the old Downing Street fur rug spread over our four knees.'

Asquith wrote with mixed connotations to Venetia two years later: 'I agree we had a very good time in Sicily. I wouldn't go so far to say "it answered every requirement". I can imagine even more ideal conditions – but I fear they are not likely to be realised in the way I should picture them' (9 January 1914).

Names in my past, like 'Birkenhead', kept reappearing in the texts I was reading, but I needed to investigate the other childhood fascinator: the illustrated name of 'Beaverbrook'. If Louis's first job had been as a photographer with the *Daily Express*, I needed to know more about Venetia's affair with its proprietor. The year was 1919.

Edwin was officiating at the Paris Peace Conference and was billeted at the official government hotel. While he worked around the clock, Venetia enjoyed herself at the Paris Ritz. Even Diana Cooper was shocked. She wrote to her future husband,

> It's a disgusting case...Venetia's face lights up when that animated deformity so much as turns to her...they are living in open sin at the Ritz in a tall silk suite with a common bath and unlocked doors while poor Edwin is sardined in the Majestic unknown and uncared for.

Later Diana reports after dinner that 'the shocking, shocking Crooks', as she called him, turned to her and said,'Don't you think she [Venetia] is being very attentive to Edwin nowadays?' Diana was stunned that Venetia was.

The Canadian-born Beaverbrook came to Britain as a young lad and his progress up the ladder of success had been phenomenal. By 1911, at the age of 32, he was already enjoying the high life as a multimillionaire. It was at this time that he brought new glamour to the Coterie. With his 'odour of genius' (Diana Cooper, *The Rainbow Comes and Goes*) he created a 'wide magnetic field' (David Farrer, *G for God Almighty: a personal memoir of Lord Beaverbrook.*). that attracted all types of women. He, in turn, was attracted to brilliant, creative and dynamic women who enjoyed excitement, and wanted to flirt with danger.

Beaverbrook bought the defunct *Daily Express* and turned it into one of the most powerful newspapers in England. But this was not enough for his controlling personality. He wanted power, so he turned to politics and was elected to Parliament in 1910. Beaverbrook was also known to be generous. It is said that he would write any woman a cheque for £100 as long as she had wit, beauty or position. Certainly he lavished gifts on Venetia and put all his worldly goods at her disposal. Later, he provided funds for the Asquith family and gave money individually to both Edwin and Venetia when they fell short. So had he helped Louis when he was vulnerable?

Venetia, like many women, found the gnomelike billionaire with piercing eyes irresistible, but many historians have wondered if Beaverbrook had his affair with her just to get his hands on the Asquithian love letters. Others think he used Venetia as his spy at the Peace Conference. Was either of the two theories true? Perhaps not, as there was always a special affinity between the two and they remained good friends for the rest of their lives. They were also both long-standing friends with Winston Churchill. Venetia, it appears, was one of the few people who could lighten Churchill's 'black dog' moods, as he called them, and the records show that both Venetia and Beaverbrook were two of the very few who were invited to his intimate birthday parties.

Venetia, a keen gardener, influenced the design of the gardens at Chartwell and, when the Churchills were homeless twice in the 1920s, she offered – and they accepted – lodgings in her London house in Onslow Gardens. The much younger Churchill was an important minister in Asquith's Cabinet and he was invited to stay by Venetia's parents at both Alderley Hall and Penrhos as early as 1909.

So perhaps Winston knew Asquith and Venetia were lovers. Indeed, Churchill later wrote of his strong disapproval. He was irritated by their inability 'to draw back from the delicious thrill of being in each other's company' while Asquith's endless letter writing was 'England's greatest security risk'. As to the coalition, Churchill resented and criticised Asquith's pathetic loss of will. Churchill had his own opinion of Venetia's marriage to Montagu and called it 'utterly disgraceful' (Morgan).

Churchill memoirs show he was impressed with Asquith's abilities, but he heavily criticised his need for alcohol, as it was Churchill who had to rescue him when he was so drunk in the Commons that he collapsed on the floor. Churchill referred to the incident in a letter to his wife: 'On Thursday night the PM was vy bad: & I squirmed with embarrassment. He could hardly speak: & many people noticed his condition.' He continued, 'He is most friendly & benevolent, & entrusts me with everything after dinner. Up till that time he is at his best – but thereafter! It is an awful pity & only the persistent freemasonry of the House of Commons prevents a scandal' (22 April 1911).

Venetia's friendship with Winston reminded me that Churchill's wife Clementine and she were first cousins. When young, the two girls were quite different, but the cousinly bond held strong, and Venetia was selected as one of her cousin's bridesmaids. When they were older, they became much closer and went on holiday together. Had Clemmie known of the Prime Minister's illegitimate baby?

Intriguingly, in later years, the Churchill and Montagu families continued to be linked with Winston's daughter, Mary Soames, becoming best friends with Judith Montagu. Both chose to serve in the women's ranks together in the Second World War.

As I read, I recalled a childhood memory. When the country was in mourning for Winston Churchill there were huge queues outside Westminster Hall. We were in London and Mum looked at the lines of people who snaked around Parliament Square to honour his memory and said, 'I think we should be in that queue, if only we didn't have to drive back late tonight to Cambridge.' Louis kept quiet. I remembered he had not often said kind words about Churchill.

Later, when we were having dinner at the Dorchester, Louis pulled a new toy out of his bag. It was smaller than any other camera I had ever seen before. In shape it was a Havana cigar tin, with the shutter mechanism being part of the lid. He then produced tickets, which allowed us to walk straight into the building where Churchill lay in state. I wondered how on earth he had swung that one. Mum was annoyed. She did not like his ability to pull strings. Maybe she suspected what I now know: Louis had a hold over a certain female in the hotel who would probably obligingly supply him with touted loot.

There had been unprecedented security and there were NO PHOTOGRAPHY signs pinned up everywhere. As we got closer to the catafalque Louis put his hand in his right-hand coat pocket, and as we reached the bottom step I heard a click. It echoed around the high empty roof. A uniformed officer pushed his way into the crowd, searching for the culprit. As soon as the policeman had returned to his position, there was another loud shutter click. The policeman instantly made another search, roughly pushing me aside. I was sure Stepfather would be caught, but he wasn't. As far as I know he never used the photographs; it was just part of a game for him.

For historians, Asquith's illegitimate child might be the fascination, but to me – the groomed stepdaughter of the grown man – the mystery runs far deeper. I wanted to know what he did in his secret life before he met my mother. There was a joy in unravelling what he and others had so carefully hidden. I enjoyed slowly unpeeling his outer shell, leaving him little by little more exposed. Part of my fun was also to strip the shady politicians of their exquisite frock coats, take off their tall top hats and exposed them for what they were.

The Aga Khan's name came up again and again in the texts as I was reading. I hardly need mention how this man's name fuelled my fascination as a child. He sounded so exotic. But now I had a connection – this time with Edwin Montagu. For Aga Khan is a hereditary title in the Shia branch of Islam, a branch highly respected by the British in India. Edwin, when Secretary of State for India, worked closely with the Aga Khan and they became firm friends both in India and at the Peace Conference. Did this mean that Louis, at the age of 10 or 11, had met the man? If so it would mean that Louis had known Edwin Montagu, his stepfather. I decided it was more likely that it was the son of that Aga Khan, known as Aly, that Louis had been acquainted with. He was Louis's age and was known as an international playboy. Double-decker buses supported an advertisement for a brand of chocolate that bore the slogan RICH, DARK LIKE THE AGA KHAN. He was the owner of six houses and when he married the actress Rita Hayward in 1949 he filled the swimming pool at his house on the Riviera with 200 gallons of eau de cologne for the wedding reception. But Aly never felt fully accepted by his upper-class contemporaries and said of them 'they called me a bloody nigger and I paid them out by winning all their women.'

I found another link in my growing chain. One of Aly's lovers had been Thelma, Viscountess Furness, a flirtatious American. That familiar surname! This was no coincidence, for Thelma Furness had married Stepfather's first wife's uncle, Marmaduke Furness in 1926 but was divorced seven years later. It was she who became the mistress of the Prince of Wales, later Edward VIII and subsequently Duke of Windsor, before Wallis Simpson.

Thelma had loved the Dorchester's social group, for she continued the lifestyle of a divorced English noblewoman and persisted in using the name Viscountess Furness even though she was divorced. So, by supposition, Thelma would have socialised with both Venetia's and Diana Cooper's friendship groups. This supported my earlier guess that Stepfather could well have met his first wife's family when he lived in the Dorchester Hotel.

In Matthew Sweet's book *The West End Front* I found some less complimentary comments about life in the Dorchester Hotel during wartime. The diplomat Charles Ritchie cast an eye around the hotel in 1940 and spotted the remnants of London society embarking on a luxury liner in the midst of a storm. He saw it as 'a fortress propped up by moneybags'. Cecil Beaton was equally shocked by the clientele's behaviour. Lord Halifax, the Foreign Secretary had a suite of rooms in the hotel as had Oliver Stanley who was Minister for War and his wife, Maureen, was been the daughter of one Hitler's most enthusiastic British cheerleaders. (Lord Lonondderry)

When I was a teenager Stepfather had mentioned royal connections. I had dismissed his ramblings but when I read about Prince Edward's mistresses I remembered Louis's secret mumblings about a flight to France for the Duke of Windsor's birthday party. I remember thinking it strange because Louis did not boast in his usual manner. As far as I know he never told anybody outside the family. My stepfather's only boast to us was that he had sat close enough to the old prince to hear that he was always questioning his friends about what life in England was now like. Oddly, my mother was not invited. She was not part of Stepfather's life at that time but the invitation was strange because it was perhaps the only event at which she did not accompany him.

I thought about this again. Why had Stepfather been invited? He was so reticent about the momentous event. This time I was sure he had not been lying. I read more. Windsor was mad about golf and, as Prince of Wales, had often played at the Royal Liverpool. I thought of Stepfather's boasts of living opposite that prestigious course and realised the Prince of Wales's social group had contained all the names I had discovered before. Beaverbrook, as the prince's 'friend', was instrumental in trying to prevent the royal from continuing his relationship with Mrs Simpson and when he failed he masterminded the British newspaper conspiracy of silence over this romance. The *Daily Express*, for which Louis was working, supported the Prince of Wales throughout the crisis. Was Stepfather the royal correspondent? Certainly within the prince's circle were names familiar from Louis's boasts. A golf partner of Louis, Walter Monckton, had been the Prince of Wales's aide and later worked in the Ministry of Propaganda and Information. Had Louis been pushed out in the cold because he had backed the wrong side, since those who supported Edward were ostracised by many politicians after he abdicated?

I was compelled to dig deeper into the Montagu family. Edwin's older sister Lily was becoming significant to my studies. I learned she was as famous in her own field as her brother. Lily, like Edwin, had found their father's demeanour and religious fervour overbearing, so much so that she suffered a nervous breakdown in her teenage years. On recovery she set her heart on reforming the Jewish religion. Testament to her success is the Montagu Centre in Central London, where she is credited with founding Progressive Judaism.

I remembered that it was Lily who had asked the liberal Rabbi Joseph to solemnise Venetia's wedding. I looked further and found that Joseph and Lily had collaborated in writing children's prayer books. But, even more significantly, Lily also collaborated in Jewish reform with another familiar fancy name, Montifiore. His forename was Claude (see Chapter 16), and he had been my religious tutor's father.

This got me thinking. Edwin Montagu and Claude Montefiore had worked closely together at the Paris Peace Conference. I was sure there was a link. Perhaps Lily, as a feminist, social worker and leader of the new 'Liberal Judaism', had helped to find a suitable mother for Louis.

With my investigative ferreting pulling me in so many directions, I felt like an octopus with too many tentacles. Now I was pulled back into the political scene. Asquith's illicit love was not just a family secret: it was possibly a political cover-up.

Interestingly, three Asquith females were in denial for his liking for women. Margot did all she could to restrict the public's knowledge of Asquith's friendship with Venetia after he died in 1928. Five years later, when Desmond MacCartney published *Asquith's Letters to Hilda Harrisson*, Hilda was portrayed at the time as 'a non-passionate' confidante of HH, but the book still caused a furore among nonconformist Liberals. (Ottoline Morrell, who socialised with both the Asquiths and the Harrissons, knew that HH poached Hilda from her husband Gilbert and in the socialite's view the affair was far from platonic. – Seymour).

Margot had not wanted the book published because the womanising nature of Asquith had been a complete revelation. The public uproar caused her to write hastily to J. A. Spender, who had been in the process of writing Asquith's biography. She pleaded with him to keep references to Venetia to a minimum (Bennett). Spender, in deference to her, accepted her plea and agreed to write that Asquith discovered 'a need for some receptive and sympathetic female intelligence, outside the circle of his family, to which he could communicate as a matter of routine...a whole succession of women friends responded to this need.' Of course Spender might well have been accommodating, as his co-writer was another of Asquith's sons, Cyril!

Daphne Bennett, Margot's own biographer, admitted how keen Margot had been that Asquith's letters to Venetia remain a secret. In addition, in her autobiography, Margot failed to mention

Venetia's importance to her husband, so much so that Hilda Harrisson got one paragraph and Venetia only a few words. Margot amusingly wrote, 'The very fact that he [Asquith] did not care for women in the accepted meaning of the phrase made him attractive to them.' Margot made a mint out of her memoirs and she was known to mould a good story to her advantage, so historians do not rate its accuracy.

The second woman in denial was HH's daughter-in-law Cynthia, whose biographer dreaded her red pen, as she scored out any words that suggested Asquith had been attracted to girls or drink.

The third woman lived in Downing Street in her formative years and as a teenager took her best friend to follow HH everywhere, even to the House of Commons. Many historians have recognised the unusually close bond between father and daughter. Churchill wrote,

> Violet adored her father uncritically and even after he had been dead for eighteen years her veneration for him never died. When criticism might arise her redoubtable champion's lance was ever ready to be drawn in his defence, at one word of criticism – or even lack of appreciation.

The journalist and politician Arnold Ward commented, '…rarely have a father and daughter been united by such a perfect unbroken love and understanding.' Roy Jenkins summarised, '…no father had a more faithful daughter. In the ranks of filial love and loyalty Violet's remains pre-eminent.'

Asquith's sentiments were in agreement with this and he wrote to his daughter on her wedding day, 'We have never failed one another: thank God…you have always understood me and I believe I have understood you. It has been a perfect relationship…' (It was fun to note that quoted, in Clifford's book on the Asquiths, there was a pre-wedding letter from Margot to her stepdaughter where she raised the possibility of infidelity – hardly the moment to raise such an issue, unless it was on her mind of course!)

I now had more evidence of how the Prime Minister's daughter reacted when she was first shown her father's letters. Mary Soames was my written source. When Violet was first told of their existence she spent the next months in shock and 'her distress was palpable'. Violet, Soames reports, poured wrath on her son Mark Bonham Carter, who clearly did not understand why the letters had made his mother so angry. She wrote pleading letters to Mark, asking him not to publish their intimate details. She had been especially keen to avoid revealing that many had been written in Cabinet meetings. Violet's diary entry for 6 March 1964 supports Soames's words: 'I cannot believe that Mark could have contemplated publishing it [the letters of May 1915]. It is a betrayal of intimacies of private life second to none. I am appalled that anyone should have read them.'

The editor of Violet's diaries adds his own thoughts: 'Readers of this volume will be forced to conclude that Violet was a victim of selective memory or self-deception [when challenged by Jenkins]...there can be no escaping the written evidence that proves, almost beyond a shadow of a doubt, that Violet knew the truth at the time.' (John Grigg).

Grigg supports his belief by quoting Margot's letter (dated 7 June 1915) to Violet: 'Father is happier over Venetia's marriage though not converted – he thinks he would mind deeply, as he has been very much in love.' Grigg argues, 'It is inconceivable that Violet could have overlooked those words.' Margot, he writes, would not have written this if Violet was not fully aware of her father's love for Venetia.

I put myself in Violet's shoes. She had a formidable intellect and had been called by Colin Coote, a parliamentary reporter of those times, as 'the best politically equipped person who never went to parliament'. However Violet, when young, had no alternative but to be supportive to her father, even if she had known about the sexual nature of the affair. Later, when older, Violet seemed to be the sensible type who might have taken the young Louis under her wing. As he grew up, Violet may have recognised her responsibility as half-sister to Louis.

Violet did fall out with Venetia when she announced her engagement in May 1915. Years later their friendship was renewed, although they were never so close again. When Venetia was dying of cancer in 1948 Violet reminded her of their fun in Sicily in a draft letter: 'You were an inseparable part of those years shared with me, all the wild joys and black sorrows of Archie's death and *so* much else.'

Violet's published diaries were helpful in other ways. I discovered that Gilbert Murray had been great friends first with Raymond and then the rest of the Asquith family. Murray had been chairman of the League of Nations. That was another institution bandied about in my childhood. Murray was also known to have a soft heart. How much had he helped Louis? I found two supportive suggestions: 'It is well known that Murray was very tolerant and incapable of ruthlessness' and 'He always turned a deaf ear in the right direction.' I turned again to Stepfather's book on the Dorchester, where he claimed he worked with Murray over a period of months in 'a House of Commons committee room'. This led me to find another link in my chain of names, as the chairman of the authors of *Germany After the War*, Eric Drummond (Lord Perth), was the first Secretary General of the League of Nations. Not only this but he had been another parliamentary private secretary to Asquith.

Had Drummond, chair of the Committee on which Louis served, known all along about the illegitimate birth in 1912? Was he the one who had allowed Stepfather's name to be added to the report?

The most unexpected woman motivated the next exciting twist to my research. Her name was Helen Melland and she had been

Asquith's first wife. She had died some years before 1912, so I had not thought her worthy of any particular study, but my extended recreational reading was bearing fruit again, as I spotted she had hailed from Didsbury, a southern Manchester suburb. Now that I was more familiar with the area I instantly recognised that this village was a vital clue. I realised I should not have ignored the family Helen had left behind after her death. I kicked myself. Of course, Helen's father, Dr Frederick Melland, was the grandfather of Asquith's first five children. The children and their father would have kept close links with this eminent medical practitioner. Maps and relationships rang alarm bells. Louis would be the half-brother to Dr Melland's grandchildren. Had Melland been involved in the scheming? Perhaps he had attended the birth.

My fingers firmly gripped the mouse in anticipation as my computer slowly gained access to the 1861 census. Where had this good doctor resided? 'Park View, Didsbury Road, Rusholme'. I studied the map. The road was a stone's throw from where Alfred Applegate lived and was even closer to Brinks Way, where Auntie Mamie was born. Amazingly, on the 1889 map, close to the Mellands, were buildings called Stanley House and Stanley Villa and the road Stanley Grove.

But a feeling of unease came over me again. Had it been Dr Melland who had created the connection between the wealthy Stanleys, the Prime Minister and the poorer Applegates? Frederick Melland's obituary told me that he and Asquith maintained a close bond throughout their lives. Melland Sr, a keen Liberal, was a popular local dignitary, and through his large number of contacts helped create work for the unemployed by using them to construct a lake in the local park. His widest circle of friends was to be found among his old patients.

But the good doctor would have been 93 in 1911, probably too old to help directly. Had it been one of his two medically trained sons who had created the link? His elder son (Violet's cousin) set up a medical practice in Bowden, close to Venetia's home, while a younger son became a physician at the Ancoats Hospital in the poorest part of Manchester. It was built to serve those living and working in the cotton industry. Not far away was the impoverished suburb of Beswick. It was here that Mary Ann had lived with her parents after moving down from Carlisle. More research revealed that the Ancoats environs attracted the good works of the Methodists, the Salvation Army and Beatrice Webb. They had all worked to improve the lot of the destitute. Did I need to study these good works more?

I reassessed the life of Alfred Applegate, the hardworking warper who had lost two cotton-working wives. As we saw in Chapter 16, his first wife died of typhus fever after only 15 months of marriage. Typhus, at that time, was responsible for the deaths of many cotton workers and was spread by the body louse. The young Alfred was left to fend for his young baby of just eight months. A year later he married Mary Ann's mother, Mary Holmes. More tragedy was to hit him: two of their babies died before they were two, then his second wife fell ill with abdominal cancer and was dead by January 1886. He now had to care for five children on his own: Mary Ann, 15, Fred, 8, William, 7, Alfred James, 3, and Charles, a tiny baby. Seven years later Charles died. To gain medical treatment cotton workers in those days would have been dependent upon a charitable trust. Had the kind-hearted Melland doctors taken a special interest in the Applegate family?

Further map work now told me that the Mellands, the Applegates and the Stanleys all lived within ten miles of each other. In the early days of my research Rusholme, Didsbury, Reddish, Beswick and Cheadle Hulme had seemed like separate places. Now I knew they were all very close. Their identities have been swallowed up by the rapidly Manchester, but they were places of extremes. Rusholme was wealthy with a stylish theatre, while Cheadle Hulme and Reddish, where the extended Applegate family lived, had appalling housing and bedraggled tenants whose children toiled in the nearby mills.

Rusholme had always been an area of deep political unrest, the suffragette movement having started down the road from the Melland household. Many famous politicians have represented the area, including Churchill and Gladstone. It was in 1866 Gladstone voiced the now famous words showing his commitments to reform: 'I am come among you unmuzzled.' However the actual constituency was not created until 1923 and a name familiar to me from childhood – Charles Masterman – became its first MP. He was a Liberal, a friend of Asquith, and had taken a deep interest in the urban poor.

The fascination to me, though, was the MP who had served in the area prior to Masterman. He was called Robert Burdon Stoker. At first this meant nothing to me, but then I read his *Wikipedia* page. It gave me all the details I needed to know. Stoker had once been made a director of the Furness Withy shipping line, which was run by Kate Furness's uncle. So I had another connection: Stepfather's first wife's family had their own links with this part of Manchester.

I ferreted more. Asquith, a Nonconformist, had married Helen Melland in Rusholme Congregational Church. Lloyd George, coincidently born in this area, was also heavily influenced by the local Nonconformists.

I had more work to do. Michael and Eleanor Brock were the editors of the Asquithian book of letters to Venetia Stanley that had created such a furore in 1982, and, as they were both quite elderly, I decided I wanted to meet them. Michael had been a distinguished academic and warden of Nuffield College, Oxford. I arranged an interview.

Chapter 18

Digging Deeper

Michael Brock had recently moved to a sheltered home, where his room was stacked with rows of erudite books. He appeared a charming gentleman. His wife, who had helped edit the Asquithian letters, was out shopping. The table was laid for morning coffee and, as we chatted, he boiled the kettle in his kitchenette. After pleasantries he agreed to keep the conversation confidential. I explained that I was doing further research on the relationship between Asquith and Venetia. 'My dear,' he said, 'you can ask whatever you like and I hope I can be of assistance.' He brought over the coffee and biscuits; a spotless tablecloth covered the tray.

I moved quickly to my topic of interest. 'Did you think that the Bonham Carters held any letters back from you?' He looked slightly bemused, so I clarified my question. 'Do you think you were given all the letters?' I asked.

'I don't think the family has any more letters,' he replied, perhaps a little hesitantly.

'What do you think about the relationship? What about the possibility that it was sexual?' I continued. 'You suggest it wasn't in the introduction to your book. Can you tell me what makes you think that?'

He took the questions in good heart and with a kind of dry laugh replied, 'I'm not at all surprised with whatever is suggested these days. The things people get up to nowadays, it just wouldn't surprise me. Nothing would surprise me.'

He had not directly answered my question. So I took a deep breath and dug deeper. 'Well, what if I said I believe the relationship was sexual and I'm suggesting that there was a baby born from this relationship?'

I was not prepared for his visible shock. Even though he had been a leading academic he was only able to stutter, 'Well I can't comment on that – that's something I can't talk about...' There was a long pause while he struggled to compose himself. 'That's confidential to the' – he again paused for thought – 'the fam—' He didn't finish his sentence.

I was also startled. I had not expected such a telling response.

There was a long silence while he looked into space and I tried to work out what to ask next. Then in a kind manner he broke the silence: 'I think that's the end of the road for our discussions.' And with that he rose stiffly with a sigh from his chair. Once standing, he remembered his manners and continued in precise language, 'You can of course finish your coffee and I thank you for coming.' It was obvious the short meeting was over and he wanted me to depart. I had been there only ten minutes. His discomfort embarrassed me but I could not let this vital opportunity go by, so I asked, 'Oh, is there nothing else you can say?'

He was now on his guard and fidgeted while I drank. But I also needed time to think, so tried to slow my drinking, but it was no good. I had clearly unsettled him and he remained upright and silent. As I got up to leave his gentlemanly manners overcame his discomfort.

'I'm sorry I can't help you and I wish you well in your research.'

Still reeling from his clear discomfiture, I replied, 'Well, it's unfortunate. But I think you've answered my question.'

His embarrassment returned and he quickly turned his face away on the pretext of reaching for my coat. He spoke in almost a whisper, his eyes to the floor. 'Yes, I believe you have got your answer.'

I made as much use as I could of the few yards to his front door. After all, he had signed my confidentiality paper. 'Do you know the name Louis Stanley?' I asked as we reached the door.

'Louis Stanley,' he repeated. He manoeuvred himself around the door so that I could not see his face. 'No...I don't think that name means anything to me.' It was a slow, measured response. He was now acting much more like a learned professor, so, from the tone of his voice, I wasn't sure what he was really thinking.

I later discovered that Michael Brock had been a zealous member of the Liberal Party and a close friend of the Bonham Carters.

On my drive back home I thought of the unpublished letters held at the Bodleian Library but securely closed to any prying eyes until the year 2015. What did they contain? Who knew what they could reveal?

I went back to speculating. Where might more evidence come from? I still needed to discover what Louis Thomas Stanley's lifestyle was like in his twenties and thirties – it seemed so mysterious.

My studies were not like regular research. I had turned into a sleuthing detective in the Hercule Poirot mould. I was constantly retracing my footsteps. Once I retrieved a new snippet of information I had to retrace my readings, observations and map work. Information that was skimmed over or did not seem relevant on a first read often became more pertinent once a new detail in his background became available. I was ducking and weaving through piles of paperwork.

I contacted the BBC to see if they could tell me which years Louis had featured on the show *The Brains Trust*. Eventually the corporation found his name. He had been on the programme just the once, in May 1949. I was disappointed that they no longer had the recordings but found that the first official *Brains Trust* had been broadcast from Winchester in September 1948 and Violet had been on that first panel. (The programme had originally been broadcast on the Forces radio service from 1941). Something made me look further. I was rewarded. In May 1949 Violet had been due to be on the panel but was indisposed. Had a half-sister given her illegitimate brother the chance to be part of the programme?

Stepfather had written more than sixty works. Most of them, I was sure, would have little of interest to me. The attraction of his writing appears to be that he was hard-hitting and controversial. In his early golf writing he gave tips on avoiding scheming females in golf clubs' social areas: these female golfers, he said, were 'designing women making their last bid to avoid spinsterhood. They know nothing about golf and care even less...Every one of these females is a potential threat to a bachelor.'

And his yearly Grand Prix books attracted the motoring correspondent for *The Times* to write '...this swarthy writer snaps and snipes fearlessly at everyone...calling the BBC commentators "a pastiche of vapidity" ' (1963).

This same review confirmed that he had attacked my Uncle Alfred in print. What prompted him to be so rude about his brother-in-law? But maybe, as another *Times* correspondent wrote, he just loved to ridicule others: 'Louis Stanley's stripping of the Grand Prix scene creates (among those who dare admit it) more tremors than a Cape Kennedy blast off.'

Did I need to read more of Stepfather's books?

I had skimmed through his title *Public Masks and Private Lives* earlier but found nothing to arouse my suspicions. But with new evidence one of his subjects took on a whole new meaning. The name was Viscount (Herbert Louis) Samuel (1870–1963). It was not a name I remembered from my childhood but Louis maintained he was one of his earliest friends. I researched.

Of course, Samuel was a Liberal, in a cotton-town constituency. He was selected by Asquith to be the first practising Jew to serve in any British cabinet. He later became Home Secretary and in 1931 leader of the Liberal Party.

Louis's written words on the man mesmerised me: 'I recall a day when Lord Samuel, who was one of my sponsors for The Royal Institute for International Affairs, lunched with me in Oxford.' I recalled my initial call to the esteemed office of the club. They had told me Stepfather had never been a member. Had something gone wrong with his sponsorship?

Another thought was far more compelling. Viscount Samuel was Edwin Montagu's cousin. It was their grandfather who had swapped their surname around from Samuel to Montagu all those years before.

The elder cousin was born in the family home in smart Belvedere in the eastern part of Liverpool but, when his father died, Edwin's dad became his guardian. Samuel went on to appreciate his uncle's religious fervour and became the venerated leader of the English Jewry.

More connections with Stepfather appeared when I found Samuel had been a regular contributor on the original wartime *Brains Trust*. There I found another familiar name: Bertrand Russell. This philosopher (and Venetia's cousin) had been on the same programme.

However, I soon found a third reason to be spellbound by names from the past – Trevelyan. Another of those names that pleased my auditory sense – 'Trevelyan' sounded like a huge bounding dog to my childish ears. Previously, the connection with the family name had been slim: George M. Trevelyan, the Cambridge historian, was the author of a biography of Asquith's colleague Grey. But the Cambridge link had been a distraction, and it was his brother who was the key.

Charles Trevelyan MP and Cabinet member served as a parliamentary secretary to the Board of Education and was Lord Samuel's best friend. Again I backtracked and more delving produced more enticing links. Charles married Gertrude Bell's younger sister, Mary, another of Venetia's cousins.

If Stepfather claimed to be a 'founder member' of The Royal Institute of International Affairs, it was time to visit the club's library in St James's Square. My own search found he had indeed been a member of this esteemed club but he had not told the full truth. He had joined only in 1957 and not as a 'founder member', as this involved parting with a considerable amount of money. The club's librarian told me that the Institute prides itself on its inclusion of people who come from all walks of political life, but I could not work out why Louis had not joined until 1957 when Gilbert Murray had been his proposer. Why had he claimed Viscount Samuel was involved in his membership?

Stepfather dedicated his book *People, Places and Pleasures* to my mother. But his *Life in Cambridge*, published in 1953, was dedicated to his father: 'To my father whose love of Cambridge was greater even than my own'. For a second I was thrown but then I realised he could have written the dedication to impress my mother, whom he would have just met. Mum would have told him of her love for her own father. It would have been typical of Stepfather to try to copy her and tell her how much he had loved his 'father'. In those years he would have been grooming her.

I was speculating again as to why Louis, at nearly ninety, had published the book *Vignettes and Memories: Reflections from a Cambridge Drawing Room*. Was it a 'safe' version of his autobiography? It appeared unedited tripe to me. But, as I had found useful material in his book on the Dorchester Hotel, I steeled myself to read his last published work. I wondered if I might be able to read it in a new light now that I knew he was a compulsive fibber. The blurb claimed that his 'professional, social and sporting activities have brought him into contact with a phenomenal number of well-known figures' and claimed he had entertained 'celebrities from all walks of life'. Yes, I thought. I can remember poor Mum over the hot gas stove. She did the preparations, the cooking and clearing up all by herself, unless one of us children was there to help.

The first question was: why had Stepfather hobnobbed with prominent clergymen?

Perseverance in sleuthing had led me to believe that Louis had studied at a clerical institution in Edinburgh called Coates Hall. This fitted in with his professed Scottish period and his boast that he had once lived in the Caledonian Hotel. In his book he maintained he had been on close terms with an Edinburgh theology professor called Brasnett. I sought an expert on the Scottish Episcopalian Church, who told me that Coates Hall had been a training establishment for wealthy Englishmen who were interested in entering the Church. On further questioning the expert advised me Brasnett took on well-connected students and tutored them in order for them to enter an Oxbridge college. I speculated again. If he had been educated 'at home' this all seemed quite likely.

However, Louis also claimed he had worked on ecclesiastical committees with Bishops Bell and Temple and other religious dignitaries. What was he doing on these committees? Lambeth Palace could not answer my queries.

I decided it was his chapter on statesmen and political characters that would be the most fertile, as he tried to make out he had been a weighty political figure himself and asserted that he had attended the signing of the Austrian Peace Treaty in 1955. Why was Louis there? What had he done to be part of these celebrations? Again, for a second, I wondered whether he had been a foreign diplomat. Had he been keeping his light under a bushel? I came to my senses. He was not the kind of man to do that. Then I found the assertion that he attended the tenth anniversary of the Untied Nations in San Francisco. How did he do this? Had he worked for the United Nations? Louis also claimed that the Russian Embassy had arranged his meeting with Molotov, the ghoulish foreign secretary of the Soviet Union. None of his claims made any sense. He was tricking the reader in some way but I could not work out how.

The text appeared like an old man's delusions of grandeur and to me such nonsense that I decided I needed another view. My friend Maggie was able to distance herself and told me the book read like an old-fashioned version of *Hello!* magazine or the William Hickey/Nigel Dempster column – packed with sexual innuendoes. Maybe this was my answer. Louis had been a gossip columnist. That would certainly explain many of his boasts. Was that why he attended those august meetings? The photograph he published in his book on the Dorchester Hotel – had I missed a clue? It had been taken on Prince Philip's stag night. The royal party had played a 'fun' role-reversal game. They had taken the assembled press members' cameras and taken snaps of the photographers. Louis was one of those men.

The royal wedding now interested me, as Stepfather gloated he had attended, and implied he was a dignitary. The Windsor Castle records helped. A childhood mystery had been solved. He had not been a dignitary himself: he had only reported on them. My theory was confirmed when an airline faxed me the list of dignitaries on the inaugural flight of a commercial plane from LA to Copenhagen over the North Pole. Stepfather had always been so proud of this trip and showed us a photograph of himself beside the plane. The fax confirmed that his name had not been on the guest list but there were two places reserved for a photographer and a reporter from the magazine *Newsweek*.

I went back to The Royal Institute of International Affairs' record books. Louis's 'phenomenal list' of celebrities had all been members. Edwin Montagu had been one of its first members when it was formed in 1920.

But there was still the mystery of his movements in wartime. I worked on a new theory. Had his photographic skills been useful to the intelligence? He certainly knew how to develop his own films and that strange postbox at Emmanuel College still intrigued me. Why had he kept it so long after he had graduated?

I crisscrossed back to Stepfather's chapter on literary artists. How had Louis known so many men of letters? Mystified, I looked at more closely at the life of Malcolm Muggeridge and discovered he was responsible for writing morale-boosting articles in 1939. Finally I had the link. All those on his literary list worked for the intelligence services in wartime. During the conscription period those men with the 'right contacts' and 'standing' were dragooned into the Intelligence Corps. They were trained in the craft for the first year or two of the war, then posted to MI5, M16 or other 'M' departments. So maybe Stepfather had been trained in snooping in 1940 and 1941 and then sent to Cambridge University to spy on others. Whom had he spied on: undergraduates or dons? I contacted the leading spy expert Philip Knightley. He thought it was highly probable that a man 'studying' theology and matriculating in 1942 would have been a spy. His email explained more: 'There are lots of precedents for M15 planting people in universities to report on the political persuasion and activities of fellow students. John Le Carré has admitted he did that himself.'

Muggeridge's own memoirs expand on the 'fun' he had in early wartime. He had so little work that he enjoyed London's nightlife, while the memoirs of the writer Compton Mackenzie (another of Stepfather's names) amusingly tell of the dense cloud of intelligence officers who had little to do but sleuth each other. However, in June 1942, the intelligence services were tightened and Muggeridge was sent abroad. Had Stepfather in the same year been sent to spy on those at Trinity College, a breeding ground for double agents? The master of the college was the historian George Macaulay Trevelyan. The other strange name Stepfather had occasionally mentioned just by surname had been Masterman. At first I thought the connection must be the Liberal MP of the

1920s, Charles Masterman, but then I found another famous Masterman. This time his forename was John and he had been head of MI5 in wartime.

So perhaps Stepfather used Cambridge as a base for his spying exploits around the country. Was this when his appalling 'traffic accident' occurred? It seemed so strange that in the world of motor racing he spent his time in the passenger seat. The 'special' postbox at Emmanuel for Stepfather must have originally been an intelligence dropbox. I asked my cousins, who had also studied at the college. Maybe they could dig deeper than I. But the brick wall was still in place. The authorities were not going to reveal anything about this past student. However, the registrar's written reply got me thinking: why had she and the Master been invited up to the Old Mill House only months before Louis died? This was odd. Were there papers that needed attention? I had further confirmation when I discovered that Edwin's nephew, Ewen, had been the naval intelligence officer who organised Operation Mincemeat, the plot to deceive the enemy with a dead body. Montagu had first written up the story in his book called *The Man Without A Name* in 1953.

The author of the famous adventure novel *The Thirty-Nine Steps* had come up in my reading. John Buchan was friendly with Raymond Asquith while up at Oxford. Gilbert Murray, as a young don, was an important part of their social group. It was at this time that HH Asquith wanted to join with his elder children's social life.

As I tossed and turned in bed one night I recalled my son Rupert coming to me after he had looked through a haul of videos that I had bought from the sale of goods from the Old Mill House at an isolated East Anglian saleroom, as Stepfather seemed intent on denying our inheriting any family mementos. They had sold for a song and my children were delighted to have a few mementos of life with 'Granny'.

Rupert anxiously told me he had found a note pushed into the *Thirty-Nine Steps* video case. Doreen, the last nurse, had scribbled, 'Do not show this film. Mr Stanley gets very sad.' At the time I had been too traumatised to bother about the significance of the note that had fallen from the box but now I wondered if it took on a whole new meaning. Why this video? I feel that the story is worth recording.

At Christmas, when Stepfather was away from the room, my mother liked to play this classic film. He did not choose to watch it. So she huddled up to her grandchildren pretending to be as frightened as they were as the hero, Richard Haney, ran over the moors of Scotland. I thought, why had the film made him particularly sad? Had he always refused to watch the film when we were younger because it reminded him of his early life?

Maybe John Buchan helped Louis find a job in the intelligence services. Buchan had helped both J. B. Priestly and T. E. Lawrence (both names on Louis's list) to do just this. More reading bore fruit. This famous author had lived in Fife, Asquith's constituency, and had been hired to write for the Prime Minister's First World War Propaganda Bureau under Beaverbrook. There were other connections: Buchan must have known Professor Brasnett in Edinburgh, for the Scottish author liked to keep in touch with young people in the town's many educational establishments when he was the Liberal MP for the Scottish Universities. Buchan's biographer details how he kept in touch with his previous Great War intelligence contacts and would 'occasionally pass on the name of a suitable recruit'. Further links were even more exciting: Edwin Montagu's nephew, Ivor, was associate producer on the famous 1935 film of *The Thirty-Nine Steps* and Buchan worked with Anthony Asquith (Puffin), the last of HH's legitimate sons and a notable film director, when he was appointed to the Board of Directors of British Instructional Films. I had rather ignored studying Puffin because he was much younger than the other four sons.

By some strange coincidence I picked up *Life Around My Father* by Penny Junor, the daughter of John Junor, a former editor of the *Sunday Express*, for relaxation. This book helped me to understand Louis's life better. John Junor had come from a relatively poor home and when he was 11, so that he could earn some cash, he became a caddy for the wealthy guests at Turnberry Hotel. At night Junor used to press his face against the windows of the hotel and watch the rich and famous. These nightly events drove his ambitions. Was this how Louis learned golf? Had he as a small boy carried the clubs for the wealthy players at the Royal Liverpool Golf Club? If he had been educated at home he would have had plenty of time to do so.

The name of the MP Duncan Sandys, a Cabinet minister, and the actor Douglas Fairbanks had been bandied about in my childhood. Disturbingly, I found that both had been involved in a sex scandal in the 1960s. This famous case, discussed in the House of Commons, concerned a compromising photograph of the married Duchess of Argyll, who was involved in what was described as a 'disgusting sexual practice'. The national interest in the photograph was the head that had been cut off to prevent identification. The case was investigated by Lord Denning for the government, and he found that there was not just one man but two in the sexually explicit photograph. The men were found to be none other than Sandys and Fairbanks. I also found that Sandys had married into the Churchill family and one of Fairbanks's ex-wives (he had four) married Venetia's nephew in 1940. So Stepfather's seedy and sorry connections with names from my childhood came alive again.

I broadened my search on the Applegate lineage. Could the footprints of the ancestors of Mary Ann give me any rationale as to why Venetia Stanley had selected her as the trusted foster mother? I was convinced both the Asquith camp and her own parents would have given the choice considerable thought.

I had resisted making rash judgements when it came to place names, but now I knew I had been too harsh on myself when it came to distances. So many of the names of the communities I had discovered in documents were so close they all merged into the urban sprawl of Manchester and Stockport. Cheap public transport, mainly in the form of trams or trains, could also take workers from one part of the conurbation to another. Reddish, a suburb of Stockport, had been a thriving cotton city with two huge mills, and it was here the extended Applegate family lived in the nineteenth century. So now I could turn my attention to the yearly directories that local libraries usually stock. I was to study them alongside the regional and historical maps.

On the 1908 Ordnance Survey map I found that Oxford Street, the home of Alfred Applegate, was the same thoroughfare as Oxford Road. Since the Peterloo Massacre it had been a place of political unrest and Oxford Street was extended to improve communications to Rusholme, where the Mellands lived.

Then I made another geographical discovery. So many times I had been slow to spot the significance of the county of Lancashire. Now I knew why. Stockport was historically part of Cheshire, but the boundary between the two counties ran through the built-up suburbs. No wonder I had been slow to see the significance of some of the early census returns. To add further confusion, Reddish, the Applegate family's hometown, had agreed to change from Manchester's to Stockport's jurisdiction. Reddish desperately needed new drains and Stockport was willing to improve the town's sanitation in return for some cotton wealth. So it was little wonder I was confused about boundaries.

The history of Manchester had not appeared relevant but now I was also learning more about the poor of the city. The industrial heart of Manchester had been a place of division between the great wealth of the cotton owners and their poor workers. Conditions deteriorated when there was a cotton famine in the early twentieth century. Thousands had been out of work with hundreds sleeping rough in the brickfields. It was reported that some were so destitute the men searched for human bones from burial sites and ground them up for flour. With squalid housing, extreme poverty and a high death rate Manchester was compared to the Dickensian East End of London. Many of the aristocratic wealthy families felt the need to do 'good' works in the most densely developed industrial landscape in the world. The cotton-producing area of Ancoats was the most deprived. Reddish, the home of the Applegates, was just as destitute. It grew so fast it had six times more people in 1901 than in 1861.

In the cotton famine of the 1870s nearby Stockport (not yet having included Reddish in its boundaries) was the most affected town. With so many families evicted from their homes for failure to pay rent, the town became the subject of a grim national joke and was called 'Stockport to let'.

I had not appreciated how destitute some of the Applegate family must once have been. In the mid-nineteenth century Engels, the famous socialist, was appalled by the conditions he found in Stockport. Alfred and his family lived, as Engels described, in 'one of the duskiest smokiest holes in the whole of the industrial area...even cottages and cellar dwellings of the workers are unpleasant to look at' (*The Condition of Working Class in England*, 1844).

Years later things had not improved much. In 1901 Alfred still lived in a deprived area with closely packed housing close to two cotton mills, each one employing nearly 500 workers. Alfred's relatives lived in the nearby roads, where there was a large brick factory.

Which of the Applegate relatives should I study in more depth? I reminded myself that Mary Ann had been born in 1870. Her elder half-sister was seven years older, while her brother Fred was seven years younger. Another brother had died when young but, from the information on the censuses, Mary had another two brothers: William (eight years younger) and Alfred

James (thirteen years younger). I thought about the family logistics and pondered.

It was time to send for more birth and marriage certificates. It was brother Fred's family that produced the juicy reward. The one-time unemployed Fred married a 23-year-old local woman. Their eldest child was called Mary Eliza Applegate! Could this be my 'Auntie Mamie'? I already knew this was an unusual combination of forenames. Did I finally have a vital link between the two women who had lived in my childhood house? Could it be that the woman I had dismissed as irrelevant to my search might just be the pearl?

Sure enough, when the birth documentation arrived there was the confirmation: Auntie Mamie, that annoying woman who had been so dippy and driven us all mad, had been born into Fred's family on 28 May 1898 at Jackdaw Court, Brinks Way, Stockport. Auntie Mamie had been Mary Ann's niece!

Before I found Fred's family, the only documentation I had on Auntie Mamie was her death certificate. It had recorded her correct day and month of birth (28 May), but it stated she was born in 1900, and in Wallasey, not Stockport. So Mamie had been two years older than Stepfather had told the registrar. Had Stepfather purposefully lied to the registrar at the time of her death? Or perhaps he never knew the truth. Then I recalled that Stepfather claimed she was his 'cousin' on her death certificate, so, if he had really been born into the Applegate family, this part of the certificate would have been true.

I noted that Fred's marriage had been a shotgun affair, as they wed in January and Mary Eliza had been born only four months later. The couple went on to have at least five more children.

Had Mary Eliza moved in with Mary Ann to help her aunt when the baby was small in 1911 or 1912? It would be an exciting venture for a 13-year-old girl about to leave school. Maybe Fred was keen to lighten the load of his growing family and was happy for one mouth fewer to feed?

Fred's details had originally not been important to my searches but, now that I knew he had been the father of the jewel to my sleuthing, Auntie Mamie, I devoured his census entries. He had been registered as unemployed in 1891; ten years later he was recorded as working as a brickmaker. My history books told me there was a wave of unemployment of brickies in 1903–4. With so many thousands sleeping rough, there was a regional outcry, so Fred must always have been living on the breadline. Perhaps Fred received aid from the Wood Street Mission, whose base was just around the corner from where he and his father lived. The mission was started to help relieve the suffering of the poor in the area.

When did Mary Eliza drop her Applegate surname and become known as Mamie Stanley? Why did she change her name? My mind went to Venetia. Why did she want her baby to keep her family name? Was it easier to create a trust fund if the offspring took her surname? Or was this cocky aristocratic behaviour?

Interestingly, in the Cheshire Kelly's Directory for 1914 a 'Miss Stanley' is recorded as living at 22 School Lane, Heaton Chapel, just around the corner from Oxford Street, where Alfred and his second wife Jessie were living. Was this Mamie or perhaps even Mary Ann? Maybe Mary Ann stayed in Stockport in those early years of 'motherhood' to be near her family. I was speculating again. Perhaps Jessie, the longstanding Glaswegian stepmother of Mary Ann, had encouraged her to take in the baby when the cotton industry was in steep decline. I could not help wondering if Stepfather, as a child, had known 'Uncle' Fred and his other 'cousins'. Had he continued to visit when he got older? Stepfather was at his most authoritative when we talked about Stockport or Wilmslow. He knew best when it came to this part of Manchester. That was fine with me, because I certainly knew nothing about the place; but, looking back, I realise that his authority did seem strange. Was I detecting a tinge of nervousness when a brother of mine moved near and started to be more knowledgeable?

There was another mystery. I could not find Alfred's death

certificate. My genealogist and I could not find his death registered anywhere. It was of no great importance, but as the search went on, it became more mysterious. Eventually, after months of frustration, we realised he must have been recorded as Frederick Alfred Applegate. For some unknown reason his wife Jessie had recorded him dead with the wrong name! Was this a strange slip by the grieving Jessie or was it part of the mystery? Why had she added the forename Frederick?

Once again, I took stock of my reasoning. Louis Thomas Stanley was born earlier than his birth certificate states, in late 1911, possibly at Penrhos. He perhaps was not expected to live, so the family delayed registering his birth. Asquith/Stanley found Mary Ann and agreed a cover story after a trip made to Sicily. They registered Louis in a house not yet completed to stop gossip, invented a cotton merchant father to fit in with Mary Ann's background. Edwin set up a trust fund with his brother-in-law, Walter Louis D'Arcy Hart.

Mary Ann perhaps not responsible for Stepfather until he was six months or older. She later moved to the Wirral area, maybe in a house owned by the Stanleys – first Rake Road, then Seabank Road, both in the Liscard area, so that Louis could walk to Somerville Preparatory School. He was sent first to Winchester College but was bullied about his illegitimacy, so, in order for him to attend Birkenhead School, Mary Ann moved to Hoyle Road. Then, either because of more bullying or through lack of funds, he was later educated at home. At some stage in his early education he was sent to Edinburgh.

Louis played golf at an early age, as Mary Ann herself liked the sport, perhaps first hitting a ball at Lytham St Annes. Being tutored at home, he had time to hone his golf skills by caddying for the elite members of his local club. During this time he met Venetia in London. Louis was impressed with her high-flying lifestyle. She got her son a job with her lover's newspaper as a photographer. He perhaps used his photographic skills in wartime. He progressed to writing articles on high society in the vein of William Hickey. Through this he met many celebrities.

He met his first wife at a party at the Dorchester Hotel. When war came he became a member of the intelligence services, perhaps working for the London Controlling Office based in the same hotel; then perhaps he was sent to spy.

At the hotel he was introduced to many Liberal dignitaries, easing his way into the team writing the pamphlet *Germany After the War*. He may have wanted to become a politician but with his background this was too risky. He inherited money from Venetia but blew it.

The earlier Stanley–Asquith trust enabled Mary Ann, Mary Eliza and Stepfather to live in the large semidetached house in Hoylake, but when Stepfather turned thirty the trust fund ceased. In 1942, when he was supposed to be studying for a theology degree, he moved his so-called 'mother' and 'sister' to Cambridge and bought them a flat with the help of his first wife's funds. Then, when he was penniless in the 1950s, he had two female mouths to feed, so he moved them into my mother's house.

CHAPTER 19

HOW HAD HE ACHIEVED THE IMPOSSIBLE?

Now that it is a few years since my mother's reburial I can retell my dispute with the Church with more dispassion, but my quarrel with the Home Office remains sore.

Initially I had asked lots of questions. What was the role of the Church in this reburial? Why had the rector been allowed to perform it? Was this normal behaviour? Even though I was not brought up as such, I was a clergyman's daughter. Would my father have agreed to undertake such a dastardly act?

I rang David, my cousin's husband, who was a retired cleric, and asked him what he thought.

'Bobbie,' he said, 'In my view, thinking priests would never have done such a thing. Reverend Ambrose should've known it was morally wrong not to consult with you. I really think he should have rung his superiors for advice. A secret reburial was against the Church of England's policy.'

'I just don't understand why he did it,' I cried, 'I am even more perplexed about his silence.'

'Well I don't know either,' replied David, 'But I do know Ambrose also read theology at Emmanuel College.'

'What?' I exclaimed.

'Yes, he told me in the vestry at your mother's funeral.'

My mind went back to the dark hours in my mother's kitchen the night she died. Ambrose and I had sat at the old kitchen table drinking brandy as I told him once again of my terrible experiences with my stepfather. When he left to cycle home as dawn was breaking, he had wound the once familiar navy scarf with fuchsia stripes around his neck.

David's voice jerked me out of my trance. 'I think you should pursue his inability to apologise,' he said.

'But how?' I asked.

'Start with the parish's churchwardens,' he suggested, 'though I must warn you: the Church will probably close ranks.'

An opportunity soon presented itself because I wanted to visit my mother's grave on her birthday. I asked if Ambrose could say a prayer over the grave after the morning service, explaining that I wanted to be sure she was at peace. He agreed.

I waited by the new grave but, instead of coming over as agreed, he crossed the gravel and entered the vicarage. After waiting probably half an hour I went to his front door and reminded him of his promise. He hesitantly followed me out but his words of platitude made no reference to her new resting place or her eternal peace, as I had requested. Why could he not even say a few words over my mother's grave that might help me come to terms with her displacement?

The next time I visited Trumpington I searched for the list of churchwardens. Hidden among old notices only one churchwarden, and that was the vicar's wife! I went back to my cousin for advice.

'Well, that tells you something,' said David. 'You'll have to go to his superior, the archdeacon.'

I was only just beginning to learn how the Church of England operated.

As I dialled the number of the archdeacon, the rain started to come down in torrents. During the initial platitudes I noticed my gutters were unable to cope with the unusually heavy flow of water, so I hurried got to the point of my call to this stranger.

'I'd like to tell you a story and ask your reaction.'

After my outline he responded in a fusty but friendly voice. 'That's certainly a very unfortunate story. Is there something I can do? Would you like to tell me the name of the vicar involved?'

My mood changed from hope to despair in seconds as the archdeacon made no immediate response. After my chivvying, he managed to speak these words: 'I expect you've experienced his quick temper.'

'No,' I answered, 'but he doesn't seem to comprehend what he's done to our family. I'd like you to ask him why he agreed to do this.'

'I'll try,' he mumbled.

'How can I tell my children that their grandmother's not in the place where they buried her?' I explained. 'All her family were there at her graveside. Then, in the middle of some dark night, she was dug up and secretly reburied. It was, as you say, gruesome. I don't…' I felt tears well up, but I managed to finish the sentence. 'I don't want this to happen to any other family.'

'Rest assured. This could never happen again, my dear.' He had changed to a soothing tone. 'My dear'! Do all clerics fob their parishioners off with false endearments?

'But it did happen, and so it could again,' I cried.

As I put the phone back in its cradle the water was still overflowing down the outside of the downpipes rather than staying within them. The archdeacon had promised to speak with Ambrose and then get back to me as soon as he could.

I heard nothing for three weeks. So I rang him. This time he was not forthcoming. 'Th-there's little I can do,' he said, 'even though I'm his superior. It may sound stupid, but he has a freehold in that parish. If he decides to ignore me he can do so. He has not broken Church law.'

'What about writing me a note of apology?'

'He w-won't do that. In his eyes he has done nothing wr-wr-wrong'. The stuttering got worse.

Nothing wrong! I couldn't believe my ears. What about his moral duty?

'There is n-n-nothing more I can do.' He clearly wanted to finish the call.

'You were so friendly and so helpful until I told you the name of the vicar. You now sound frightened of talking with him.' By now I was really irate.

'He tells me he was t-tricked,' he added.

'So you've to warn others. This mustn't happen again,' I insisted. 'All vicars should be notified.' Meanwhile, the archdeacon was becoming repetitive and I was becoming more frustrated.

'The vicar w-w-wouldn't like it,' he said.

'But my mother's body was dug up in the dead of night like some petty murderer!' I shouted down the phone.

'If you insist I can write a paragraph in the diocese's newsletter,' he said helplessly.

My only option was to accept; I waited for the promised copy. No newsletter arrived. Once again, I made chivvying phone calls to the archdeacon's office.

He had changed his mind again. 'The vicar in question is allowed some privacy in this matter,' was his retort.

'You're condoning his behaviour! I want to speak to the archbishop,' I said outraged.

'He's abroad, and anyway you will be asked to speak to the bishop first.'

'OK, so I'll speak to the bishop.'

'He's also on holiday.'

I had reached the end of my tether. 'Our family is deeply distressed and you're not taking any action against a vicar who agreed to not only a bizarre act but a morally wrong one. I'll just have to go the press. I think the *Cambridge Evening News* would be a good start.'

At that a swift appointment was organised with the Bishop of Ely. At last I was given time to put my case.

As the bespectacled bishop sat in his winged chair I retold my story.

'The religious ceremony of my mother's first burial has been undone,' I chanted. 'Each of her living relatives, both young and old, had thrown the blessed red earth down into her grave.'

I then told him of the family importance of plucking the water lily from her childhood home. 'That cherished flower and those soil crumbs have been unceremoniously flung aside. To add insult to injury, she was reburied alone.'

The bishop tried not to show his shock but took the same line as the archdeacon. Reverend Ambrose had not broken Church law so there was little he could do. It was then that he explained that, as a Church body, they have little power of redress over parishes that hold a freehold.

This helped explain their inability to act, but provided no reason why they could not write some words of caution for the clergy in the diocese. Surely they could reprimand Ambrose. Again, I received a promise that an advisory notice would be written in the diocesan newsletter. However, true to form, it took another two phone calls to remind his office that the publication had not been printed. When it finally came, the long-awaited announcement was tame and obtuse.

At the same time I had been battling with the Home Office. At the beginning of 2004 I felt my life was beginning to get back to normal. The shock of the reburial had lessened. The 6th of January came and went and I reflected on the effort over the years I had put into helping my mother make it a special day for Stepfather.

Three days later I received a call from a brusque South African woman telling me that Louis was dead. At the age of 92, he had died suddenly. As she spoke, I looked out of a frost-covered window. My emotions were numb. Relief that he had finally gone came later. No longer would he order our flowers to be removed from the newly dug grave. Nor would he be able to tie me in emotional knots.

However, there were still questions to be asked. What about his funeral? What would happen to Old Mill House? The day after his death I began to be a little irrational. Was I really free of this stepfather of mine, or could it be a deception?

I decided there was only one way to put the demons to bed, and that was to go and see Stepfather's dead body. Perhaps I could get some of his DNA before it was too late. Maybe one day I could get proof of my theory. I learned that to get DNA I had to pull out a hair root or cut off one of Louis's nails. I had nightmares for days, wondering if I could do such a thing. I had only seven days to decide.

Meanwhile, a stranger rang me up claiming to be another of Louis Stanley's new solicitors. This would be the third in two years. He rang to tell me they were planning to put Louis's body in my mother's grave. The huge weight of weariness returned. The man was dead but his phantom could still disturb me. Stepfather's brain had worked on a different plane from ours, which meant he could always be one crucial move ahead. In a grotesque twist Stepfather had already secretly organised with Reverend Ambrose that his own name be added to my mother's headstone even though he was still alive! He had planned for us to pay homage to him when we visited our mother's grave. The written words disturbed us in our grief. There was no alternative but to allow the words to remain on our mother's stone, as we had a more pressing battle. The difficult vicar was demanding that Louis be buried on top of our mother. We were not going to have this. Numerous lengthy exchanges between the family and the dreaded duo of the new lawyer and vicar seemed to be getting us nowhere. Our desire to visit our own mother's grave without being reminded of the very man who had dishonestly removed her body from her beloved Sutton Coldfield seemed lost on both the lawyer and vicar. But eventually we won through, as Stepfather's own last will and testament asked for him to be buried beside, not on top of, my mother.

This family fight gave me renewed strength to visit the undertakers and witness his dead body. The ghost needed to be exorcised from my mind. But I wanted moral support. So I rang up nurse Pauline. She kindly made the arrangements and we agreed to meet up in the village of Linton. She would be equipped with rubber gloves, nail clippers and sample bags. Remembering the past, I wondered if the undertaker thought it a little odd that I wanted to see his body. I did not get a good night's sleep. Would Stepfather rise from the marble table and greet me like the corpses in the Hammer horror films? But surely this was the last unpleasant task in my long saga.

Greeted in the yard by the undertaker's son, we crossed the yard to the converted outhouse without further ado. There was an unusually high stone step into the purple-shrouded room. Louis's body had been placed in the first stall. One section of the flimsy plum curtains had been pulled back to expose the upper part of his cumbersome body. The boy departed and left us alone with the dead suited giant. His gross colourless nose grabbed my attention. The stretched skin took years off his age but it was a sallow, sulphurous colour, almost jaundiced. I stood and stared. Was it the cold that made me shiver? Pauline pulled down the blanket that was hiding his huge hands. The nails were too short to be cut further. It had to be the hairs, she whispered, and I had to extract them! I did not want to know whether taking hairs from a cadaver was legal or not. I just knew I had to touch his cold body and pull at least one out. Pauline was more controlled and started to peel open the surgical gloves. But as she pulled them apart a piercing tearing noise echoed around the chapel of rest. We stared at each other horrified. Would we be rumbled? She indicated that we would not be able to use the gloves because of the noise they made. I would have to clutch his hairs with my fingers. On my first attempt I tried to pull a hair out without touching his head. That was never going to work. Time was passing and I still had nothing to show for it. As I pulled again the door opened and strong boots climbed the step. We exchanged worried glances.

'We'll just be a little longer,' Pauline said to the undertaker's assistant, her voice calm and controlled.

I knew I had one last chance to pull hard enough to yank a root out of his decaying skull. I was now able to touch his head, but whoever had laid him out had made his hair all slimy. So the more I pulled the more my fingers slipped. The undertaker spoke and our time had run out.

No funeral is pleasant and this one I knew would be tough, but if I wanted to shut the door on this chapter in my life I had to attend. As the day drew near I realised I felt a certain fascination to see who might attend. My children were angry that I should even have contemplated attending, but when my son Rupert quizzed me about Louis's deceit over Granny's reburial he was so angry he vowed to escort me.

Once again I approached the drive to Cambridge with a sense of the unknown. What would happen at his funeral? Surely this really was the last hurdle. I found the whole occasion so soon after my mother's reburial harder than I had anticipated. Jackie Stewart was surprised to find he was the only representative from the world of motor racing, although the wreath from Bernie Ecclestone was grossly massive. I wondered whether Barbara, the woman he had rung late at night, was there. I had since discovered that she had been the manager of one of the shops in the hallway of the Dorchester Hotel. I did not want to meet this floozy, as I had been told she was the cause of mother's stroke. My mother had become all flustered by Stepfather's behaviour in London that fateful morning. The driver who had driven them to London had overheard their conversation. Stepfather must have promised my mother he would never visit her again, but Mum had caught him out. Her suffering over two very long years had been brought on by Stepfather's infidelities.

Louis's wake was held at a hotel on the bank of the River Cam close to the graduate building that had once snubbed his application to join. Ambrose once again officiated at the service.

I feared greatly for what might happen to the beloved Old Mill House, as now we had a stranger dealing with Louis's affairs, and, as we had suspected, he had drawn up a daft will. It was open-ended, so the executors could do what they liked, and Stepfather had asked for what remained of my mother's money to be left to unnamed charities, which was his last joke, because he had hated all charities, calling them all scams. However, when the solicitor turned to me and revealed that Ambrose had asked for £10,000 from Louis Stanley's will for new church toilets I was offended. The vicar's behaviour had seemed so illogical: even if he had been taken in by Louis's amazing persuasive powers, surely he should have listened to his parishioner's children. How had he the gall to ask for money for such an act?

However, the answer came three years later. The parish of Trumpington had seriously fallen out with their vicar. As Ambrose had a church 'freehold' they found, just as I had, that his Anglican superiors would do nothing to compel him to obey. The parishioners were so angry with his antisocial and rude behaviour that they took Ambrose to the Church Court – the first time it had been held for two hundred years. The case attracted a good deal of publicity and the convened court found that he should be relieved of his post and asked to leave the village, 'as relations had broken down with his parishioners'. He left the parish in disgrace in September 2008. The national press deridingly called him the 'spitting vicar', because of allegations that he had spat at his parishioner when he had disagreed with the priest on some minor matter.

It was our bad luck that this vicar was the clergyman in our mother's parish. But that was not the case with the Home Office.

Again, I had to face that word 'exhumation', the word that gagged in my gullet. I had to ring the division of the Home Office that dealt with burials and exhumations.

An officious young man answered the phone. His manner surprised me. It was too casual. I felt I should perhaps be asking about my tax affairs rather than the process of digging up dearly departed bodies. I got straight to the point but skirted round that word: 'How does one go about a reburial?' I focused on the photo my son had recently given me. Mum, sitting sideways on her favourite chair in the hall, with the yellowing receiver pressed to her ear, her spare hand holding a pencil. She was doodling as usual. Her mauve shirt brought a glow to her skin and the gilt that peeped out below her softly backcombed hair belonged to her favourite clip-on earrings.

The man's Lancastrian accent was matter of fact. 'Well, first I must warn you that reburials are not normal and it's a complicated business. Can I ask why you want to do this?'

'I'm just making a general enquiry.' I tried to sound relaxed.

'Well, it takes a long time and is very difficult to organise.' His brusqueness led me to believe he had a pressing pile of paperwork that needed attention.

'How difficult?' I ventured.

'Most applications are unsuccessful because so many factors have to be taken into account.' He was getting chattier.

'I see,' I fibbed. 'Well, I've recently heard of a case where a body was removed soon after the original burial.'

'I assure you that's just not possible,' came his prompt response – 'madam,' he added as an afterthought.

His confrontational manner augmented my bravery. I told him I knew of an anonymous case where a body had been removed within three months. Without warning I was promptly passed to his manager. 'Madam,' said the new voice, 'we can't talk about individual cases. Would you like us to send you an exhumation form?'

My body trembled. I needed to focus on my mother's photograph, as the information dripped into my brain – so there was a standard procedure for removal applications.

'You'll need to fill in our form,' the voice continued.

I could not let this opportunity go past, so I summoned the emotional strength to ask, 'Is there another way of applying?'

'There's no other way. We cannot agree to exhumations unless you fill in a form.' He threw all his authority behind his voice.

I left the brown envelope unopened on my desk for days as I wondered if I had the courage to venture further. There were a number of boxes that applicants needed to complete. My eyes were arrested by one question: 'To the best of your knowledge and belief does any person object to the proposal to remove the remains or would any person be likely to do so?'

So Stepfather must have lied to the authorities. What had he put in this box?

I asked my solicitor for advice. She told me there were no legal precedents, so there was no advice. There was only one last avenue open to me. I could contact the MP for Winchester, the well-liked Mark Oaten. But, before I did, I had to be absolutely sure of my facts. I gathered the courage to make another call to the Home Office. The officer in charge reiterated that the only way for a reburial to be considered was to fill in their form.

'We don't think it's a good thing to make this process easy, Madam. It's a difficult decision and we like to leave families plenty of time to think through all the ramifications,' he added.

My MP grasped the nettle straightaway and promised to investigate why the Home Office had agreed to the reburial. As part of our submission we gave evidence of my mother's final wishes. The first letters we received from the department were evasive and dismissed our specific questions. We persisted and wrote again, and then again. Finally, we received a reply that claimed that, in this particular case, no form had ever been filled in! The Home Office had tied themselves up in knots. They insisted it was a mandatory rule that every applicant must fill in their form. But now they were saying Mr Stanley had been allowed to be an exception. Why? And how was this organised?

The admission that no form had been filled in encouraged Mark Oaten to write another flurry of letters. But the replies were unhelpful and avoided our direct questions. They refused to address the issue that my mother's children and extended family had not been told there would be an exhumation and a reburial of her remains. They blindly refused to answer our explicit questions while their letters reiterated, 'The form already seeks to obtain the consent of all members of the family who are considered to have a close degree of kinship to the deceased.' Well, they had clearly failed in our case!

Even after months of wrangling, the Home Office would not address the clear fact that our applicant had either lied on their mandatory form or been allowed to be an exception!

Only MPs can request the services of the Parliamentary Ombudsman, whose job is to investigate complaints with government departments. So, when the case dragged on, Mark Oaten involved him in our case. We wanted a clear-cut answer from him as to whether this exhumation had been permitted under the correct Home Office procedures or not.

We had three outstanding questions: (i) How had the application been made, if it was not on the usual form? (ii) Who in the Home Office authorised the departure from the usual procedures and on what grounds? (iii) How many times in the last three years had the Home Office authorised exhumation without completion of the application form?

As with the Home Office, it was hard work to get any sensible answers from the Ombudsman with many months of delay; and then, as in so many other situations concerning Louis Stanley, the letter had its surprises! Counter to the previous letters from the

Home Office, the Ombudsman's investigations asserted that Stepfather *had* filled out a form. The reburial licence had been issued on 25 September 2002, just 78 days after my mother's burial, and the member of staff who processed the application clearly remembered the application, for Stepfather had included a photograph of the two of them together. The clerk had never received any photographs before.

Further information from the Ombudsman revealed that only 900 reburial licences were issued each year. Each member of staff was instructed to follow strict procedures according to 260 pages of 'lengthy instruction'.

The letter provided no answers as to how my mother's licence had been issued and just increased the complexity of our case. We knew the only way forward was to insist on a photocopy of the form that stepfather was meant to have filled in.

The reply to this request was almost laughable: 'The application form completed by Mr Stanley has however been lost, along with a sack of other files in November 2002, when some Home Office staff moved to different offices.'

I was dumbstruck. Strange, I said to myself, that they moved offices in the very month that we started asking serious questions. I was disillusioned. However, I was even more incredulous when we found out the Home Office was not the only official body to 'lose' the form. The burial authority had 'lost' their copy as well! Most convenient.

Once I had recovered my composure I couldn't help smiling at the typical official wording of the Ombudsman's letter: 'But for the loss of the forms, it would have been routine Home Office policy for them to be retained and archived for a minimum of five years.'

In over 18 months of enquiries with the Home Office, all we received were falsehoods, evasions and probable cover-ups. My MP was happy to continue the battle to learn the truth, but I felt I had to admit my family's battle with the Home Office was over. They held the strings. I was never going to get an honest answer.

However, I agreed for Mark Oaten to write one more time to the Home Office asking the authorities to review their exhumation procedures. They were more open on this and agreed that future measures taken should be clearer, and they agreed to reassess their application form. Also, as the law on reburials was ripe for review, the problems incurred in my case would be made a precedent. They further comforted me that they did wish that the law be altered so that a living spouse would be unable to overrule their dead partner's wishes. Was this a sop? I could only wait and watch. I just hoped I had stopped the possibility of any other family going through our experience.

CHAPTER 20

THE 1911 CENSUS

It was with mixed feelings that I learned that the 1911 census was available online two years before its 100th anniversary. What would it reveal? Would I get firm evidence one way or the other? I had solved many mysteries, but the ancestral roots of that granny, Mrs Mary Ann 'Stanley', who had joined us around the large fireplace for salmon-and-fish-paste rolls on Sunday afternoons, continued to tug at my inner soul. Her family *had* to hold the final secret of Stepfather's past. In the earliest days of my investigations I had imagined I might find her surname on the estate list for Alderley Hall. But of course my research had progressed in great strides since then. I understood the situation far better and I knew it would have been far too risky to allow sloppy tongues to wag on the Cheshire estate.

The census details dripped through my brain's aquifer. I was surprised and puzzled. Even by April 1911 Mary Ann Applegate was calling herself Stanley. Why? Not only this but she was residing at the same address as Mary Eliza (my 'Auntie' Mamie). Even more surprising was her surname – Stanley. Why had both Mary Ann and Mary Eliza taken on the name Stanley as early as 1911? My previous research had led me to believe that the Asquith–Stanley baby had been born in October–November 1911 or possibly as early as July–August; but why were both of them using the surname as early as April? Had the baby arrived even earlier than I thought? If so, why had they delayed for so long before registering the birth if the conspirators already had a scheme in place and a suitable foster mother waiting?

In the marital status of the census column Home Granny had entered that she had been married for four years and had no children (she had recorded Mary Eliza correctly as her niece). Why enter four years? Of course, there was no *Mr* Applegate on the form and she did not claim to be a widow. Intriguingly, she had entered 'wife' in the required column of 'relationship to head of household'. This had not satisfied the checking enumerator, who had crossed out 'wife' and had written in 'head' of household. Why had Mary Ann made this slip? Why did the enumerator correct her entry? Did he know more?

I gave the details further thought. Surely it was Mary Eliza who was giving the game away. Why was the unmarried niece also calling herself Stanley in 1911? Perhaps her name change was the conspirators' flaw. I thought again. Mary Ann had never claimed on paper that Mary Eliza was her daughter, so, if the older woman really had married a man with the surname Stanley, her niece would not have taken on his name. I think I had the situation sussed out. The surname change of her niece Mary Eliza was all part of the shadowy plan. In public, the two women probably acted as mother and daughter in an area where they were unknown. Then, if and when a new baby arrived, the neighbours would not be suspicious.

Why had Venetia's family made plans for a foster mother so early? Maybe Venetia had fallen pregnant before.

It had occurred to me much earlier that perhaps Stepfather had not been the only fruit of the Asquith–Venetia affair. I remembered Michael Brock, the academic, and his reaction to my question about offspring. Had there been more pregnancies? Maybe the first baby had not survived. Maybe there had been miscarriages. And from all the evidence it is quite probable that Asquith had other sexual relationships outside marriage. I remembered one of Venetia's letters written to Edwin when she was in France deciding on the course of her future life: 'I know quite well that if it hadn't been me it would be someone else or a series of others who would have made him just as happy' (20 April 1915). Was she admitting to herself that Asquith was a womaniser? Had she always suspected he would turn to another when she left him?

I think she had been right to worry, as Asquith restarted writing to her sister immediately after her fateful letter arrived on his butler's plate (see Chapter 16). It amused me that the married sister, Sylvia, acted with more reproof and gave Asquith a reprimand for composing letters to her during Cabinet meetings. However, her sturdiness, I discovered from more reading, did not stop Asquith making her a sexual proposal. In June, a month before Venetia married, Sylvia must have received a clouded invitation on the lines of his request to Diana Cooper. We don't have her rebuke but in his reply to her letter Asquith appears to throw up his hands in innocence:

'That you could *ever* have suspected that I should be tempted to convert our wonderful relations of love and confidence into – what shall I say – an erotic adventure? Perfect love, as the scripture says, casteth out fear and still more distrust' (20 June 1915).

I reconsidered Venetia's position. If Asquith was trying it on with Venetia's married sister of 33 years in 1915, what hope had there been for the young woman of 18 in 1906? It must have been almost impossible for this slip of a girl to stop his passionate advances.

In the Bodleian Library, I had my own look at Sylvia's letters written to her husband, Anthony Henley, who was at the time fighting on the front. She, like Venetia, often stayed at The Wharf, but there were a number of things that shocked me about her letters.

First, Asquith's alacrity alarmed me. He immediately turned his attention from one sister to another and without delay began to divulge cabinet secrets. Sylvia, rather than keep the state confidences to herself, told her husband, who was a soldier. We don't have Venetia's letters, so we don't know how she dealt with these important matters of state, but it does show that the accusation of Asquith's taking of security risks – potentially allowing the nation's secrets to get into enemy hands – was certainly valid. Sylvia was not a secure confidante.

Second, two days after the formation of the coalition (26 May), Sylvia reports that she does not like 'the Prime's' behaviour, for when they depart from each other's company he tries to steal a passionate kiss. Sylvia tells her husband that she does not like this but two days later she complains about it again. On the following day she is so worried she refuses to sit beside 'the Prime'.

Sylvia's justification of why she stayed with Asquith perhaps gives us an insight into why Venetia remained attached to him for so long. Sylvia wrote that 'it is manifestly my duty' to stay listening to the Prime Minister. She rationalises that she must do this because Asquith has pleaded with her to stay close to him, as she is the 'one person' with whom he can relax.

Anthony Henley's letters have not survived but we can deduce the scale of his worry from hers. On 31 May Sylvia has to explain she is not 'in love' with the Prime Minister. She admits she likes Asquith's attention and his important confidences, but the emotional stress he places on her is obvious by 20 June. It must be just before this date that Asquith suggests sexual relations. Sylvia responds strangely. For, rather than run from Asquith and stop meeting him, she continues to agree to go on long drives with him.

The third revelation was the strange relationship between the two sisters. Sylvia becomes jealous when her husband sends Venetia a letter, just days before her wedding (15 July). This causes an angry scene as Venetia refuses to tell her sister of its contents. This makes Sylvia furious with her husband and she accuses him of fancying her sister.

But enough of speculating about the two sisters' jealousies. Let's return to the 1911 census. With great excitement I now had completed the missing link. I had made the connection with the city of Liverpool. The 'Stanley' women's address was a house with six rooms to the east of the city and the street map told me Newborough Avenue was close to a park. Friends familiar with Liverpool told me this area had once been a wealthy and predominantly Jewish area.

Once again a visit to the area gave me handsome rewards. The neighbourhood has changed dramatically since the early twentieth century. Toxteth is now deprived but the past grandeur of the buildings that once surrounded Sefton Park is easily identified. On the park's doorstep was the house where the two women lived. More interesting for me was the once grand district of Belvedere. It was a stone's throw away and here the Montagu family's house, Claremont, had once stood. Viscount Samuel had been born in the mansion and his family had made their millions by trading silver bullion. When I read that the family went to the Liberal Progressive Synagogue in nearby Princes Road I recalled details of Venetia's wedding. Joseph Morris, the rabbi who had agreed to marry her, had come from this synagogue. All that separated Claremont, the synagogue and the two Marys' lodgings were short walks through the park.

My drive to Birkenhead also proved fruitful. I looked in the yearly Gore directories for Newborough Avenue. Mary Ann was absent but interestingly number 8 had no registered tenant for the period 1910–14. Had the many local rabbis used number 8 as a 'safe house' for pregnant ladies?

In the library, as I waited for further requested documents, I amused myself by turning the pages of the 1911 directory in a haphazard manner. As I did, I spotted a road called Claremont, presumably named after the Montagus' former home (which had been demolished). Then, as I nonchalantly turned further pages, my eyes rested on 1 Claremont Road. This was just too big a coincidence to be chance – the building was the headquarters of the Liberal Club!

I used the 1901 census to trace more members of the extended Applegate family. For the first time, I found Mary Ann's younger brother Alfred James. He had moved to Shoreditch in London and was working for the railway company that served the line to Alderley Edge. Older brother Fred was still living in Reddish with three more children since the last census.

The world of research is changing very fast and so much more information is uploaded each day on the Internet. There is so much more available than when I started, so I had begun some new searches. But it was not until I returned from my visit to Liverpool that I found my pearl.

First I discovered that Marion, another of Edwin's sisters, was known as Mamie. Then I found that his sister Lily was a pioneer of youth work, setting up the first Jewish Club for Girls. But this was not all. An academic paper gave me more details. Lily had modelled her work on a former youth worker. This woman had been a groundbreaker in work with girls from poor homes. Her name was Maude Stanley! (Sometimes spelt Maud). Again I was staring at a black-and-white script with incredulous eyes. Maude Stanley (1833–1915) was Venetia's aunt, sister of Lord Sheffield! She established her Girls Club Union, the first nonreligious body to help needy young girls.

Maude was not the aristocrat 'playing at' helping the destitute: she worked with impoverished teenage girls in the Five Dials district of London and published her first book about her work in 1878. Maude documents her visits to the poor and describes how she dealt with drunkenness, overcrowding and starving families. Her text, *Work About the Five Dials*, still highly readable to the modern reader, demonstrates her real understanding of those in a less fortunate position than herself. Later, in 1890, Maude Stanley instructs other philanthropic ladies on how to deal with girls who leave school at a tender age and work in poor conditions.

The excitement was complete when I discovered that one of her earliest clubs was near the home of the Applegates in Didsbury. It opened in 1882, when Mary Ann was 12. I read Maude's book in more detail. She tells of clubs being so popular that the girls often stayed on as members for over ten years with individual girls making such great strides forward that she can find them positions way above their station. Maude's words reveal more:

> The clubs were formed because of the lack of occupation for the girls driven from the countryside. All public buildings were closed at 6.00 she [the working girl] probably does not care for reading, the only music to be had is that of public bands and picture palaces however cheap cannot be indulged in an evening – nothing remains for choice but a probably stuffy home with sewing to do or aimless perambulating of the streets with a girl friend or young man.

Then, on p. 222 of the same book, I see a sequence of words that flash like beacons from the page:

> When I first began to work in London, I met a family who had come from the north a few years before, and they would often speak to me of the happy day they had spent at Alderley Park when they came over there from Manchester, being brought by the manager of a Sunday School.

Could this be the Applegate family? Was it Alfred and his wife and the children who had gone to the Alderley Estate as a treat to get away from the drudgery of warping? Even if this family was not the Applegates, it proved Maude knew many destitute families living in the vicinity.

It was obvious: whom else would Venetia tell when she found

herself pregnant but her kindly aunt, who knew so many suitable girls willing to care for a child in exchange for a new lifestyle?

Had Rusholme's Congregational Church, where Asquith married Helen, organised the Sunday school outings to Alderley Hall? Certainly the three families – Asquith, Melland and Applegate – were all Nonconformists. Had the church also been the catalyst for their acquaintance?

Aunt Maude (perhaps working in tandem with Lily Montagu) finds Venetia a proven reliable woman with Mary Eliza in tow. Maude then moves the 'expected foster mother' to a safe house that is perhaps owned by the synagogue near Lily's family home in Liverpool. Both Mary Ann and Mary Eliza are advised to call themselves Stanley in time for the 1911 census. All the preparations are carefully organised not to raise any suspicions.

How close had the relationship been between Aunt Maude and her niece? (It was strange it was the same family relationship as between Mary Ann and Mary Eliza.) Interestingly Maude died on 14 July (at Alderley) from a heart condition thought to have been brought on by the stress of the war, just 12 days before Venetia's wedding on 26 July 1915. The death caused the ceremony to be delayed.

Venetia's father had been interested in education and, remarkably, I found that Stockport's Sunday school was said to be the biggest school in the world! In 1905 it was four storeys high and had 58 classrooms. Was this the Sunday school that visited Alderley Hall?

Maude's connection with the Liberal Party was easy to find. Her brother and nephew were both MPs and she held a literary and political salon in her house close to the Houses of Parliament in Smith Square. Amusingly, Nancy Mitford, her niece, once described her as 'very ugly'. Of course she entertained those familiar names that Stepfather used so often in my childhood. They reappeared as reliably as a ticking clock; many were related to Venetia Stanley. Each time the hands moved on, so did my connections. I was satisfied I had found the answer to my puzzle.

The conundrum that had fascinated me for years was solved. I had leapt over the final hurdle. It amused me that I had not only stripped Louis naked, leaving him exposed like a pickle in a pot, but I had also laid bare an encrusted Asquithian secret. The two women whom Stepfather had so cleverly coerced my mother into housing all those years ago had finally spewed out their secrets. Their lives had changed for ever when they agreed to look after Louis Thomas Stanley.

I reflected on the name Applegate. I had been auspiciously lucky. If the plotters had selected a female with a more commonly occurring surname the devious untruths would never have been detected.

Now we faced probate. But before that there was more disturbing news. Mr Stanley's third lawyer, who had been appointed at the last minute, to deal with his daft will had found that his previous lawyer, Mr H, had left Louis's state of affairs like 'a dog's dinner'. He continued, 'I am horrified – quite, quite horrified – in disbelief at the amount of overcharge.' We were not surprised. Louis had corrupted all those around him. The man had been completely taken in with his manipulative nature, but where he had gone wrong was his refusal to listen to us or Diana, our lawyer. All we could do was report Mr H to the Law Society.

As we had received nothing from our mother's estate, Stepfather's third new solicitor approached us. He had a proposal. Each of us would be allowed to take one object worth less than £1,500 out of the probate arrangements. It seemed odd to thank a stranger for 'allowing' me to own a single article from my own mother's estate.

I selected the Japanese lacquered grandfather clock that had stood in the hallway close to the entrance to Home Granny and Auntie Mamie's flat. It was strange to think that both these two women had held the key to my personal detective story. They were not history on a page. They had lived under the floorboards of my bedroom when I was a child. It was Stepfather's bragging of names that had intrigued me but their profiles had fuelled my fascination with political and social conspiracies.

The timepiece had been on the threshold of Stepfather's two worlds. At eight o'clock each day he walked away from the two women who had harboured him and his secrets, walked past the clock and across the hall and entered into the exposed world of our family. When I was very young the front door in the hall was flung open, but he didn't like this. He wanted it kept closed, so that the blue gate with its jangly bell became the only entrance to our house.

I wonder what shade of blue the gate is now. I can't imagine it any other colour. But I will never know because I shall never see it again. I can't face the pain.

And that's not the only pain. I can't find the inner peace I once had beside the plot where I buried my mother. I miss the grave with the tall hollyhocks sagging over pebbles from the beach.

Despite the misery I do have one treasured memento. I found it jumbled up in a box full of household junk that I managed to buy at the secret auction: a tiny blue-and-white pottery musical box shaped like a windmill with nickel sails. It now stands lopsided on just three bead-like legs. Stuck with decayed Sellotape on its upturned base is a withered yellowed notelet. By turning the little model upside down I can just make out my mother's printed script. She was not in the habit of writing on her possessions. This was a one-off. We had teased her about her appalling handwriting, so she must have wanted us to know this worthless musical box was important to her. She had made the effort to write in capitals: GIVEN TO US BY THE MANAGER OF THE HOTEL WHEN WE WON THE DUTCH GRAND PRIX. The race was won by Jo Bonnier in 1959 on the seaside track of Zandvoort, our first win in the World Championship.

The tiny memento of her past life sits on my desk and catches my eye as I struggle to encapsulate on paper what life was like behind the blue gate and why the search to explain its mysteries became a such an absorbing tale.

EPILOGUE

How apt is my story to the lasting fame of Shakespeare's four compelling words spoken by a servant in his play, *The Merchant of Venice*: 'The truth will out'?

Too often for my comfort the directory, the map or the document I was scanning fell inexplicitly open at an unlikely place as if the paperwork were encouraging me to find another crucial link and expose more of the truth. If the pages had fallen open in another haphazard way I would never have discovered the full story.

Similarly, my last piece of good fortune arose only when I was rounding up my story. Having nearly completed the Applegate family tree I found the telephone number of a living descendant and wondered if there was anybody alive who could remember back to the 1910s. That first relation was too young and was hesitant to reveal family details to a stranger, but she cautiously gave me the email address of a family member, living in Australia, who was working on her own version of their family tree.

I was disappointed not to get a reply. I tried numerous times. However, three years later when my research was coming to an end, I looked at the untied ends and decided it was worth making one more effort to contact her. I used the same message and the same email address but this time a response arrived. I did not want to prejudice any family memories so I did not tell her all the details. Nevertheless, the descendent gave me permission to visit her 90-year-old mother, who now lives in Wales. She had married into the family and was Fred Applegate's daughter-in-law.

Anne Applegate knew of family secrets and, as we talked, my suppositions of how the family came to take in my stepfather came alive. It was strange to listen to Anne talk of the characters who had for so long been historical details on outdated pieces of paper. We discussed Fred, her father-in-law, who had become my story's fulcrum. Why had he and his wife not brought up their daughter, Mary Eliza (my Auntie Mamie)?

The elderly Applegate remembered the family's gossip and confirmed my side of the story. Although she had not known which relative had taken in Mary Eliza she did remember more significant stories about the unnamed relative. She was the wealthy one who had 'done well for herself' by marrying a cotton broker who worked in Liverpool. Significantly, nobody in the family knew anything else about him, nor had anybody ever met the man. Even more spectacularly, Anne remembered she had a son who the family assumed was her own.

My paperwork was confirmed further as Anne chatted. Fred got his girlfriend, Elizabeth, known to the family as Lizzie, into the 'family way'. Mary Eliza (my Auntie Mamie) was the baby and was the reason for their hasty marriage. So the family must have been sympathetic to the Stanley family's problem of potential illegitimacy! How significant was this?

Anne Applegate did not know at what age Mary Eliza left her parents but the paperwork suggests she was about three when Fred was unemployed and Lizzie was expecting her second child.

Interestingly, I later investigated Lizzie in the census and discovered she must have been friends with Mary Ann, many years before, as both had lived and worked in Bollington when they were teenagers. This all made sense. Fred had fallen for his sister's best friend and got her into 'trouble', and then, when things got tough, Lizzie's best friend, and aunt, took the child in.

According to the family, Fred was a colourful character – attractive but a scoundrel and a rotten husband. Having hurriedly married Fred, Lizzie had a tough life. She was forever pregnant and she continued to produce many more children, one of whom my research had failed to spot. Her youngest was born an astounding 21 years after the birth of Mary Eliza.

It appears that Mary Eliza may have been fortunate to live away from her natural parents, as Fred liked his drink and ended up an alcoholic.

Anne was keen to recall a family story about Fred and Lizzie, which had never made much sense to her. She had been in her mid-twenties and the year was 1938. It was a story to confirm many suppositions.

Newly married Anne and her husband were the first in the family to buy a car. When the vehicle arrived her mother-in-law, Lizzie, pleaded with the young couple to take her (and her husband, Fred) to see their long-lost daughter in a place by the sea called Hoylake. They set off excitedly from Reddish early in the morning and marvelled at the newly completed Mersey Tunnel as they travelled through its winding passages. When they arrived in Hoylake and saw their relative's house they were surprised by its grandeur. To my utter surprise, Anne described the house in Hoyle Road just as it stands today as if she had visited it yesterday.

However, the event turned out to be a disaster. When the excited group knocked on the door only Mary Eliza, who was in her early forties, was at home. Her aunt and 'brother' were in London, as they often were. Before Mary Eliza could welcome them into the house an almighty row developed on the doorstep.

Lizzie flew into a rage demanding to know why her daughter had not been in contact. Fred, equally angry, stormed off to the pub. Distraught Lizzie charged down to the beach to clear her mind.

Anne found herself alone in the large house with Mary Eliza. They chatted as they cleared dishes from a party held the night before. Mary Eliza proudly showed Anne a truly magnificent bureau on the landing of the house. She told Anne that her aunt, Mary Ann, was a companion for the elderly or sick. Her last client had given her this amazing piece of furniture.

Anne had always speculated why the reunion had gone so badly. Nobody ever talked about it again. It remained a family secret. I have my own thoughts.

Anne's most supportive news was still to come. She talked of her husband's early life. In his boyish days, his best friend and playmate was a 'cousin' called Louis! Finally I had heard the name. It was all I needed to confirm my theories. Stepfather from an early age had lived with Mary Ann Applegate and had often visited the extended family. This was why he knew Stockport so well. Further confirmation came when Anne told me Mary Eliza's sisters used to visit her and her aunt when they were young. When the sisters returned from their trips to the Wirral they talked of Louis but never of their nonexistent 'uncle'. Had anybody in the extended family ever suspected who Louis's parents really were? Had they been intrigued by it all? Anne, having married into the family, didn't know the answer. The Applegates had kept their side of the conspiracy of secrets.

Imaginary scenes from the past still circulate in my head as my stepfather's life still fascinates me. His two feet had never been planted firmly in one camp or another for he hopped from one social and cultural class to another. His cousin and Louis, being the same age, were natural playmates but as they advanced in years they were brought up in different worlds. I thought of Stepfather's more lonely life with a private tutor and a mature sister living a secluded life by the seaside while his 'cousin' lived in a crowded terraced house with outside toilets and bulging with both older and younger siblings. They all had to contend with an abusive father. The elder sisters toiled in the local mill but Fred (the younger) didn't join them. On the day he reached his 14th birthday he left school to become a butcher's boy.

I had one last question for Anne. Had her husband, Fred the younger, ever played golf? She laughed and laughed. Of course he had always loved the game. But he was not a playboy and as her husband matured he turned to pursue a career. He joined the locally founded Co-operative Society and rapidly progressed up the hierarchy to become its national vice-president. Had Fred ever looked back to his childhood and wondered what had happened to his golfing playmate? Had he ever speculated about what his friend had made of his more 'privileged' upbringing? As close pals, had the boys confided with each other about their problematic and absent 'fathers'? Perhaps their bond was strengthened when the two young lads maintained their own conspiracy of secrets.

My quest has been a fascinating historical search for many reasons, not least to satisfy my own curiosity and put childhood uncertainties to bed. When I reflect on the historical details and look back on that era, a hundred years ago, I see that life for all social groups was radically different from today's society. Now that I have researched those times I can imagine myself playing each role in the story and I can appreciate how the series of events unfolded. But there is a part of me that still says, 'Wow!' What goes around comes around.

Today's world has moved on and sexual relationships of all sorts are more open and birth control has put an end to the social stigma of unplanned pregnancies, but the social division between high society and the rest of the population is as wide as it was a hundred years ago. Men with powerful positions still exploit their prey, just as young Venetia's life was ruined by a powerful older married man. He abused his position and demanded that others conspire with him to protect his name.

Little has changed.

People who have helped me

I thank all those who got involved in my story.

There were times when I was in the depths of despair and I could see little good in human beings. Close friends rescued me from wallowing in this belief. Without their support I would not have completed this book. They listened, supported, gave their time, read drafts and cheerily encouraged me to keep going even when I appeared to be walking through thick treacle that stuck to the soles of my boots. Their belief in my ability to finish the task stopped me from letting them down.

Three of my friends, Annie Smith, Jenny Plastow and Margaret Hamer, sadly died in the last months of my efforts to complete the task but their valuable support will never be forgotten.

Conspiracy of Secrets was a particularly lonely writing task. Most of the material I was drafting had to remain undisclosed. I had to keep my thoughts, my research and my writing to myself for nine lonely years. My friends provided me with a much needed outlet. Different friends helped me in different ways but I am particularly grateful to those who offered to read my lengthy, rambling first drafts. I knew I could trust my friends to read sections without personal judgement and the pure fact that I knew my words were, at last, being read motivated me to improve. The thrill for me was being able to share my thoughts aloud with others. I am not sure any of my friends realise the depth of joy and release these conversations gave me. So once again I salute you my faithful friends: Henrietta A, David A, Maggie T, Patrick T, Sonia C, Peter E, Helen H, Vanessa P, Dot G, Peter G-C, Jill P, Alan P, Leila P, Frances C, Kathryn R, Penny C, Brian B, and Ann L.

I would also like to thank all the nurses and carers who looked after my mother, often under intolerable circumstances. I would like to thank especially Pauline, Eleanor, Georgina, Bonnie and Pam.

I would like to say thank you to all those who were once involved with the renowned motor racing team of BRM and kindly made time to see me. Special thanks go to ex-mechanic Dick S. I am only sorry that I could not include more of the tales I was told.

Thanks go to my local librarians who worked so hard to retrieve the vast amount of material that I requested. I would also like to thank the other sources of research data and ephemera that I used. Each librarian's help was invaluable.

Stephen T did a thorough job in pursuing my outlandish genealogical requests. Together we tracked the most unlikely and often most veiled families with a limited budget. Particular thanks go to my friend Henrietta who listened so attentively to my tales of woe. From one whispered conversation she picked up my stepfather's surname and then spotted the same name on the cover of a book – that knowing glance at a title sparked my in-depth investigation.

More thanks go to the relatives of Mary Ann and Mary Eliza Applegate, who allowed me to pry into their family even though they had no idea why I was so interested.

Special thanks go to Maggie T, who regrettably had to share some of my ordeals. The plan was for her to come to my house two or three days a week in order that we could work together on creating exciting materials that developed children's literacy skills. All went well for nearly a year but then disaster struck and from then on each time she entered the house I started with the words: 'You won't believe what's happened', then later 'Guess what I found out'. Maggie provided me with a post on which to lean and her good sense and Yorkshire humour got me through that long and difficult period.

I am sorry that my children did not escape the emotional anguish of this tale. But now with my task completed we can move forward and remember Grannie as she would have wished. Thank you Tom, Rupert and Hannah for your patience, love and support.